BOURBON

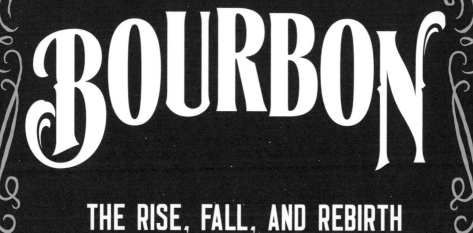

BOURBON

THE RISE, FALL, AND REBIRTH
OF AN
AMERICAN WHISKEY

Fred Minnick

Foreword by Sean Brock

VOYAGEUR
PRESS

Inspiring | Educating | Creating | Entertaining

© 2016 Quarto Publishing Group USA Inc.
Text © 2016 Fred Minnick

Photography © Fred Minnick except as otherwise noted.

First published in 2016 by Voyageur Press, an imprint of The Quarto Group, 100 Cummings Center, Suite 265-D, Beverly, MA 01915, USA.
T (978) 282-9590 F (978) 283-2742 Quarto.com

Voyageur Press titles are also available at discount for retail, wholesale, promotional, and bulk purchase. For details, contact the Special Sales Manager by email at specialsales@quarto.com or by mail at The Quarto Group, Attn: Special Sales Manager, 100 Cummings Center, Suite 265-D, Beverly, MA 01915, USA.

13

ISBN: 978-0-7603-5172-7

Library of Congress Cataloging-in-Publication Data

Names: Minnick, Fred, 1978-
Title: Bourbon : the rise, fall, and rebirth of an American whiskey / Fred Minnick.
Description: Minneapolis, MN : Voyageur Press, 2016. | Includes bibliographical references and index.
Identifiers: LCCN 2016009158 | ISBN 9780760351727 (plc)
Subjects: LCSH: Bourbon whiskey--United States--History. | Whiskey--United States--History. | Whiskey industry--United States--History.
Classification: LCC TP605 .M567 2016 | DDC 641.2/520973--dc23
LC record available at http://lccn.loc.gov/2016009158

Acquiring Editor: Erik Gilg
Project Manager: Madeleine Vasaly
Art Director: James Kegley
Cover Designer: Faceout Studios
Layout: Wendy Holdman

On the endpapers: *shutterstock/Tischenko Irina*

Printed in China

To OLM, and the geeks.

CONTENTS

Foreword | 6

Introduction | 8

CHAPTER 1 Father of Bourbon | 12

CHAPTER 2 And the Bourbon Shall Flow | 30

CHAPTER 3 Government: Friend and Foe | 54

CHAPTER 4 "Whiskey Is the Devil's Own Brew" | 76

CHAPTER 5 The Fight for Prohibition's Medicinal Whiskey | 86

CHAPTER 6 Big Business: Post-Prohibition Growth | 118

CHAPTER 7 Distillers vs. Nazis and US Government | 138

CHAPTER 8 The Boom of the Bourbon Image | 160

CHAPTER 9 Rise of White Spirits | 176

CHAPTER 10 Success in a Red Dress | 188

CHAPTER 11 To Beat Jack Daniel's | 198

CHAPTER 12 Bourbon's Return and Potential Fall | 212

Bibliography | 236

Index | 238

Acknowledgments | 240

FOREWORD

BY SEAN BROCK

James Beard Award winner and *New York Times* best-selling author

Almost a decade ago, the bourbon bug bit me: I had my first taste of Pappy Van Winkle, and I haven't been the same since.

Over the years, I've dedicated my career and life to studying and celebrating southern culture. My restaurant, Husk, serves as the church where we give our daily sermons in the form of food and drink. We want to share all of the seminal things that belong to the South with the rest of the world, like cornbread and fine whiskey.

When I tasted twenty-year-old Pappy Van Winkle for the first time, the world stood still. I was struck with an incredible sense of pride as a southerner. This stuff is ours, I thought—it was born here and belongs here, and it is world class. My mind started to ramble, and I realized I didn't know anything about the history of our great spirit or what contribution liquor had truly made to America. Its taxes have helped build roads and schools, funded wars, and birthed our beloved sport of NASCAR. I knew it was my responsibility to learn as much as possible about a subject that contributed so significantly to our culture, so I started digging. I bought every book I could find with the word *bourbon* in the title and sat in front of my laptop Googling for hours and hours on end. I quickly realized that the story of bourbon was as confusing and clouded as a presidential election.

Nearly every story I read seemed like a fairy tale made up for the sake of marketing. That's when I discovered Fred and his incredible passion, not to mention his almost dangerous breadth of knowledge on these subjects. It takes a special person to dig this deep and discover truths that so often seem to be hidden on purpose. The book that you are about to read can easily transform you into a bourbon history buff. I read it in two days. I wish I could have had this information in front of me ten years ago, but it simply didn't exist before Fred poured it all out in this all-encompassing bourbon encyclopedia. Within these pages are some facts people don't want to hear, like the story of the reverend Elijah Craig and how he invented bourbon. It is filled with stories about the tangled history of whiskey production that ultimately help us realize bourbon's place in American history. Bourbon is not just about getting intoxicated; its role in medicine, politics, society, and economics are important to our country. This is a textbook for those who have always wondered about the true history of bourbon and will serve as a foundation for those who are interested in what the future holds. It provides a deep understanding of how bourbon became the worldwide phenomenon it is today. It's allowed me to have a different respect for bourbon, caused me to take in the flavor a little slower with every sip I take, and enabled me to speak with more confidence in spreading the gospel. It occurred to me that Fred may have written this book so people like me would stop texting him random bourbon history questions at odd hours of the night.

Sit back, pour a healthy glass of liquid history, and soak up all this knowledge that Fred so generously shares with us.

All of us bourbon lovers have our moment when the brown spirit captivated us, moved us, and brought us into the fold. For renowned chef Sean Brock and many others, the Van Winkle bourbons were their first love. The bottles pictured are supremely rare and tasty.

INTRODUCTION

ourbon is more American than apple pie, existed before baseball, and has built more roads, schools, and government infrastructure than any non-petroleum domestic product. That's saying a lot for a style of whiskey made predominantly from corn. Since its birth, bourbon has transcended its status as intoxicant liquor, has become an American symbol used in political circles and popular culture, and has endured harsh economic times. From the statesman Henry Clay saying he'd use bourbon to "lubricate the wheels of justice" to the 2015 Obama-McConnell saga known as the "Bourbon Summit," bourbon is woven into the dealings on Capitol Hill; and through Paul Newman drinking J. T. S. Brown on the *Hustler* and the *Saturday Night Live* parodies using the spirit, bourbon is embedded in America's pop culture.

Although bourbon's American importance is often relegated to its role as nothing more than a drink, as you will see in *Bourbon: The Rise, Fall and Rebirth of an American Whiskey*, bourbon helped build the United States of America. Today, 60 percent of the average bottle goes to tax; thus, bourbon builds schools, roads, and government infrastructure. Health groups and anti-drinking leagues would vilify distilleries for saying such, but I'm not affiliated with a distillery, so I speak the truth: bourbon is good for America. And it's time we understand the historic intricacies that make it so unique.

This book offers an illustrated narrative to an iconic and under-rated spirit that has connections to such celebrities as Mila Kunis, Sean

Sean Connery endorsed Jim Beam bourbons in the 1960s. Bourbon brands have enjoyed a rich history of paid and non-paid celebrity endorsements. Ironically, Connery played James Bond, who ordered a martini shaken and not stirred and impacted the white spirits movement. Starting in 2014, the company, now Beam Suntory, brought back its celebrity connections with actress Mila Kunis. *Beam Suntory*

President Barrack Obama (right) and Senate Majority Leader Mitch McConnell (Republican, Kentucky) captured the bourbon world's heart with the suggested "Bourbon Summit." It all began when Obama said he'd enjoy Kentucky bourbon with McConnell. The meeting never happened, but the bourbon industry enjoyed several months of press regarding the Bourbon Summit, ranging from *Saturday Night Live*'s skit with a bottle of Woodford Reserve to the social media hashtag #BourbonSummit. *White House*

Connery, and Sophia Loren, and that has motivated the US government to convene many times over what to call it, how to tax it, where it should be made, and whether its distillers are defrauding the government. The characters—ranging from James Beam to Schenley Distillers—are real, yet seem every bit as fictional as soap opera drama. Bourbon offers astounding American Dream business stories, making the Beam legacy as strong as that of the Ford family and the United Distiller failures as sad as that of Studebaker automobiles. But because it's an intoxicating spirit and not a car, bourbon's historical importance is dismissed in the high school and collegiate classrooms. Full disclosure: *Bourbon*, the book, will not get you drunk. So there's no excuse to not use this or other great bourbon histories in the classroom setting. The modern era of bourbon learning has begun, and consumers have spoken through cyberspace to prove that bourbon matters beyond the casual drink.

When President Barack Obama said he "would enjoy having some Kentucky bourbon" with Senator Mitch McConnell (Republican, Kentucky), the Senate majority leader, in order to show the two sides can work together, social media blew up with the hashtag #BourbonSummit. Every major news outlet seriously covered the so-called Bourbon Summit, with citizens hoping it would become a catalyst for compromise.

The Bourbon Summit didn't actually happen, but Obama visited the makers of Cleveland Bourbon as part of his tour with the Manufacturing Advocacy and

Kentucky distilleries offer some breathtaking views. But few things are more pulse-quickening than that of a simple warehouse. Behind those walls are coveted barrels of whiskey at the Buffalo Trace Distillery.

When it comes to spelling the spirit *whisky* or *whiskey*, there is zero consistency. Congress spelled it *whiskey* in one sentence and *whisky* the next. American whiskey is traditionally spelled with an "e," but many outlier brands choose to omit the E.

Growth Network, a nonprofit manufacturing advocacy. The Cleveland Bourbon visit was highly noted as a snub toward Kentucky bourbon and to McConnell. The *Washington Times* wrote, "President Obama visited a bourbon bottling company Wednesday at a small business incubator in Cleveland, where a new process ages the beverage in about a week. His visit served as a reminder that Mr. Obama still hasn't held a promised bourbon summit with Mr. McConnell as an icebreaker for their increasingly frosty relationship."

The Bourbon Summit narrative essentially lasted from November 2014 to May 2015, giving the distilleries free publicity in the political and pop-culture pages of the newspapers and constant airtime on BBC, CNN, Fox News, and MSNBC. The Bourbon Summit never made bourbon a prominent topic of discussion, but the spirit was potentially a vehicle for political compromise and illustrated how deeply ingrained it is in the American culture. For the students of bourbon history, the Bourbon Summit was just the latest political snafu. Past presidential whiskey blunders include President George Washington federalizing troops against distillers and distillers defrauding the government to pay for President Ulysses S. Grant's reelection campaign.

In *Bourbon: The Rise, Fall, and Rebirth of an American Whiskey,* you will learn about bourbon through legislation, lawsuits, and trends. This bourbon history combines business, genealogy, Kentucky, lawsuits, legend, marketing, and an occasional patent. My goal is to offer new history that changes what we know about this spirit and to dig deeper into subjects we know little about. The subjects are presented in illustrated vignettes to make it an easy-to-read history, interesting to those who do not even drink bourbon. From President Obama using it in his November 2014 speech to many appearances in movies and television snows—ranging from *NCIS* to *The Internship*—bourbon is everywhere, all the time. For the love of all things American, fast-food restaurants are even cobranding bourbon hamburgers.

Thus, bourbon is no longer just liquor. It's a slice of Americana.

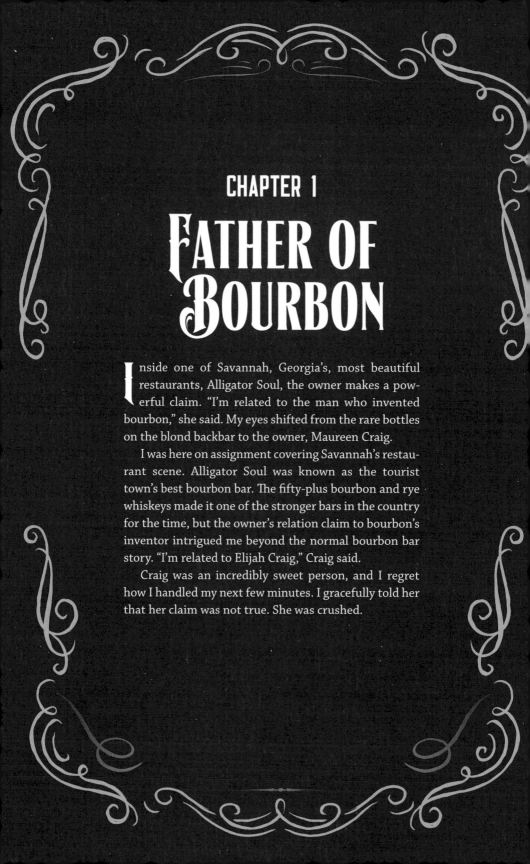

CHAPTER 1

FATHER OF BOURBON

Inside one of Savannah, Georgia's, most beautiful restaurants, Alligator Soul, the owner makes a powerful claim. "I'm related to the man who invented bourbon," she said. My eyes shifted from the rare bottles on the blond backbar to the owner, Maureen Craig.

I was here on assignment covering Savannah's restaurant scene. Alligator Soul was known as the tourist town's best bourbon bar. The fifty-plus bourbon and rye whiskeys made it one of the stronger bars in the country for the time, but the owner's relation claim to bourbon's inventor intrigued me beyond the normal bourbon bar story. "I'm related to Elijah Craig," Craig said.

Craig was an incredibly sweet person, and I regret how I handled my next few minutes. I gracefully told her that her claim was not true. She was crushed.

To some, bourbon is just an intoxicating liquor. For them, bourbon's inventor is no more important than the price of tea in China on any given day. But we passionate bourbon lovers fret over bourbon's regulatory definition: whiskey distilled from a fermented mash of at least 51 percent corn, off the still at no more than 160 proof, and entering a new charred oak container no more than 125 proof. Oh, and it must be made in the United States, but not just Kentucky! Beyond these rules, bourbon, more than other spirits, evokes a curiosity in enthusiasts to the point that we actually care and argue about who invented this spirit made predominantly of corn and aged in wood. Does anybody care who invented vodka, gin, or rum? Perhaps some do, but glorifying the inventor of bourbon is the American way.

This country loves crowning inventors of things, from Alexander Graham Bell's invention of the telephone to Eli Whitney's creation of the cotton gin. We love staking claims so much that Henry Ford was named the automobile creator, even though Karl Benz beat him to it. We know who created such great foods as the potato chip (George Crum in 1853), cotton candy (William Morrison and John C. Wharton in 1897), and the chocolate-chip cookie (Ruth Wakefield in 1930). But we've been sold a big, fat lie when it comes to Elijah Craig inventing bourbon, and we accepted this intoxicating nontruth one shot at a time—because Americans love a good story and regularly accept legends as fact, ranging from tales of Bigfoot to claims that Presidents George Washington and Abe Lincoln never told lies. And for whiskey lovers, well, it's even worse. Both Ireland and Scotland have nonverified legends crowing their whiskey inventors.

Unfortunately, Elijah Craig's claim to inventing bourbon was based on legend. All those inside the bourbon circles know this, books have published this, and distillers have outright told the media that Craig did not invent bourbon. Yet for nearly a century, the legendary Baptist minister Elijah Craig was considered the "Father of Bourbon."

Craig was considered the "most popular preacher in Kentucky" and elected and consecrated an Apostle of the Baptist General Association of Virginia (before Kentucky became a state in 1792). He was credited with founding Kentucky's first fulling mill and first paper mill in 1789 and 1791 respectively. The book History of Kentucky (1874) by Lewis Collins lists bourbon whiskey first being made at the fulling mill in 1789 in Georgetown, but the title did not specifically connect the Baptist minister with the creation of bourbon.

At the time of Craig's alleged creation, thousands of settlers were moving to Kentucky, which was a part of Virginia until 1792. Virginia encouraged settlement in Kentucky. During the first years of the American Revolution there was no way for these settlers to legally claim their land, but the Virginia legislature permitted settlement in Kentucky before 1778 to anybody who could claim four hundred acres, also offering them an option to purchase an additional thousand acres adjoining their settlement at a reduced price. Religious encouragement seemed to work, too. Both the Catholic and Baptist leaders encouraged the migration of their people to Kentucky.

The first American distillers were farmers, who distilled whatever grain surpluses were around them. In the Northeast, it was rye. Early distillers didn't think corn offered the same high quality as rye, but settlers were encouraged to plant corn as they moved west and would eventually distill with corn. In Kentucky, they found pure water that had been naturally filtered through limestone, such as the ten-acre spring-fed lake at Maker's Mark in Loretto, Kentucky. The early distillers used pot stills, such as the pictured 1807 still stored at the Woodford Reserve Distillery in Versailles, Kentucky.

In 1785, Anglo-Saxon Catholic Basil Hayden is credited with leading twenty-five families down the Ohio River to Kentucky. Reverend Father John Carroll, Superior of the Jesuits in the United States, wrote favorably of Hayden, "with whose character and virtue I am well acquainted. . . ." Hayden became a Kentucky pillar and established a significant distillery in Marion County, making whiskey from corn and rye. His grandson would later create a brand named after his grandfather, calling it Old Grand-Dad, and more than a century later the company Jim Beam created the Basil Hayden brand.

There was also the matter of taxation.

After the United States of America won the Revolutionary War, the country needed revenue to mend broken cities and build new towns. Treasury Secretary Alexander Hamilton suggested a whiskey tax to help fund a self-supporting and effective government. In 1791, President George Washington accepted Hamilton's excise tax, but distillers felt betrayed, and western Pennsylvania farmers and distillers scoffed at the new country's audacity in seeking to take their money. How could the government demand taxations after Pennsylvania distillers supplied American soldiers with medicinal whiskey for the Revolutionary War? Rebels took arms against the government in what was known as the Whiskey Rebellion. Washington retaliated, federalizing troops against the distillers. This conflict lasted until 1794, and many moved to Kentucky seeking to avoid it. While this may be true, there were five hundred stills set up in Kentucky when it became a state, indicating that the Whiskey Rebellion likely had a nominal impact on the state's distilling industry. But many distilleries claim their Kentucky roots begin with the Whiskey Rebellion.

According to his descendants, Scottish-born Robert Samuels was one of those distillers. In the 1780s, Samuels found a slice of whiskey-making heaven in Kentucky, where his bloodline continues to run a whiskey business now known as Maker's Mark. The first Samuels received a land grant of four thousand acres in the small town of Deatsville, a quick horse ride to the larger Bardstown and a few hours from Louisville. He established a gristmill and later distilled corn. Jacob Beam, the first of the long line of Beams, also settled in Kentucky in 1795.

However distillers came to Kentucky, the state's natural resources kept them there. The water and grains were splendid for raising cattle and horses and making whiskey. The state's wheat, tobacco, and corn consistently ranked the highest in quality among the states, and this led some to believe that it was the Kentucky ingredients, not the people, that led to great bourbon. This point was prominently made in the 1880 annual report of the Kentucky Bureau of Agriculture:

> In the production of Indian corn, Kentucky has always stood the equal of any in acreage yield, and in its qualities superior to that of any other state, north or south or west of it. It has long borne the soubriquet of the Corncracker State and not without just grounds to the distinction. Its corn, as do its wheat and barley, and oats and grasses, partakes of the

elements of the soil upon which it is raised, and of the water that percolates through them. How conclusive of this fact is it, that Kentucky Bourbon whiskies in an open market and in the face of a free competition, are able to possess themselves of an exclusive market in the United States, Great Britain, France, and Germany. The whiskies made in no other States have or can come in competition with them, and because the corn of which they are made and the water used in their distillation lack the essential qualities and ingredients possessed by Kentucky corn and Kentucky water. Herein lies the reason of it. Kentucky distillers possess no art or skill or superior knowledge above other distillers.

Of course, many men and women distillers of past and present would sharply disagree with the agricultural department's assessment. Skill and talent go a long way toward good bourbon, but who was originally distilling these ingredients? Despite three major distillers—Beam, Hayden, and Samuels—settling into Kentucky during the first wave of migration, none of them are credited with inventing bourbon. "These pioneer distilleries were crude and cheap affairs and processes used in operating them were the most primitive," wrote John G. Mattingly in 1903, eighty years old at the time. Mattingly's grandfather, Leonard, was an early distiller who made whiskey and brandy. "From about the year 1820 up to 1845, a majority of the leading and well-to-do farmers of central Kentucky owned

ABOVE: To make bourbon, the spirit must enter a new charred oak container. The earliest known record of this charring technique specifically used for whiskey comes from 1826, when a Lexington grocer requested barrels with burnt insides. Legend offered a trumped-up story of how this technique came to be. The truth lies somewhere between legend and record.

OPPOSITE: Daniel Boone arrived in Kentucky in 1767 and carved out roads and established early Kentucky settlements. He's considered America's most important frontiersmen. His cousin, Wattle, was one of the men linked to early Kentucky whiskey. *Library of Congress*

and operated small distilleries and from every section of the state from one thousand to three thousand barrels of copper whiskey was annually either hauled in wagons or shipped to New Orleans by the flatboat merchants . . ."

If there was a true consensus among the distillers that there was indeed a bourbon inventor, Mattingly's grandfather, Leonard, would have known and John likely would have mentioned it.

After Mattingly died, the bourbon industry crowned Craig as bourbon's inventor and offered a backstory involving barrels damaged in a barn fire. According to former TV actor George McGee, who portrayed Craig in a one-man play in 1982, the legend goes like this:

> There was a small fire behind one of the mills where they were storing barrels. It burned some barrels and scorched the inside of some others, and the workmen went to Pastor Craig and said, "Some of the barrels are ruined. What do you want to do?" He seemed to have always been over-extending himself financially, and he told them not to throw them away, just to go ahead and put the corn whiskey inside and see what happened. And after awhile they discovered the color was different. And, of course, the taste was different. I think the Baptist term for that was it didn't taste good, but it was more mellow.

As I told Maureen Craig, this claim is too fantastic to be true, but the legend had to start somewhere. Who gave credence to this myth? An early mention of Craig inventing bourbon is in the February 13, 1934, *Louisville Courier-Journal*, in which the story attributes Collins's book: "The historian points out that the first bourbon whisky was made at the mill of the Rev. Elijah Craig, at Georgetown, in 1789 . . ." Mentions of Craig's bourbon invention increased in the 1960s, when the industry was campaigning to make bourbon a unique product of the United States. From 1958 to 1968, the Bourbon Institute executed a public-relations campaign using the Craig legend constantly, saying Craig invented bourbon on April 30, 1789, the same day President George Washington was sworn into office.

The legend was invented to promote the bourbon industry. Fortunately for the distillers, the Internet didn't exist in 1964 and they could get away with the fib.

It's true, though, that Craig's accomplishments were many, including owning a distillery and establishing the first school and paper mill in Kentucky. After his passing, Craig's great Baptist faith was discussed, but not his distilling prowess or bourbon invention. In the known records of 1800s-era distilling pioneers, there is no mention of Elijah Craig.

Nonetheless, Craig accomplished in legend what nobody has every truly done—he served as the bourbon father.

The 1800s were a bustling time of invention for distillation. This steam coiled mash tun patent is still used today.
Oscar Getz Museum of Whiskey History

Who Really Created Bourbon?

Finding the provenance of bourbon begins with a look at corn.

As settlers moved West to Kentucky, they were encouraged to plant corn, a versatile grain that could be used for flour, eaten whole, fed to animals, and provide hygienic secondary use. For the New World, corn equaled feeding a population. And Kentucky's soil "exceeded belief" for corn plantings, according to a 1792 *American Gazetteer* account. It was such a treasured foodstuff that King George II issued in *The Statutes at Large from the Magna Charta* (1765) "a discouragement of the distilling of spirits from corn." Great Britain wanted corn used for food and limited its distillation use under the American colonies and prohibited in Ireland.

Thus, as Kentucky became a state in 1792, corn was not a preferred grain for distillation. Whether through their restrictions or preference, Northeasterners distilled rye, and the earliest forms of American whiskey were rye, not corn based.

But whiskey's evolution into a Kentucky spirit that can reliably be identified as bourbon, and coming to an educated guess as to its creator, requires some examination of the time period from 1813 to 1818. This is the period corn distillation gains notoriety in the Northeast.

It was in 1813 that the Northeast preference for rye-based whiskeys had given way to spirits made predominately with corn. Expert distillers of the time were already considering corn to "have more spirit than any other grain," wrote Harrison Hall, a renowned Northeastern distiller, in 1813 in *Hall's Distiller*. If one were keeping up with Hall's distilling recommendations, they would distill a product of corn and rye. Hall wrote: "I have ever considered the union of rye and corn in mash, as productive of more spirit and of a purer quality, than can be obtained from either grain alone; and if the proportion of one fourth part of rye can be obtained, it is enough."

In fact, the New Jersey-based Hall promoted Tennessee and Kentucky whiskey to a population that had a bias toward Atlantic state spirits. Hall's adoption of corn in distilling in a rye-centric Northeast gave the western states more credence, and he flat out said that Kentucky and Tennessee distillers:

> . . . have already made considerable progress in the art of distillation and the vast quantities of grain which are produced by their fertile lands, beyond the necessary consumption, cannot be so well disposed of, in any way as in pork and whiskey. Hence we already find Tennessee and Kentucky whiskey in our sea ports, and it is generally preferred to that made nearer home; this by the way, is a powerful argument against the common prejudice against using corn, as the western whiskey is chiefly made of that grain. . . .

As advertisements in the major East Coast newspapers appear requesting copper-distilled whiskey and Kentucky whiskey, the Pennsylvania rye distillers certainly felt the market pressure. However, in Hall's writings he never uses the word *bourbon* to describe whiskey.

But his later works reference the production methods that are without a doubt bourbon-production techniques. In his 1818 book *The Distiller*, Hall notes a style of fermentation we would consider sour mash today:

> [T]he mode of mashing adopted in Tennessee and Kentucky . . . It is not uncommon in some of the distilleries in those states to use dirty casks, into which the requisite quantity of pot ale in a boiling state is thrown, corn meal is then added, and well stirred; in this state it is suffered to stand three, four or five days, when a small portion of rye meal and malt is added, and the whole is cooled off. No yeast is added, and the stuff is ready for the still in about four days more.

Hall advised against this technique for rye mashing and said he must do more experimentation, but there are numerous references in his work to burning the inside of casks with straw, indicating the distillers were using bourbon-production techniques. But Hall did not advise storing the corn-centric whiskey inside a charred cask.

The earliest known record of a charred oak barrel for storing bourbon is in 1826, when a Lexington grocer requests whiskey stored in "burnt" barrels. It's quite likely we'll never find an earlier reference to the charred oak. Distillers did not keep logs or journals, and recipes were passed down via handwritten notes in their family bibles. Thus, a scholarly identification of the true father of bourbon might be impossible. But it's not without reason or reach to name the most likely inventor of bourbon.

Although his is the most common name associated with bourbon, Craig wasn't the only name offered as its creator. Among others, the following people have been named inventor at one time or another, though newspaper clippings, family history, or oral history: Daniel Shawhan, Jacob Spears, Wattle Boone, Daniel Stewart, John Hamilton, Marsham Brashear, and John Ritchie. There were also many slave distillers and women making whiskey, but none have been documented as creating bourbon.

Jacob Spears's family moved to Kentucky in the late 1780s. According to an 1897 account, Jacob Spears's Bourbon County Distillery was known as the "famous Peacock Distillery" standing hillside near Kiserton, a former community along Stoner Creek, five miles north of Paris. The article titled "Oldest Distillery in Kentucky" credited Spears with bourbon's creation: "In this rude distillery was made the first bourbon whisky ever distilled—the product which was destined to make famous in the remotest parts of the earth the names of Bourbon and Kentucky." These 1800s-era newspaper accounts say Spears moved from Pennsylvania to Kentucky to avoid "bloodshed by the troops sent by President Washington during the Whiskey Rebellion," but this could not have been true, since tax records place him in Fayette County in November 1789.

There was also Jacob Spears in Lincoln County in 1790, but this Spears was married to an Abigail Huston in 1791 and passed away in 1818. Spears the noted distiller was married to Elizabeth Neely and died in 1825. That Spears, a Revolutionary war soldier, appears on the second census as a Bourbon County resident in 1800 and was credited as the first Bourbon County distiller in the "Statistics of Bourbon County" section of *History of Kentucky*: "Mr. Spears cut the timber into suitable sizes, distilled, went to the mill, and also attended a fine stallion he had brought." The book said he first set up the still around 1790.

FIRST PUBLISHED

The first mention of bourbon whiskey is in 1821 in the *Western Citizen Newspaper* with Stout and Adams advertising "bourbon whiskey by barrel or keg." This author searched through hundreds of pre-1821 newspapers to find an earlier reference. None were found.

Before the *History of Kentucky* was published, in an 1869 New Orleans *The Times-Picayune* article, Spears is linked to bourbon's history: "The first whiskey manufactured in Bourbon county was made by parties who emigrated from Pennsylvania about the year 1790. The first distillery was erected by Jacob Spears a short time afterwards."

Confusing matters, the other Jacob Spears's sister, Catherine Spears Frye Carpenter, wrote the first known sour mash recipe in the back of the family bible and dated it 1818. Could the past newspapers have been wrong? Did they mix up the Jacobs? It's doubtful. In all later references it's the Bourbon County Spears who is discussed as bourbon's creator.

After Prohibition, during a 1935 Congressional hearing over the regulation of food, drugs, and cosmetics, Congressman Virgil Chapman, a Kentucky Democrat, said when relating to the origins of American whiskey, "I do know that as an accurate, historical fact, in the year 1790, 2 years before Kentucky was admitted to statehood, a man by the name of Jacob Spears, in Bourbon County, Kentucky, where I reside now, made straight Bourbon whisky, and because it was made in Bourbon county, that type of whisky, Wherever made in the world, has been called Bourbon whisky ever since."

Chapman's commentary is the first time a congressman mentions a bourbon creator. Chapman offered a statement of "historical fact"—but since when do we trust congressmen for facts? The Jacob Spears trail soon goes cold and there's little additional effort to revive his name or look into his history.

Daniel Shawhan was born in Kent County, Maryland, in 1731 and was a part of the distilling culture in the area. After serving in the Revolutionary War, his rye whiskey was noted for its quality. In 1788, the Shawhans left Maryland and settled in what is now known as Bourbon County, Kentucky. His family claims that he set up a still and began distilling corn. Shawhan passed away in 1791, one year before Kentucky became a state, but he passed on the distillery to his son, George, whose distillery was cited for owing the government money in 1794. Daniel's grandson (and George's son) George Shawhan became a well-known distiller and an important figure overall. After serving as a confederate in the Civil War, George Shawhan

Given all the facts we have, Jacob Spears is bourbon's most probable creator. His descendants say he is the one who at least came up with the name *bourbon*, after Bourbon County, which is supported in Abraham Spears's obituary from the 1860s. Pictured is Jacob Spears's grandson, Jacob. *Catesby Simpson*

OPPOSITE: Jacob Beam settled in Kentucky in 1795, and his wife, Mary Meyers, received inheritance to start what would become the Beam legacy. The Jim Beam brand rose to the top of bourbon sales in 1970 and hasn't looked back.

There's a strong connection between President Abraham Lincoln and Kentucky bourbon. Lincoln's father, Thomas, worked for a known Kentucky distiller.

left Kentucky in 1872 for Missouri. In fact, it is a Missouri history that brings the Shawhan name into the conversation as an inventor of bourbon. According to the *History of Jackson County, Missouri*, published in 1881, Daniel Shawhan built the first still and manufactured the first whiskey in Bourbon County. The Shawhan name also appears in the 1875 *San Francisco Chronicle* newspaper story as the bourbon creator.

But since it's clear that Daniel Shawhan did not move to Kentucky until 1788, Shawhan would have been nearly a half decade behind the other distillers in the area. It's highly unlikely that a Maryland rye whiskey distiller would have moved to Kentucky and immediately started distilling corn, when rye was available, and simultaneously had the idea of maturing in a charred barrel. It's also suspect that the strongest piece of historical evidence comes from Missouri and not Kentucky. It's more likely that the story derived from George Shawhan's wish to preserve his grandfather's distilling legacy in order to bolster his own distilling prowess.

The 1794 government record opens the door of possibility that indeed the Shawhans owned a distillery. But other than family legend, there's nothing to indicate that they distilled corn and used charred barrels.

Wattle Boone, also identified as as William, Wattie, and Waddie Boone, was a cousin of Daniel Boone, and was likely proposed as bourbon's inventor because of his employee—Thomas Lincoln, the father of President Abraham Lincoln. The future president's father worked for Boone, who resurrected a distillery in Nelson County, at the intersection of Pottinger's Creek and Knob Creek. According to the Lincoln papers held at the Library of Congress, Boone was said to have built the first Kentucky distillery in 1780, but other published accounts have said the distillery was built around 1770.

Boone's distilling prowess is murky. His descendants believe that it was Wattle's father, Walter, who actually set up the distillery. In fact, Wattle's distillery seems to take a backseat to the fact the father of a future president worked for him and that he was a related to the famous Daniel Boone. Case in point, according to an 1897 *Louisville Courier-Journal* story: "Thomas Lincoln was engaged by Wm. Boone, a distiller, as mash hand, which was then in operation upon nearly the exact spot where the big Atherton distilleries now are. . . ." By the time of this story's publication, both bourbon's and Abraham Lincoln's legendary statuses were well known. It stands to reason that if Boone were the first distiller or the inventor of bourbon, newspapers would want to publish this fact.

Daniel Stewart operated a distillery in Fayette County, Kentucky, in an area known as Madison Station. He is credited with one of the earliest Kentucky still advertisements. Published in June 1789, Stewart advertised "a copper still of 120 gallons capacity, with a good copper and pewter worm." Two hundred years later, the US Alcohol, Tobacco, and Firearms agency circulated a memo naming Stewart as one of bourbon's possible inventors. National Distillers also advertised Stewart's bourbon distilling roots in a 1950s campaign called "400 Miles Westward They Brought Their Old-World Skills—and Bourbon was Born in Kentucky." But Stewart's strongest argument comes from the fact he sold a still, not that he distilled with it. In *The Social History of Bourbon*, author Gerald Carson theorized Stewart might have used the still in 1788 to 1789. Perhaps. He was in the right place at the right time. Unfortunately, Stewart's distilling legacy doesn't carry on to future generations in Fayette County, so his true contributions remain a mystery.

John Hamilton has several significant mentions of either inventing bourbon or at least being a contender, such as the 1939 *Sesquicentennial: A Record of the One Hundred and Fiftieth Anniversary of the Founding of Bourbon's County Seat* and a 1957 *Kentuckian-Citizen* article: "Captain John Hamilton, who ran away from Pennsylvania on account of his participation in the whiskey insurrection, distilled in Bourbon before Spears. . . ." Hamilton is mentioned in the same National Distillers advertisement as Stewart, as well. But the best piece of evidence comes from court records. In 1799, George Culp sued John's brother, Daniel. Culp was to pay Hamilton in whiskey for bear and deer skins. According to the lawsuit, John Hamilton of Bourbon County, Kentucky, was to validate the whiskey. Culp paid, but did not receive the skins. There are also two property transactions by a John Hamilton from 1790 to 1794 in Bourbon County. One was three hundred acres on Main Slate Creek, a part of the two-thousand-acre tract owned by Jacob Myars and John Golkg in July 1791; and the other was four hundred acres on the "waters of Coopers Run" in March 1793. In the *History of Kentucky*, the author states Hamilton lived to be one hundred, and people often said he was the first Bourbon County distiller.

John Hamilton was an extremely common name, and there were several John Hamiltons in the whiskey trade. For example, in Belfast, Ireland, a well-known whiskey salesman John Hamilton sold barrels of whiskey in the early 1790s. There were also John Hamiltons in Pennsylvania. According to an 1819 *Pittsburgh Weekly Gazette* report, John Hamilton's wagon was robbed and he posted a $100 reward for the captors. Even without a possible name confusion, word-of-mouth promotion of Hamilton's contributions was not strong enough to spark a bourbon connection in the 1800s.

Marsham Brashear, on a May 7, 1782 deed, purchased land from Benjamin Pope and James Patten with 165 gallons of whiskey. In *Kentucky Bourbon: The Early Years of Whiskeymaking*, author Henry Crowgey writes that this transaction suggests Brashear made the whiskey, and he has since been referenced as one of the first distillers. His family also moved to Kentucky from a major distilling region. The Brashears moved to America from France in 1658. They settled along the Monongahela River where Brownsville, Pennsylvania, is today. This was a hotbed area for rye whiskey.

The Brashears became iconic Kentuckians and have landmarks named after them in Bullitt County, Kentucky. If Marsham truly invented bourbon, there would likely have been a greater awareness and mention of it in the evidence of the time. The Brashears were arguably more important and legendary than Elijah Craig.

John Ritchie was one of the earliest people connected to inventing bourbon. Ritchie is in the first federal census as a Nelson County resident in 1792. Born in Scotland in 1752, he died in Nelson County in 1812. The venerable Dr. M. F. Coomes, a historian for the Filson Club, wrote in 1895 that Ritchie's distillery in Nelson Country was where the first of "Kentucky's famous red liquor" was created. Subsequent papers described Ritchie's distillery as a little still house eighteen square feet with puncheon floor. "The old furnace on which stood the copper worm still stands, the only monument to Ritchie's memory," R. E. Hughes and

BOURBON, THE NAME

From the 1600s to 1800s, not many names had more worldwide awareness than "Bourbon," usually tied to the powerful ruling family that simply became known as the House of Bourbon. The House of Bourbon begins its power reign in the 1200s, when Robert, Count of Clermont, sixth son of King Louis IX of France, married Beatrice of Burgundy, heiress to the lordship of Bourbon. Their son, Louis, became Duke of Bourbon in 1327 and his line led to Bourbon-Vendôme, a branch that became the ruling house of first Navarre (1555) and then of France (1589), under Henry de Bourbon. Bourbons ruled France until 1792 and again in 1830, but their name had far greater meaning than just a family crest. Bourbon Street in New Orleans and multiple counties, including Kentucky's, in the New World were named after them. Products were also named after the family, commanding greater prices and known for superior quality. Bourbon coffee, Bourbon sugar, and Bourbon cotton were considered the best in their respective categories, with traders advertising this fact in newspapers. Whoever decided to name this whiskey *Bourbon* almost certainly did so knowing that there would be immediate name recognition.

Some people theorize that the whiskey was named after Bourbon County, while others think the namesake was Bourbon Street in New Orleans, but Richard Campanella, author of *Bourbon Street*, says the connection between the street and the whiskey is purely coincidence. He writes:

> Then there is the name: that America's most famous locale for libations shares a sobriquet with America's most famous distilled spirit was pure serendipity. Bourbon the street and Bourbon the whiskey do, however, have a common origin: both salute the royal House of Bourbon, the former in the 1720s and the latter in the 1780s, when a county in Kentucky was so named to honor King Louis XVI's aid to the American Revolution. That region would later specialize in the distilling of a fine American whiskey and lend its name to it. It would also send a steady stream of flatboats and steamboats loaded with whiskey and other commodities down the Ohio and Mississippi to New Orleans in the nineteenth century, and it's fair to say that Bourbon whiskey has been flowing on Bourbon Street for the better part of two centuries. The coincidence by no means explains the latter's fame, but it certainly didn't inhibit it.

C. C. Ousley wrote in the 1901 Louisville and Nashville Railroad magazine *Kentucky the Beautiful*. The house still stands, with the marking "J.R. 1780" on a rock in the chimney. Family historians say Ritchie loaded flatboats and sent them to New Orleans in 1780, and his descendants still believe Ritchie created the first barrels of bourbon, based largely on the Filson Club essay in the 1890s.

Evan Williams built his small distillery on Louisville's Fifth Street near the Ohio River, but he "claimed the right to sell his product without license" and was indicted by a grand jury for this offense. Williams's infamous reputation doesn't stop there. His neighbors frequently complained about the distillery's smell, and it was eventually declared a nuisance to Louisville. But Williams is never considered the inventor of bourbon, and it is difficult tracing his roots, as there are two men named Evan Williams in Louisville at the same time. Williams the distiller was an early board member of the Louisville trustees. According to an early account of Williams, he attended every board meeting with a jug of his whiskey. All the members drank the whiskey before the meeting was adjourned, but it's never referenced as bourbon.

Vague cases have also been made for men named William Calk, Henry Hudson Wathen, Jacob Meyers, and Jacob Forman.

Bourbon historian Michael R. Veach has also made the case for a pair of French brothers—John and Louis Tarascon—for introducing the charred-barrel technique into bourbon in the 1810s and for calling it corn brandy instead of whiskey. While this is plausible, corn brandy was also a term used in Iceland, Sweden, and Norway for a popular rectified spirit made of corn.

From a scholarly approach, archeological digs near the homes of all these alleged inventors would help. Somebody had to have come up with the idea of charring barrels. There is evidence, too, that there's truth to the legends. According to an April 29, 1900, *Louisville Dispatch* article: "There are men now living and actively in business who have seen the manufacture of whisky in this state developed from an incident in farming to one, if not the greatest, industry in Kentucky." This article is published more than thirty years before Elijah Craig's name is connected to inventing bourbon and more than fifty years before the barn fire legend is born. Perhaps the legend of a farm accident was true; we've just had the legend wrong. Perhaps the staves were accidentally burned and used in the construction of the barrel, which coincidentally yielded a premium whiskey. Of course, this conjecture leads to the legends of Elijah Craig and his barn fire. Given the fact that European coopers were charring the inside of barrels for brandy, it's most likely Veach's theory is correct—that somebody brought this technique to the New World. Some 1700s-era American coopers also discussed using flame to clean barrels from past contents, such as fish heads, but they did not purposely char them to intentionally add flavor for whiskey. In the court of conversation, it's plausible that the accident was not from the trumped-up barn fire, but from a distiller mistakenly filling a charred barrel to transport down the river.

The question of *how* could also start with *who*. I place a lot of stock into the 1800s-era accounts that name Spears, Shawhan, and Ritchie, because they were distilling at the right time. Shawhan was in Bourbon County and Ritchie in Nelson County. But if we take Collins's book as fact, we'd have to dismiss both men because they were not distilling in Georgetown, which was a part of Fayette County from 1780 to 1789. Georgetown became the Scott County seat in 1792. Since tax records list Spears as a resident of Fayette County in 1789, the year bourbon was allegedly first created, it places one of the most-commonly referenced inventors inside county lines at the time of bourbon's creation. But since Spears moved to Bourbon County and started distilling there in 1790, his Fayette County contributions, perhaps, were never discussed. Furthermore, Kentucky is a very territorial state; people place great pride in their counties, and it's likely the Scott County founders wouldn't want to credit a distiller who left their district.

The key facts for me suggest Spears as the true father of bourbon: the 1860s newspaper articles, Collins's *History of Kentucky* naming him the first Bourbon County distiller, the 1789 tax record linking him to Fayette County, and Congressman Virgil Chapman speaking under oath that Spears invented bourbon. Of all these, I find the Chapman oration the most interesting. What does Chapman have to gain by speaking of Spears? He was not known for spinning fantastic tales and stated Spears's bourbon creation was a historical fact. That means Congressman Chapman, a Bourbon County resident, would have heard about Spears in coffee shops, at church, or wherever the community gathered. This word-of-mouth history cannot be dismissed. His testimony also offers a glimpse into Kentucky politics: Chapman was trying to stake Bourbon County's claim on bourbon's creation. The heck with Scott or Fayette County!

For unknown reasons, Spears's claim as the father of bourbon was dropped. It's possible that many people came to the conclusion that a charred barrel made great whiskey, or that the distillers of the time just didn't think the process was important enough to write down; thus, their children and grandkids and or neighbors came to their own conclusions on who invented bourbon, leading hearsay to become fact.

Spears's claim also could not overcome a sexy legend. For some the Elijah Craig legend, likely born in an advertising meeting room, was too good to pass up.

Even if Spears was not the first bourbon distiller, he was most certainly one of Kentucky's first and most important. He was among the early Kentuckians who loaded his whiskey onto flatboats and floated to New Orleans, where bourbon's marketing power begins with the stroke of a pen—when President Thomas Jefferson signed the Louisiana Purchase.

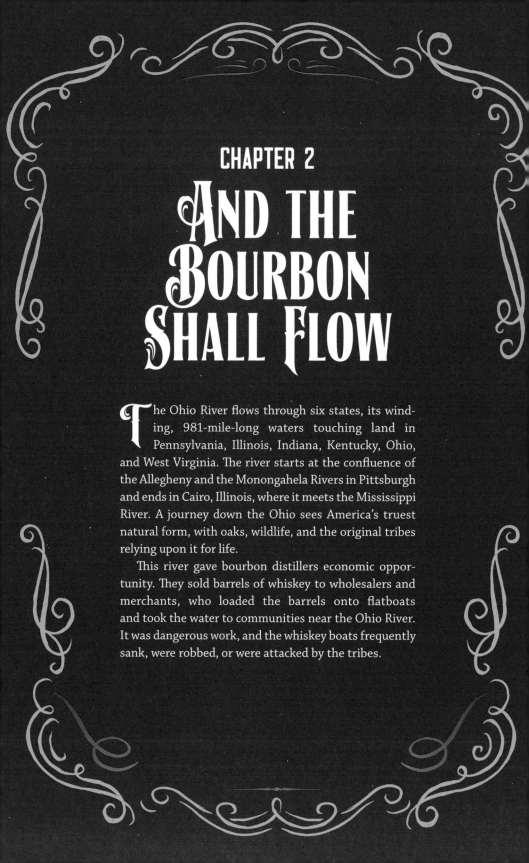

CHAPTER 2

AND THE BOURBON SHALL FLOW

The Ohio River flows through six states, its winding, 981-mile-long waters touching land in Pennsylvania, Illinois, Indiana, Kentucky, Ohio, and West Virginia. The river starts at the confluence of the Allegheny and the Monongahela Rivers in Pittsburgh and ends in Cairo, Illinois, where it meets the Mississippi River. A journey down the Ohio sees America's truest natural form, with oaks, wildlife, and the original tribes relying upon it for life.

This river gave bourbon distillers economic opportunity. They sold barrels of whiskey to wholesalers and merchants, who loaded the barrels onto flatboats and took the water to communities near the Ohio River. It was dangerous work, and the whiskey boats frequently sank, were robbed, or were attacked by the tribes.

Early accounts of whiskey transport along the Ohio River often carried stories similar to this:

> As a Mr. Pryer was descending the Ohio River with a boat load of whiskey, he was so unfortunate as to get his boat sunk in a violent storm on the 28th near Wilkinsonville. When he had by his exertions regained some barrels of his whiskey, there came 15 Mohawk Indians . . . in canoes, who abused Mr. Pryer, and took 12 barrels of his whiskey, put it in their canoes and descended the river.

This particular event in the early 1800s led to the eventual deaths of the four Mohawks and was one of many skirmishes between whites and natives over barrels of whiskey. Add these attacks to scurvy, wild animals, and the unknown, and early bourbon whiskey salesmen and distillers faced a dangerous world that required whiskey. Lots of whiskey. When President Thomas Jefferson repealed the whiskey tax that caused a mini rebellion, he did so with America's health in mind. Jefferson, who did not personally care for whiskey, was against the whiskey tax that caused the rebel uprising and considered it a prohibition on the "middling class of our citizens and a condemnation of them to the poison of whiskey . . ." The proponents of the whiskey tax said it was merely a tax on the rich, and they were not happy when Jefferson repealed it in July 1802. The *Newport Mercury* reported in 1802:

> The lords of the ancient dominion, and all the aristocrats who follow in the train of Virginia, now ride in their coaches without being taxed for this luxury—there are no longer any taxes on making whiskey, and the Virginians, and the Virginia Colonists [the Tennessee and Kentucky men] now enjoy the luxury of getting drunk for a few cents. This first year of Jefferson's Republic, the Virginians call the first year of liberty: It may seem to be a reign of liberty in the great state of Virginia, but it certainly is not for the New England a reign of equality.

The newspaper said the repeal of the whiskey tax took away from the true necessities of life, namely tea, sugar, and coffee. The rich drank whiskey, the poor relied upon tea and coffee: "that in Virginia 'tis the fashion for men to employ hours of leisure in horse-racing, card-playing and drinking whiskey—here [in Rhode Island] they tarry at home in the evenings, observing our good old fashion of drinking tea with their families." Those who opposed the whiskey tax's repeal seemed to think the government encouraged whiskey drinking over the more refined tea drinking, that teas still paid prewar duties, and that the new country's whiskey policy really only served Virginia.

The whiskey tax repeal naysayers said, "It is a fact, that there is more whiskey drank in Tennessee, or in Kentucky, than in all New England. It is a fact there

INDIANS AND WHISKEY

There are multiple accounts of whiskey traders making unscrupulous deals with tribes. Unsavory whiskey traders were the first white men many tribes met. These white men would often make one-sided deals or steal from the natives, and the Indians retaliated on all pioneers, thinking all white men were alike. "The whiskey traffic is a great drawback to the welfare of Indians," US Indian agent A. D. Balcombe said in 1863.

Early on, the US government forbade traders from selling whiskey to the tribes, but to no avail. By the late 1800s, whiskey had taken an unfortunate toll on the tribes, leading one chief to say: "Fire water can only be distilled from the hearts of wild cats and the tongues of women, it makes my people at once so fierce and so foolish."

is more public income, derived from the duties paid on brown sugars, imported into Newport and Providence, than what the National Treasury receives from the states of Kentucky and Tennessee. Indeed it may be said Kentucky and Tennessee contribute nothing towards maintenance of the national government."

While this statement of Kentucky whiskey's contribution to the nation was accurate in 1802, President Jefferson was planning another move that would not only bolster the country's economy but also give lifeblood to bourbon distillers.

Louisiana Purchase

The Louisiana Territory ranged from the west of the Mississippi River to the Rocky Mountains and from the Gulf of Mexico to Canada. The land encompassed 828,000 square miles and would double America's size. But the real value of the Louisiana Territory was a single city—New Orleans, an integral port to the New World. Whoever controlled New Orleans dictated South America, area islands, and even some European goods.

Spain had controlled New Orleans since 1762, and in 1795 signed the Pinckney treaty that allowed the new United States to safely navigate the Mississippi and to transfer goods through New Orleans. But the cost of controlling New Orleans was just too much, and in 1800 France acquired Louisiana from Spain and took possession two years later. President Jefferson was concerned about the more powerful French holding New Orleans, saying, "There is on the globe one single spot, the possessor of which is our natural and habitual enemy. It is New Orleans." James Monroe and Robert Livingston negotiated with Napoleon Bonaparte, offering $10 million for New Orleans and West Florida. Jefferson was prepared to create an alliance with England for military action, but instead Monroe and Livingston bought the entire Louisiana Territory from France for $15 million in August 1803.

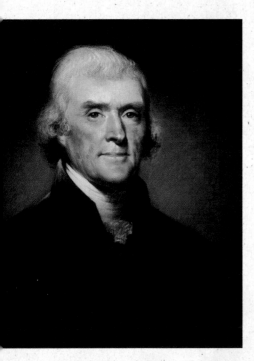

One could make the case for President Thomas Jefferson being the greatest whiskey president of all time. He repealed the whiskey tax and signed the Louisiana Purchase that opened the markets for bourbon makers. *Library of Congress.*

Now, Kentucky, Maryland, Ohio, Pennsylvania, and Virginia flatboats and eventually steamboats carrying whiskey could freely enter the New Orleans ports to sell barrels to Louisiana merchants such as Wallace & Pope, a New Orleans retailer that is frequently listed in the early 1800s *Price Current* as a purchaser of barrels of whiskey. They would also sell to other ships carrying goods to destinations all over the world. Whether these ships were planning to give whiskey to their crew for merriment or medicinal purposes, or were instead planning to sell to the blending houses of London or Belfast, is unknown. But early New Orleans ship records indicate that ships leaving for Europe frequently contained barrels of whiskey.

In fact, whiskey was one of New Orleans's most prized commodities. According to newspaper accounts from the early 1800s to 1831, whiskey traded with other spirits along with cattle, cotton, tea, and sugar as important goods. During this time, the wholesalers differentiated gins, brandies, or rums based on type, advertising the spirit's geography or production style to give consumers better purchasing information. Gin was specified as Holland gin; rum was either from Jamaica or New England. They did not classify whiskey based on country, grains, or style. However, whiskey was cheaper than most other spirits in New Orleans, perhaps signaling that consumers preferred gin and rum. Whiskey was a mere 24 cents per gallon in 1825, while New England rum was 38 cents per gallon and Jamaican rum 90 cents per gallon. The bulk was coming from Kentucky and Ohio—specifically Maysville, Kentucky; Louisville; and Cincinnati. In one week in 1825, the port analysts at a major newspaper wrote, "The only transaction [of whiskey] during the week was a sale of 50 bbls. [barrels] on order at 24 cents. This article continues very heavy, owing to a stock on hand from 9,000 to 10,000 barrels if not more. We cannot expect any improvement on this article for some time . . ." Whiskey interests began to increase a few years after this proclamation.

FAST FACT

A total of 250,000 gallons of whiskey entered New Orleans in 1817.

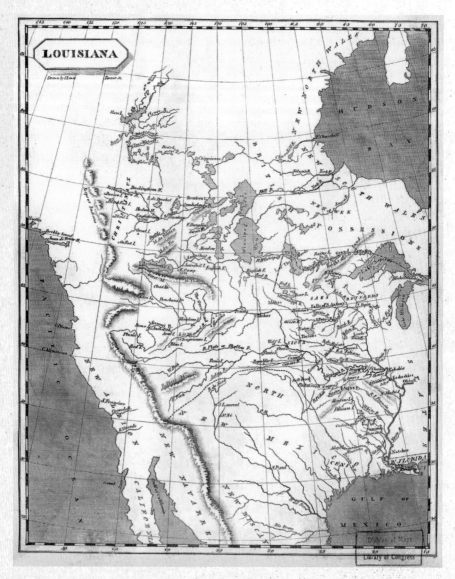

Louisiana was a territory unlike any other of the New World. But its most valuable asset was its port city—New Orleans. *Library of Congress.*

There is direct correlation between price increases and a greater number of whiskey-laden boats arriving from Kentucky. In 1829, whiskey prices passed those of Jamaican rum, which had dropped significantly, and were neck and neck with gin at near 30 cents per gallon. By 1830, New Orleans's whiskey demand was extremely high and the city actually experienced the occasional shortage. "The stock is light, the receipts small, and the article continues to improve," the analysts for the *New Orleans Commercial Intelligencer* wrote in 1830. "Sales of copper distilled barrels were made on the wharf in the early part of the week at 30 cents [per gallon] and more recently at 31 cents."

Whatever whiskey didn't stay in the city moved on to wherever the ship captain landed next. Recreational drinking and medicinal usage led the demand for whiskey from early American distillers.

Of Corn, Medicine, and Taxes

Distilled spirit was an essential part of living. If you had any malady, the common domestic medicine was whiskey.

After finding a rattlesnake-bitten man unconscious, former congressman William Maryant said he gave the man a glass of whiskey with a spoonful of powdered red pepper and poured it down his throat.

> In a few minutes, it was puked up, as were also three or four more doses. After the fourth glass, it remained on his stomach. His pulse improved greatly in a short time, and after getting five or six glasses to remain, I ceased giving him any more, until the pulse fell very fast, and nearly ceased beating. I again commenced giving him the whiskey and pepper, and soon discovered that on the ceasing the stimulants, his pulse would again sink to nothing. After taking more than one quart of this liquor, a copious stool followed; the spirit was again administered, until his pulse became steady. During the night, he took three quarts of whiskey; in the morning he was much better, but very week [*sic*]—he finally recovered.

If you faced death, your caregiver's job was to open your mouth and pour quart after quart down your throat. If you lived, it was because whiskey saved the day. If you died, it was because your caregiver needed better whiskey. This was the belief of most households in the 1820s and 1830s. Businessmen capitalized on this medicinal demand, as well as on the market that offered promising clients in brothels and taverns alike.

After Jefferson repealed the whiskey tax, whiskey-related business drastically increased. Distillers did not feel the need to hide from the taxman, and businesses that serviced distillers came out of the woodwork.

TARGETING DISTILLERS

Based on the political outcry after the whiskey tax repeal, distillers were seen as an affluent target for inventors. The owner of the J. Old's Patent Bark Mill made bold claims about his mill, saying it would crack the corn just right and grind the cob for excellent food. But he was especially proud of one fact: "I have already sold several to distillers and considerable farmers in West Tennessee and Kentucky."

The early distillers and whiskey salesman transported barrels on large flatboats like this. *Library of Congress*

Henry Watters and John Hogg advertised in the *North Carolina Journal* a new still design, recently patented under the United States government for "the distilling of spirits upon a new principle and an improved plum of stills by means of a condensing tub." The salesmen claimed that adding the condensing tub on a fifty-four-gallon still could yield fifty to fifty-four gallons of spirits per day—over 1,500 gallons if employed three hundred working days—selling the fact it offered still longevity. The condensing tub was invented and patented by H. Witmer of Lancaster, Pennsylvania, a renowned distilling area. In 1803, Kentucky's Samuel Brown received a patent for using steam in wooden and other stills. In 1810, New York's Phares Bernard received a patent for steam stills, the first to be introduced into the United States. Hall suggests early distillers were also experimenting with spirit filtration:

> As my whiskey could not be made worse, I determined to take this opportunity of making an experiment, and according threw into the still, a quantity of each, agreeably to my expectation, produced a spirit free from the empyreumatic flavor, thought not perfectly pure. I have repeated the experiment since, and am now convinced that a perfectly pure spirit may be obtained by distillation of any whiskey, however impure, with fresh coal; and that charcoal not good enough for filtration may yet be used with advantage in the above mentioned manner.

Active distillers were always looking to improve upon procedures.

By the 1820s, bourbon whiskey became a known commodity, but was also referred to as *copper distilled* or *Kentucky whiskey*. Just as whiskey began to receive recognition, the temperance minds began picking apart whiskey's effects on society: "You are creating and sending out the materials of discord, crime, poverty, disease, and intellectual and moral degradation. You are contributing to perpetuate one of the sourest scourges of our world," according to a *Carlisle Herald* editorial in October 1830. Around the same time, dairy farmers were also questioning the business of distillers. The Milkmen's Benevolent Society members once fed their cows still slop—the leftover grains from distillation—but now the temperance milkers believed if they stopped buying still slop, the distillers would go away and so would the "wretchedness" of whiskey.

Even while temperance groups increased in numbers and pursued the end of whiskey, bourbon was increasing in popularity and its distillers were becoming legendary. People fell in love with the sweetness, the rich caramel and vanilla flavors

FLATBOAT ARRIVALS

On any given day in the early 1800s, more than a dozen flatboats arrived in New Orleans. Flatboats typically carried whiskey and other freight, while the steamboats carried large groups of people or livestock. According to the archives of the *New Orleans Price Current*, these flatboats all arrived in October 1825:

Three flatboats of Mr. Buckner, from Louisville, Kentucky, with 1,300 barrels of flour, to W. and J. Montgomery.

Flatboat of Mr. Burnett, also from Louisville, with five hundred barrels of flour to Thomas F. Townsley, S. W. Polk, and Charles Byne and two castings to Gordon & Forestall.

Two flatboats of Seth Cutter, from Cincinnati, with 742 barrels of flour.

Flatboat of Mr. Turner, from Louisville, with 220 barrels of flour and 300 kegs of lard.

Flatboat of Mr. Coarse, from Louisville, with 188 barrels of flour and 140 barrels of whiskey, to Charles Byrne and M. F. Maher & Co.

Flatboat of Mr. Kean, from Cincinnati, with 130 barrels of flour and 30 barrels of whiskey, to M. F. Maher & Co.

Two flatboats from Missouri with six hundred barrels of corn and flour and forty-five kegs of butter to Mr. Carey, plus eight barrels of whiskey.

Flatboat from Kentucky with four hundred barrels of stone coal.

they cannot quite describe, and constantly mentioned its pureness and quality. But the common whiskey of the day was rectified whiskey—spirit that was adulterated after distillation.

Distillers sold barrels to the wholesaler or so-called rectifier, who might add prune juice, water, or tobacco spit to add color and volume to the barrel, thereby allowing them to make more money per barrel. It also created a side business for assayers who tested bourbon for purity. In the 1850s, John. H. Cutter, of Louisville, encouraged consumers to send his whiskey to the state assayer office, and he published the comments from agents. "Dear Sir:—I have made a chemical analysis of the same of 'Old Bourbon Whiskey' you brought me, made by John H. Cutter, of Louisville, Ky., and find that it is free from all poisonous matters, and has 49 percent of absolute alcohol in it—and about 4 ounces of saccharine matter to the gallon. It is a pure and unadulterated liquor, and is suitable for medicinal use," attested Massachusetts's state assayer Dr. Charles T. Jackson.

Such pure accolades not only built bourbon's acclaim, but also grew individual brands. Consumers trusted bourbon as a whiskey type and became familiar with particular brands. In the 1840s newspapers advertised bourbon available at a local merchant as Old Bourbon Whiskey, but gradually bourbon became so commonplace that the merchants separated their offerings from others. For example, Louisville merchant James Cromey advertised Old Bourbon "2 to 6 years old" for sale, offering a unique age differentiation from his competitors. In the 1840s, Cromey's competition, Walker's, advertised his barrels' vintage, such as 1833 or 1834. Merchants would publicize the whiskey as *superior, old, and pure*, always trying to get the competitive edge.

The most powerful promoter of whiskey, though, was Crow. Not the bird, but James C. Crow, whose distilling procedures revolutionized the industry. Crow added thermometers and saccharometers, cleanliness standards, and the industrialized methods of sour mashing, and he made sure all his whiskey was aged in charred oak. While all these methods likely occurred elsewhere, Crow put them all together and made them standard operating procedure for Kentucky distilleries. It made his whiskey widely revered.

In an 1857 *Courier Journal* article about a fire destroying much of the city, John Raine, of the Galt House, lost 230 barrels of whiskey, some of which was "genuine Crow whiskey, 12 years old, for which he had frequently been offered five dollars per gallon." To put this in perspective, regular whiskey sold for 28 cents per gallon in New Orleans in 1857. If Raine's claim was true, it was selling for the equivalent of $15,000 a gallon in 2016 money, according to the historical value of the dollar. So revered and respected was this spirit that it was known as Crow whiskey rather than simply bourbon. Because Crow helped industrialize the bourbon distilling business, and his name and brand of whiskey meant so much, the spirit called bourbon could well have been named after Crow instead.

MASTER DISTILLER

The term *master distiller* is used a lot these days, but it actually goes as far back as the 1790s in Ireland, where respected distillers were called such and were deserving of the title. In the early United States, master distiller was not a common term. It was reserved for only the very best of the trade, and you don't see it used unless distilleries are trying to separate themselves in the marketplace. Today, the term is loosely used and the modern duties include public speaking, media appearances, and bourbon pairings.

The title *master distiller* has drastically evolved. Although it was used in the 1700s and 1800s, the term really comes to life in the 1900s when distillers were referred to as *master yeast makers and distillers*. They were usually also the owners of the brands. Today, many master distillers must also conduct media and marketing initiatives. Pictured: former Four Roses master distiller Jim Rutledge.

In fact, many merchants did not even mention bourbon when advertising. When promoting his right to sell "Old Crow Whiskey," Charleston's F. W. Wagener & Co. advertised in all caps: "IT IS THE BEST WHISKEY MADE." His ad did not mention "bourbon." Old Crow also received twenty-first-century-style press.

In the mid-1800s, culturist authors would occasionally travel America and detail our alcohol consumption habits, usually saying how brash we were with our drinking, but no newspaper covered alcohol as a lifestyle topic. Except for Old Crow. "This brand of whiskey has a reputation second to none in the world, but it has become so scarce," the *Lexington Gazette* wrote.

Other significant bourbon brands would be sold and sought after in the 1800s, notably Waterfill & Frazier, E. H. Taylor Jr., Oscar Pepper, James E. Pepper, A. Keller's, Davis, Chicken Cock, Silver Creek, and Woodcock. Many were close in quality to Old Crow, but they were always branded bourbon first. There was also the issue of bourbon not always being bourbon.

No matter how well Old Crow or Chicken Cock branded themselves or how much people fell in love with their whiskey, a rectifier could take that whiskey and add whatever they wanted, and neither the quality nor medicinal efficacy could be controlled nationwide.

In 1869, the Japanese were tired of receiving rectified whiskey sold as "straight whiskey"—a common term that today means the whiskey must be at least two years old. At that time, *straight* was supposed to mean "neat whiskey," meaning that nothing was added to it and the whiskey wasn't stolen. But rectifiers marketed their adulterated products as "straight," which led to the Japanese government suing US companies over false advertising. Ohio Circuit Court judge Alphonso Taft, father of future President W. Howard Taft, ruled that a product containing neutral spirits could not be called straight whiskey. This ruling impacted only exports, but it was an important step against rectified whiskey.

EXPERIMENTATION

In addition to inventing stills, and creating barrel methods and mashing techniques, early 1800s-era distillers experimented constantly to figure out methods that worked for them. Distiller Harrison Hall wrote that in 1806 he made a batch of "still burnt whiskey." He happened to have charcoal nearby, but it was not of high enough quality to use for filtering.

Straight whiskey was such a valuable label that Kansas City rectifiers advertised their straight whiskey connections. The Pioneer Liquor House of Fort Scott, Kansas: "The only rectifiers south of Kansas City, the only house in the state owning and operating a distillery in Kentucky in connection with the trade in Kansas. Will sell straight bourbon whiskey from one to five years old in quantities to suit purchasers, either in bond at our distillery at Flemingsburg, Ky., or from our house in Fort Scott."

Rectifiers had the edge in the fight for the consumer, because there were no regulations prohibiting them from adding unsafe materials to create anything from apple brandy to whiskey. Because the term *straight* could also mean *rectified*, the liquor stores began to receive requests for "pure" whiskey. Thus, some storeowners went out of their way explaining their rectified products, advertising: "No rectified whiskey sold as a fine article, but all my best grades are purchased directly from distilleries, and warranted pure."

The rectifier wasn't the 1800s-era distiller's only problem. There was the continued temperance threat seeking a prohibition, fires that plagued the industry and its towns, and constant criminal activity surrounding the whiskey business. During the Civil War, the government imposed taxes on whiskey distillers for the first time since 1817. The Internal Revenue Service created two types of bonded warehouses. Class A bonded warehouses stored whiskey inside the warehouse connected to the distillery itself. A Class B bonded warehouse was designed as general storage of goods and was typically kept by a merchant. All bonded warehouses required an application to the tax collector of the district. The IRS on average collected about $12 million a year in liquor taxes, but multiple so-called whiskey rings formed throughout the country to evade paying taxes.

In 1867, when the whiskey tax was $2 per gallon, the *New York Times* accused the entire distillery industry of defrauding the government. Common sense

Pike's Magnolia Whiskey was made in Cincinnati and was so popular that it was frequently counterfeited. It was one of the more appreciated rectified whiskeys. *Chronicling America: Historic American Newspapers*

Continued on page 44

DOCTOR CROW

Born in 1789, James C. Crow moved to Kentucky sometime in the early 1820s. While there's no known record of Crow receiving a medical license in Scotland, 1800s-era texts refer to him as such and specify he was also a chemist. So, as a physician and chemist, Crow came to Kentucky and started working for Col. Willis Field's distillery in Millville, Kentucky. Obviously a talented distiller, Crow took his talents to Woodford County to work at the Oscar Pepper Distillery, which is now the Woodford Reserve Distillery site.

It was with Oscar Pepper that Crow built a legacy to last for centuries. Although texts credit him with inventing the sour mash technique, there are multiple references to earlier creations of that process, long before Crow moved to Kentucky. Despite not really being the inventor of the sour mash technique, he certainly caused bourbon-making to become more scientific.

For the first time, Kentucky distillers had an industrial protocol for making whiskey, largely created by Crow. The perfectionist doctor pursued quality over quantity, which worked in favor of a better product. He distilled a mere 2.5 gallons of whiskey per bushel, yielding whiskey that had drinkers thirsty for more Crow whiskey, and his methods caught the attention of other distilleries and kept many bourbon mashes from becoming bacterial breeding grounds.

Crow's whiskey was so famous that Joseph C. S. Blackburn used it as a bargaining chip during his 1875 campaign for the State House. Crow died in 1856, and Blackburn allegedly owned the final ten gallons of "genuine Crow whiskey." He decanted the whiskey and solicited his opponent's supporters for a drink.

> As you drink that, sir, I want you to remember that you are helping to destroy the most precious heirloom of my family. It is the last bit of genuine Crow whiskey in the world. Observe, sir, that you do not need to gulp down a tumbler of water after swallowing the liquor to keep it from burning your gullet. On the contrary, you know instinctively that to drink water with it would be a crime. All I ask of you is to remember that you are getting something in this liquor that all the money of an Indian prince cannot buy. Drink it, sir, and give your soul up to the Lord. Then if you can vote for Ed Marshall I cannot complain, because it will be the Lord's act!

After Crow's death, Gaines, Berry & Company (later known as W. A. Gaines & Co.) took Crow's methods and leftover stocks, and branded Old Crow. As a young marketer for Gaines, Berry & Company, E. H. Taylor seized an opportunity when a Pennsylvania judge pronounced his state's older rye whiskey better than Kentucky bourbon. A taste-off between matured rye whiskey and Old Crow ensued. Old Crow won, and Taylor sent out a press release: "After the evidence was all in and well digested, the judgment was rendered in favor of Kentucky's 'Old Crow' as being the most mellow, rich, full yet delicately flavored and surpassing in bouquet."

From this point on, Old Crow became the preferred liquor in the United States. It was in the White House, at social gatherings; poets loved it, Temperance women loathed it, and Prohibition bootleggers counterfeited it.

After Prohibition, National Distillers, the owners of Old Crow, took the whiskey to even greater heights. They introduced a chess decanter series in the 1960s, which became an iconic collector's item and set in motion a trend for ceramic decanters.

Old Crow also popularized the marketing of its master distiller. While bourbon has always had a love affair with the master distillers, Old Crow purchased full-page ads in publications like *Life* magazine to showcase George Donehoo, Old Crow's master distiller. One 1970 *Life* ad read: "He is the one man who knows all the secrets that give our country Bourbon its special character. The first scientific way of distilling bourbon was invented by Dr. James Crow back in 1835. But giving our bourbon a handcrafted taste is still an art . . ."

When Fortune Brands purchased National Distillers and, thus, the Old Crow brand, the Jim Beam parent company gutted the once-legendary bourbon. Once the whiskey presidents drank, Old Crow now sat on the bottom shelf and its best marketing feature was that it was a value brand.

But more than 150 years after Crow's death, his legacy continues to influence the industry he changed.

Old Crow was widely considered the best whiskey of the 1800s. It was the whiskey all others were compared to and sold at a premium. *Library of Congress*

Continued from page 41

suggested they might be right. After the Whiskey Tax Repeal, distillers only momentarily paid taxes during the War of 1812 to fund the war, after which they were free of federal tax until the Civil War. That's half a century of zero federal taxes. It's easy to see why some distillers would want to avoid taxes, but the *New York Times* suggested that distillers not only avoided taxes, but sold the whiskey to merchants as bonded—a trusted term. "It is the constant and well-known universal practice for storekeepers to receive and admit Western whiskey into bond without the knowledge of the [tax] collector ever have known it," the paper wrote.

The sentiment against distillers coincided with whiskey makers lobbying for reduced taxes. Starting in 1868, members of the House began preaching a whiskey tax reduction, arguing this would reduce such fraudulent activity and increase overall revenues for the country. "This whiskey tax has greatly demoralized the country; we have whiskey rings at the North, South, East, and West, but especially at Washington. The people connected with them are so accustomed to steal that they would do it if the tax were five cents a gallon. I am for throwing it off entirely," said R. S. Elliott, a member of the Union Merchant's Exchange, St. Louis, at the first National Board of Trade.

The tax-evading whiskey rings were a national crisis, as they jeopardized the government's ability to finance infrastructure. None were stronger than the distiller conspiracy that included St. Louis, Chicago, and Milwaukee companies in 1875. Agents carrying out raids discovered 1,200 barrels of illicit whiskey, ledgers, and office records for sixteen distilleries and rectifiers. As more evidence was found, it received national attention. The Treasury Department's supervisor for the area, John McDonald, received the full support of President Ulysses Grant, who said, "There is at least one honest man in St. Louis on whom we can rely—John

Women were frequently used in early American whiskey posters to attract men. Temperance leaders publicly criticized distillers for their connection to prostitution. *University of Louisville Libraries Archives and Special Collections*

McDonald. I know that because he is an intimate acquaintance and confidential friend of Babcock's." As it turned out, Orville Babcock, a former general and Grant's personal secretary, was accepting bribes from McDonald, who pioneered the whole whiskey ring scandal.

The government indicted 176 distillers, rectifiers, wholesalers, revenue supervisors, gaugers, storekeepers, collectors, and deputies. The prosecution charged that after McDonald was appointed to supervisor in 1869, he began formulating a plan to defraud the government. He began the whiskey ring in 1871, recruited C. G. Megrue from Cincinnati to be his point person, and began collecting money from distillers and distributing it to Ford, McKee, Joyce, Megrue, and the various party members. "It became necessary, after the organization of the ring, to include men of influence at Washington, who should become part of and parcel of the combination; that the ring might be properly notified of any contemplated raid by government detectives," the prosecution said at trial.

The trial became much less about the whiskey and the distillers, and more about the conspiracy that connected them and the political dealings inside. In fact, the trial learned that some of the defrauded funds were used to pay for Republican election campaigns, including Grant's, leaving many to make the same conclusion as the

During the Civil War, the North imposed a whiskey tax, while the South confiscated stills and prohibited production. Both used whiskey for medicinal purposes. *Library of Congress*

BOURBON EXPORTS

Bourbon whiskey was America's number-one alcoholic export in the 1800s. Distillers shipped to several ports in Germany, England, Central America, and Africa, where liquor dealers sold bourbon by the barrel. In 1888, bourbon whiskey withdrawals for export were nearly ten times that of rye whiskey. Distillers exported 1.2 million gallons of bourbon, with its number-one destination being Bremen, Germany.

Fair Play newspaper in Sainte Genevieve, Missouri: "The St. Louis Whiskey Ring, like all other frauds that have been discovered, is composed of Republicans."

The Great Whiskey Ring ended with President Grant pardoning McDonald and Babcock, and the scandal became a lot more about the conspiracy than the distilleries. But those major distilling areas—St. Louis, Chicago, and Milwaukee—became major brewery cities, and this was no accident. In response to the whiskey ring scandals, Chicago brewers formed a Chicago Brewers' Protective Association to advise the mayor of police corruption and connection to new whiskey rings. Brewers also used the whiskey ring history lesson in arguments for beer tax reductions.

But for the distillers, the whiskey ring was a black eye they could not escape and which made them vulnerable to attack when fighting for tax reform. Those who wanted to keep the whiskey tax unchanged were mostly temperance types who were circulating pamphlets suggesting that whiskey was only used for intoxication. The *Daily Milwaukee News* fired back at this assertion:

> It does not appear . . . that all the intoxicating liquors sold are used for the purpose of intoxication. An investigation would show that there is scarcely a man or woman in the United States who does not pay a portion of the whiskey tax. It is a tax which reaches the mechanic and the artisan, the chemist, and the serving girl, the common table and the sick chamber. But suppose all the whiskey manufactured to be consumed by the

When selling whiskey, merchants had to pay taxes and keep stamps visible to the naked eye. After distillers and Washington officials were caught in a multi-state whiskey ring evading taxes, the Internal Revenue agency heavily scrutinized all levels of the whiskey business.

intemperate. Why tax the poor man who drinks whiskey a larger proportion than the rich man who drinks high-priced wine?

The whiskey tax was raised 15 cents per gallon for all in-store sales and 30 cents on all manufactured product after the passage of an 1877 bill. Some chose to ignore this and sold without paying tax (crooked whiskey), creating a new enemy for bourbon distillers—the illicit whiskey salesmen. Leading into the 1880s, the likes of George Garvin Brown and E. H. Taylor faced government taxation that threatened to cut into profits, temperance leaders wanting to take away their right to sell whiskey, rectifiers adding all sorts of unwanted liquid to their so-called bourbon, and now, moonshiners who sold to people more cheaply than they could. Bourbon distillers knew they had to do something to survive. One of their first unification efforts was to stop making whiskey. They claimed to have been sitting on an overwhelming amount of whiskey. More production, as well as increased competition, led to fewer profits.

In 1887 and 1888, the Kentucky Distillers' Association members suspended operations due to overproduction. "We should state that this action on our part is taken solely for the purpose of doing what lies in our power to help the Kentucky distilling interest to bring the stock of Kentucky whiskies within its normal limits, and to repair the damages which have been caused by the great over-production in the past few years. We consider it the duty of all Kentucky distillers at this time to forget their personal interest, and consider the general welfare of the great industry in which they are engaged," W. A. Gaines & Co. wrote to the Kentucky Distillers' Association. "We have . . . determined to sacrifice our personal interests for the general good of the business."

The distillers came out of the shutdown with a boom on their hands. Everybody wanted bourbon, especially bonded bourbon. But new taxes and the temperance minds decreased the bourbon demand in the mid-1890s, leading to another

Continued on page 52

HOW TO IMITATE OLD BOURBON WHISKEY

There were many recipes for rectified bourbon whiskey. This one was simply called No. 274.

Take 30 gallons of pure rectified whiskey, 6 gallons pure bourbon whiskey, 3 half pints simple syrup, 1½ ounces sweet spirits of nitre; mix them all together, and color with sugar coloring.

Old Forester began with brothers George Garvin Brown and J. T. S. Brown Jr. forming a whiskey firm with Old Forester as their brand and selling exclusively by the bottle. Brothers Brown were chasing the pharmaceutical market. It's the only brand that has remained with one company since its inception. Other 1800s-era brands—Old Crow, Old Grand-Dad, E. H. Taylor, and others—have been seen numerous owners.

1800s DISTILLERY FIRES

The bourbon distilling business has no greater foe than fire. If a spark touches the distilled spirit, barrels explode and people often die.

In 1852, a Baltimore distillery fire took the lives of Hugh Fagan and Francis Timmons. Around the same time, a Louisville boy was killed in a distillery fire.

Louisville nearly turned to ashes after an Old Louisville block of businesses and a tobacco warehouse caught fire in 1864. It started when two government buildings housing saddles, harnesses, hay, oats, and Union soldier equipment caught fire. The buildings were bordered by thousands of whiskey barrels on both sides, and when the fire reached the barrels, survivors witnessed a "lurid blue flame" and heard explosions of whiskey barrels. Thousands of barrels were gone, and only one house—the Simms Furniture Store on Eighth Street—survived. Damages were estimated at $2 million.

Even in times of death and absolute ruin, the distilleries rebuilt. When the Illinois John S. Miller Distillery burned to the ground in 1877, the family lost five hundred thousand bushels of corn, one hundred thousand bushels of rye, its high wines, and its cattle. Prior to the fire, Miller had reportedly shipped barrels of whiskey to Europe and South America, but the disaster still caused $80,000 in damages. Nevertheless, the distillery rebuilt.

The fires were often attributed to vandalism or accidents, and were often a product of the times. When worker Henry Weel walked through a Gibson Distillery warehouse in 1883, he carried a lamp. When a bung reportedly popped off a barrel and scattered whiskey over the lamp and the hands of Weel, explosions then occurred one after another and burning whiskey scattered in every direction, seriously injuring fifteen people.

After the Connellsville, Pennsylvania, Overholt & Co. distillery fire in 1884, a worker tried to blame spontaneous combustion of mill dust, but inspectors believed it was his cigar butt that caused the fire leading to the loss of $330,000 of whiskey and $115,000 in equipment.

The business-oriented distilleries were typically insured, but distillery fires were so costly that the insurance companies frequently tried to skirt paying. In the case of *The Andes Insurance Company vs. Elias Shipman* (the distillery owner), the contract stipulated that the distillery would have a watchman on the premises constantly during machinery repairs. At the time of the distillery fire, the watchman was asleep in the office, and the insurance company tried to argue that this violated the insurance policy. The judge, however, awarded Shipman the insurance policy's terms, which didn't really matter since it was only $10,825, one-third of the property's value.

By 1871, nearly one thousand insurance policy cases went to court, with the insurance agencies always trying to get out of paying for reasons ranging from violation of contract (as in Shipman's case) to whiskey makers storing barrels next to open-flamed stills instead of in warehouses. Usually, the courts affirmed the distillery's claims, even giving smaller distillers the benefit of the doubt. An Arizona judge once used the distiller's social status to the plaintiff's favor." Although the complainant read over the policy before he left the office, it is hardly to be presumed that a plain countryman, unacquainted with the law of insurance, would have noticed or understood the difference . . ."

During the 1800s, America's insurance industry was becoming stronger, and the distillery business was quite profitable. The insurance firms studied the distillery business and its fire hazards more closely than did the distillers themselves. *Insurance Journal*, 1888:

> The principal danger from fire to apprehend in a distiller is from the "doubler," where direct heat is applied, and where during the filling process danger may be apprehended from collapse or explosion. But even in the event such an accident the fluid, containing about 60 percent of water, would extinguish any ordinary fire that might ensue. But usually, however, this contingency is provided for in having the doubler apart from other portions of the building, and cut off by fire walls if not altogether in a separate building . . .

By the turn of the twentieth century, fire insurance was more specific and firefighting had advanced with internal combustion fire engines. Even with the new advances, distillery fires today are just as dangerous as the 1800s. From 1996 to 2015, several Kentucky distillery fires destroyed whiskey stocks, warehouses, and stills, and even killed people.

In the 1800s, distillery fires were an epidemic. The flammable whiskey led to many deaths and encouraged the development of firefighting techniques. This painting depicts Toronto's Stone Distillery burning in 1869; it was reconstructed the following year. *Distillery Heritage District*

PROTECTING ASSETS

In addition to taxes, distillers were troubled by employee theft and improper loans to family members.

To thwart theft, the companies created bylaws that required every barrel transferred be accompanied with a warehouse receipt with a corporate officer signature. To move property at a W. A. Gaines facility in 1887, one needed written approval from the majority of the directors.

W. A. Gaines also protected itself from contract favors to friends. "All contracts for staves, hoop iron and malt shall be signed by either the president or vice president and countersigned by the treasure," according to the company's bylaws.

Continued from page 48

Kentucky Distillers' Association–endorsed shutdown. Wrote Brown-Forman's George Garvin Brown and Marion Taylor:

> The general depression in business the past two years, together with an increased government tax on whiskey, has resulted in decreased consumption of the fine whiskies made in Kentucky, as the stocks now in existence are in excess of the consumptive demand, which causes serious depression in values, affecting not only our daily transactions, but greatly lessening the value of warehouse receipts as collateral security.

This time, distillers blocked the shutdown. An anonymous source told the *Louisville Courier-Journal* that the distillers had significant holdings and expected a boom similar to the 1888 shutdown. "We are very far from a boom in the whiskey business, even should the intended lock-up occur. In fact, I don't expect any considerable change in values for two or three years, even in case of suspension," said the source that added the holdouts were for "personal advantage" and not the industry's. One month after the anonymous source made these comments, 294 of Kentucky's 300 distillers agreed to an eighteen-month shutdown.

The shutdowns showed the bourbon industry's vulnerability and that it was only as strong as the sum of its parts. During this same time, the industry's strength in Washington was shining through.

Fire continues to plague the distilling business. This downtown Louisville building was the site for the future Old Forester Distillery in July 2015. The historic building burned before a still was even inside. Firefighters managed to save the exterior.

CHAPTER 3
GOVERNMENT
Friend and Foe

With a full one hundred years of existence as a nation, American consumers still had little assurance that the products they purchased were pure. From snake oil salesmen to unsavory whiskey brands proclaiming to cure cancer, consumers had to sort through a large body of lies. But there were three words consumers trusted in whiskey circles: bond, distilled, and bottled.

During America's first century, the distillers sold barrels of whiskey to rectifiers, wholesalers, and merchants who took control of the whiskey and, often but not always, bottled it. Now, in the late 1880s and early 1890s, distillers who likely were tired of the impurities added to their whiskey started to bottle for themselves. With that change, these three words—bond, distilled, and bottled—became poetry to the ears of whiskey consumers.

That's why W. L. Crabb, president of the Fible & Crabb distilling company in Eminence, Kentucky, offered a simple promise: "Goods sold in bond or free!"

Distiller promises were not enough, though. Consumers needed assurance. The Committee on Judiciary of the House of Representatives determined that legislation was needed to protect the public from counterfeiting.

At the heart of the issue was bonded whiskey—that which was stored in government-approved warehousing and at the center of the controversial whiskey rings of decades past. Distillers were also mishandling their stocks, creating surpluses by not properly forecasting demand.

The government allowed whiskey to remain in bond before tax was paid. In 1879, there were 15 million gallons in surplus, and although the distillers were beginning to realize overproduction errors, they did not mind sitting on the additional stocks—distillers constantly campaigned for an extension for tax payments, arguing they would go into bankruptcy otherwise.

The world needed its whiskey for medicinal purposes, of course. Thus, Congress attempted to pass a bonded whiskey bill in 1884. Kentucky Congressman Albert D. Willis said, "The fact is the distillers throughout the country recognize the fact that if the bourbon whiskey is now forced on the market in such quantities, as it will be as the law now stands, that it will throw their goods out of market, or require them to sell at losing prices." The bonded whiskey bill of 1884, however, did not pass.

Distillers then began arguing to change the bonded age limit to reduce their taxation mark, but this earned them a reputation as whiny business-men. J. M. Atherton, of the Atherton Distillery, said:

> Whiskey dealers all over the country have been making laughing stocks of Kentucky distillers because of the many changes and reforms they favor, but which generally fall through after a great deal of discussion and agitation. Something is radically wrong when '94 whiskey is actually bringing better price than the output of '92. As far as the reduction of the bonded period is concerned, there should be no difference of opinion . . . whiskey improves but

E. H. Taylor Jr. purchased a distillery on the Kentucky River in 1869 and outfitted it with the finest boilers and distillation equipment. He also became an instrumental figure in the bourbon industry's fight against Canadian whiskey dealers and wholesalers, and helped successfully lobby for the Bottled-in-Bond Act. Buffalo Trace continues to use his name and likeness to sell whiskey. *Buffalo Trace Distillery*

slightly after being in the barrel more than four years, so that the eight-year period is but little help in that direction. By the present method of regaining at the expiration of four years the owner of the whiskey in bond often practically pays the government about $1.15 tax on gallon instead of $1.10.

This time distillers didn't champion solutions to their own problems. They played the victim role, protesting that under the threat of rectifiers and unsavory salesmen, whiskey makers could not assure consumers were getting pure whiskey. They also positioned the idea of bottling of spirits in bond as a way of selling whiskey exports, an enticing revenue idea for an industry that couldn't export bottles under 1896 law. According to government regulation, whiskey could not be shipped overseas unless in its original package and only if the exporter had paid the internal revenue tax. Since most US whiskey was sold by the barrel from the distillery to the

THAT OLD BLUE RIBBON BRAND

Poem, Fible & Crabb's Old Blue Ribbon Whiskey, circa 1895:

Come in, dear boy, for old time's sake,
And ruminate awhile,
I know it's just your hour to take
An after-dinner smile;
And there's my crystal in the cleft
Behind the music stand
With still two honest jorums left
Of Old Blue Ribbon Brand

Drop down in that great leather chair
And keep your eye on me

Whilst I proceed to measure fair
This real eau de vie
It's been at least a year, I think
Since I have tried my hand
To mix for you a perfect drink
Of Old Blue Ribbon Brand

You know I used to mix them well
Before that joyous day
When you and your old Sweetheart, Belle,
Joined hands and went away.

You know how many times by stealth
Our meetings here were planned to sit
    and doubly drink her health
In Old Blue Ribbon Brand

Ah Lucky Dog! You're happy now
And snugly fixed for life—
You took fine laurels on your brow,
When Belle became your wife;
The secret of your winning her,
I'm sure, I understand—
It came from true ambition's spur
In Old Blue Ribbon Brand

There never yet was a human soul,
Who drank Kentucky's best,
And failed to find the proper goal
For perfect rest.
If he was false, it made him true,
If little, made him grand—
A dwarf becomes a giant through
This Old Blue Ribbon Brand.

Frederic Stitzel patented the rack use of barrels in 1879. Also patented in this time is the use of heat cycling in warehouses to control the temperature. Both methods are still used today. Buffalo Trace pictured.

wholesaler or rectifier (distillers typically did not have bottling setups), there was no way of verifying original packaging.

Congressman Walter Evans of Kentucky introduced a bill that allowed export of bottled goods in lots of proof gallons. Internal Revenue agreed with the premise as long as there was a government's guarantee affixed across the bottle neck and there was constant government supervision of the warehouses. As Evans's bill passed the Ways and Means committee, distillers were likely anticipating the open markets, the increased protection against rectifiers, and a solid measure that would ensure consistent bourbon, whether it was made in Kentucky or Missouri. The House passed the Evans bill May 19, 1896. The distillers were tasting a victory. But opposition remained.

As the bill went to the Senate on December 16, 1896, the Liquor Dealers Association petitioned the Senate Finance Committee for amendments. A hearing was granted: John B. Thompson and T. H. Sherley represented bourbon interests, while the liquor dealers were represented by I. W. Bernheim, of all people, and W. L. Snyder, president of the National Wholesale Liquor Dealers Association. The distillers argued that liquor dealers opposed the bottled-in-bond act because they wanted to bottle the whiskey themselves in order to make adulterations.

With the passing of the Bottled-in-Bond Act, consumers could trust whiskey with the appropriate seals. It also created new jobs for women in a time when most industries wouldn't allow female employees. Men were poor bottlers, so the jobs went to women. *Oscar Getz Museum of Whiskey*

The liquor dealers fired back, with Bernheim, a distiller with numerous interests, saying, "This bill is intended solely to benefit the distillers, principally those of Kentucky. It is a sham and is only intended to drive Canadian whisky out of the market."

Shortly after Bernheim made these comments, the National Liquor Dealers' Association met to discuss the plans by some Kentucky distillers (known as "Spirits Trust") to halt production. The liquor dealers believed the production stoppage was a tactical effort to encourage the support of the bottled-in-bond act. The wholesalers held strong and managed to introduce a few slight provisions to the bill. The bill passed the House, and the following Senate hearing offered amendments that ensured that reliable firms could continue bottling whiskey out of bond and that their whiskey would not require government stamps on bottles, cases, barrels, and other packages.

On March 3, 1897, the second session of the fifty-fourth Congress introduced "An act to allow the bottling of distilled spirits in bond," becoming known as the Bottled-in-Bond Act of 1897. President Grover Cleveland signed the act into law, and bourbon distillers celebrated while the liquor dealers were relieved that they could continue to rectify bourbon whiskey. In July, the Internal Revenue commissioner made a slight amendment to the act, requiring the distillery information to appear on the strip stamp.

This landmark consumer protection legislation offered guarantees people did not have before: namely, a means to identify when and where the whiskey was produced. The product would be four years old at minimum, made at one distillery in one distilling season, bottled at 100 proof, and have distillery information on the bottle. Other, less visible requirements were also there to protect consumers. For example, exported bottled-in-bond whiskey was allowed to be 80 proof and the distiller was required to declare his bottled-in-bond intent in the bonded warehouses prior to withdrawal of whiskey. "The mixing or blending of different ages or seasons is not allowed, but those of any season between January and July and beween July and January may be mixed, the former being designated as the spring season, the latter the fall season. Nor can different products of the same distillery be mixed, such as bourbon and rye, etc.," said T. E. McNamara, of W. W. Johnson & Co., a member of the executive committee of the National Wholesale Liquor Dealers Association of America.

Bottled-in-Bond became law the same day that Congress approved lighthouse construction for Egmont Key and Saint Joseph Point, Florida, and established Potomac Flats as a public park. In that session, Congress also provided protection to national military parks, approved a bridge over the Yazoo River in Mississippi, passed regulations over the Fraternal Benefit Association, and enacted a few defense-oriented and Post Office revisions. It was a slow Congressional day, as policy goes, but the Bottled-in-Bond Act has stood the test of time, offering consumers assurance and distillers confidence their whiskey would not be adulterated after it left their warehouse.

But bourbon distillers could not rest on this victory. Other potential damaging government and consumer threats loomed. The immediate threats were within their own ranks.

Middleman Friction

During the late 1800s, liquor wholesalers and bourbon distillers were not the best of friends, since the two groups had different interests. The wholesalers wanted to continue operating as they had in the past: sell the distiller's whiskey for them, whether mixed with coloring, bonded, or carrying the distiller's brand. And the distillers wanted to move in a new direction, in which they bottled the products and received more profits rather than allow the wholesalers to earn the bulk of the money.

Wholesalers were dealt three effectively crippling blows. The first was a stoppage of production from July 1896 to January 1898, giving wholesalers less product to sell. The *Wine and Spirits Bulletin*: "Why was this agreement made? Not for the benefit of the 'middle man,' but owing to the fact that the majority of the Kentucky distillers were unable to borrow money from banks to make new crops, and the banks were calling in loans."

The *Wine and Spirits Bulletin* also saw the Bottled-in-Bond Act as a blow to the middleman; but the bill in which wholesalers went all-in and drew the line was the Thorne Bill of Kentucky, which proposed to stop distillers from making private brands for a particular store or bottler. If passed, this bill would almost

Continued on page 64

THE BOTTLED-IN-BOND ACT

In March 1897, Congress passed the Bottled-in-Bond Act, the closest thing American distillers had to a Constitution. This is the act in its entirety, including select reference headings from the original text for clarity.

An Act to allow the bottling of distilled spirits in bond.

Be it enacted by the Senate and House of Representatives of the United States of America in Congress assembled,

Bottling of distilled spirits in bond. Sec. 1. That whenever any distilled spirits deposited in the warehouse of a distillery having a surveyed daily capacity of not less than twenty bushels of grain, which capacity or not less than twenty bushels thereof is commonly used by the distiller, have been duly entered for withdrawal upon payment of tax, or for export in bond, and have been gauged and the required marks, brands, and tax-paid stamps or export stamps, as the case may be, have been affixed to the package or packages containing the same, the distiller or owner of said distilled spirits, if he has declared his purpose so to do in the entry for withdrawal, which entry for bottling purposes may be made by the owner as well as the distiller, may remove such spirits to a separate portion of said warehouse which shall be set apart and used exclusively for that purpose, and there, under the supervision of a United States storekeeper, or storekeeper and gauger, in charge of such warehouse, may immediately draw off such spirits, bottle, pack, and case the same[.]

Mingling of same spirits. *Provided*, That for convenience in such process any number of packages of spirits of the same kind, differing only in proof, but produced at the same distillery by the same distiller, may be mingled together in a cistern provided for that purpose, but nothing herein shall authorize or permit any mingling of different products, or of the same products of different distilling seasons, or the addition or the subtraction of any substance or material or the application of any method or process to alter or change in any way the original condition or character of the product except as herein authorized; nor shall there be at the same time in the bottling room of any bonded warehouse any spirits entered for withdrawal upon payment of the tax and any spirits entered for export[.]

Regulations. *Provided also*, That under such regulations and limitations as the Commissioner of Internal Revenue, with the approval of the Secretary of the Treasury, may prescribe, the provisions of this Act may be made to apply to the bottling and casing of fruit brandy in special bonded warehouses.

Stamp, how affixed. Every bottle when filled shall have affixed thereto and passing over the mouth of the same such suitable adhesive engraved strip stamp as may be prescribed, as hereinafter provided, and shall be packed into cases to contain six bottles or multiples thereof, and in the aggregate not less than two nor more than five gallons in each case, which shall be immediately removed from the distillery premises

The early Bottled-in-Bond Act was a monumental piece of legislation for distillers. This term became coveted and protected, and consumers associated words "bottled in bond" with premium quality.

Cases to have stamp affixed. Each of such cases shall have affixed thereto a stamp denoting the number of gallons therein contained, such stamp to be affixed to the case before its removal from the warehouse, and such stamps shall have a cash value of ten cents each, and shall be charged at that rate to the collectors to whom issued, and shall be paid for at that rate by the distiller or owner using the same.

Branding of cases. And there shall be plainly burned on the side of each case, to be known as the Government side, the proof of the spirits, the registered distillery number, the State and district in which the distillery is located, the real name of the actual bona fide distiller, the year and distilling season, whether spring or fall, of original inspection or entry into bond, and the date of bottling, and the same wording shall be placed upon the adhesive engraved strip stamp over the mouth of the bottle. It being understood that the spring season shall include the months from January to July, and the fall season the months from July to January.

trade marks. And no trade marks shall be put upon any bottle unless the real name of the actual bona fide distiller shall also be placed conspicuously on said bottle.

Inspection of spirits. Sec. 2. That the Commissioner of Internal Revenue, with the approval of the Secretary of the Treasury, may, by regulations, prescribe the mode of separating and securing the additional warehouse, or portion of the warehouse hereinbefore required to be set apart, the manner in which the business of bottling spirits in bond shall be carried on, the notices, bonds, and returns to be given and accounts and records to be kept by the persons conducting such business, the mode and time of inspection of such spirits, the accounts and records to be kept and returns made by the Government officers, and all such other matters and things, as in his discretion, he may deem requisite for a secure and orderly supervision of said business; and he may also, with the approval of the Secretary of the Treasury, prescribe and issue the stamps required.

The distiller may, in the presence of the United States storekeeper or storekeeper and gauger, remove by straining through cloth, felt, or other like material any charcoal, sediment[,] or other like substance found therein, and may whenever necessary reduce such spirits as are withdrawn for bottling purposes by the addition of pure water only to one hundred per centum proof for spirits for domestic use, or to not less than eighty per centum proof for spirits for export purposes, under such rules and regulations as may be prescribed by the Commissioner of Internal Revenue with the approval of the Secretary of the Treasury; and no spirits shall be withdrawn for bottling under this Act until after the period shall have expired within which a distiller may request a regauge of distilled spirits as provided in section fifty of the Act of August twenty-eighth, eighteen hundred and ninety-four.

Spirits for export. Sec. 3. That all distilled spirits intended for export under the provisions of this Act shall be inspected, bottled, cased, weighed, marked, labeled, stamped, or sealed in such manner and at such time as the Commissioner of Internal Revenue may prescribe; and the said Commissioner, with the approval of the Secretary of the Treasury, may provide such regulations for the transportation, entry, reinspection, and lading of such spirits for export as may from time to time be deemed necessary; and all provisions of existing law relating to the exportation of distilled spirits in bond, so far as applicable, and all penalties therein imposed, are hereby extended and made applicable to distilled spirits bottled for export under the provisions of this Act, but no drawback shall be allowed or paid upon any spirits bottled under this Act.

In case of loss or deficiency. Sec. 4. That where, upon inspection at the bonded warehouse in which the spirits are bottled as aforesaid, the quantity so bottled and cased for export is less than the quantity actually contained in the distiller's original casks or packages at the time of withdrawal for that purpose the tax on the loss or deficiency so ascertained shall be paid before the removal of the spirits from such warehouse, and the tax so paid shall be receipted and accounted for by the collector in such manner as the Commissioner of Internal Revenue may prescribe.

Reinspection. SEC. 5. That where, upon reinspection at the port of entry, any case containing or purporting to contain distilled spirits for export is found to have been opened or tampered with, or where any mark, brand, stamp, label, or seal placed thereon or upon any bottle contained therein has been removed, changed, or willfully defaced, or where upon such reinspection any loss or discrepancy is found to exist as to the contents of any case so entered for export, the tax on the spirits contained in each such case at the time of its removal from warehouse shall be collected and paid.

Penalties. SEC. 6. That any person who shall reuse any stamp provided under this Act after the same shall have been once affixed to a bottle as provided herein, or who shall reuse a bottle for the purpose of containing distilled spirits which has once been filled and stamped under the provisions of this Act without removing and destroying the stamp so previously affixed to such bottle, or who shall, contrary to the provisions of this Act or of the regulations issued thereunder remove or cause to be removed from any bonded warehouse any distilled spirits inspected or bottled under the provisions of this Act, or who shall bottle or case any such spirits in violation of this Act or of any regulation issued thereunder, or who shall, during the transportation and before the exportation of any such spirits, open or cause to be opened any case or bottle containing such spirits, or who shall willfully remove, change, or deface any stamp, brand, label, or seal affixed to any such case or to any bottle contained therein, shall for each such offense be fined not less than one hundred nor more than one thousand dollars, and be imprisoned not more than two years, in the discretion of the court, and such spirits shall be forfeited to the United States.

Counterfeiting, etc., stamps. SEC. 7. That every person who, with intent to defraud, falsely makes, forges, alters, or counterfeits any stamp made or used under any provision of this Act, or who uses, sells, or has in his possession any such forged, altered, or counterfeited stamp, or any plate or die used or which may be used in the manufacture thereof, or who shall make, use, sell, or have in his possession any paper in imitation of the paper used in the manufacture of any stamp required by this Act, shall on conviction be punished by a fine not exceeding one thousand dollars and by imprisonment at hard labor not exceeding five years.

SEC. 8. That nothing in this Act shall be construed to exempt spirits bottled under the provisions of this Act from the operation of chapter seven hundred and twenty-eight of the public laws of the Fifty-first Congress, approved August eighth, eighteen hundred and ninety. Approved, March 3, 1897.

No exemption from state, etc., laws.
Vol. 26, p. 313.
March 3, 1897.

THE SAMUEL FREEDMAN CORPORATION
BULK WHISKIES
BOUGHT.............SOLD
MAin 0820   MAin 3116
MERCANTILE LIBRARY BLDG., CINCINNATI, OHIO

In the 1800s and early 1900s, distillers and wholesalers were constantly at odds. Caught in the middle were the whiskey dealers who purchased stocks from distillers and flipped them at a profit to mix-happy rectifiers and wholesalers. The Bottled-in-Bond debates had to be difficult times for the likes of Samuel Freedman in Cincinnati, who had to appease both sides. *Author collection*

Continued from page 59

certainly scrub out the wholesaler. Wholesalers protested that the bill was unconstitutional, but it passed the Kentucky legislature in 1896 and gave some of the most restrictive distilling guidelines passed in American history. The Thorne Bill made it a felony for non-distiller, owner, or operator to sign warehouse receipts, with penitentiary time up to ten years upon conviction.

The wholesalers felt themselves being muscled out and encouraged their brethren to separate ties with distillers, preparing for a trade war. They believed the distillers were behind the Thorne Whiskey Bill and offered sharp words: "Let every middleman join an association where no distiller of any kind can be admitted. If this can be done—verily I believe it—the distillers can sell any kind of trade they desire, except the middleman, and in short time they will find it requires years of experience to handle trade which neighbor pays cash nor gives acceptances. . . . Arrange your businesses so that you can sell five barrels of blends to one barrel of two sampled whiskey. Let the middlemen combine and build distilleries," wrote N. M. Uri to fellow wholesalers.

But Uri and other wholesalers had to be surprised to learn that the distillers didn't support the Thorne Bill. "I believe I correctly represent the general distillery sentiment of the state in condemning the proposed registration of warehouse receipts," wrote John M. Atherton. "So far as I know, this state, and speaking broadly, the government in this country . . . at no time attempted to regulate or interfere with transactions of personal property, or with documents of title thereto by any system of registration. . . . This law imposes very severe penalties for the violation of its provisions."

Atherton and other distillers worked with wholesalers to present their case that the Thorne Bill was unlawful. They claimed Hon. William Pryor Thorne, whose Tobacco Bill was better received, slipped the law into legislation without giving the distillers or wholesalers an opportunity to object to it. "Distillers and dealers pronounce every feature of the bill as vicious in principle and as an interference without any other than selfish considerations with the operations of the wholesale laws now in force in this state, and which are ample in their judgment," the distillers testified, adding that the Senate had been misled and deceived.

When the Thorne Bill passed, the *Louisville Post* called it one of the worst bills in the state, saying it was "merely another illustration of the progress paternalism is making in Kentucky. . . . It is based on false pretenses. The Thorne Bill does not betray its purposes in title; it denies to the owner of a certain kind of property rights inherent in all ownership. It permits a man to sell his plow factory in an instant, but permits no transfer of a distillery for thirty days to heirs, creditors, or to purchases. It . . . ruthlessly violates the constitutional prohibition against class legislation."

The Thorne Bill was signed into law. Shortly thereafter, the Kentucky Distillers' Association passed a resolution to investigate distilleries allegedly operating in violation of the Thorne law. "Be it resolved, that the president and the board of managers be instructed to investigate the same and employ suitable counsel to enforce the provisions and penalties of this law."

In some respects, the Thorne Bill pitted wholesalers against distillers, who were forced to turn on their own to survive. It was a lesson in government for the distillers: Some support you, others want to crush you. It also took away a sales channel for smaller distillers. R. B. Hayden's Old Grand-Dad and the Old Judge Distillery were sold in 1899 to non-Kentucky interests. In fact many smaller distilleries were selling to larger companies, collectively organized as the Whiskey Trust.

The Trust and other distillers had a new problem on their hands. What was whiskey?

Pure

At the turn of the twentieth century, the government was still struggling with consumer protection against unsavory whiskey salesmen. Some whiskey companies oversold whiskey's status as medicinal.

Distillers frequently advertised medicinal whiskey. And why not? Whiskey was the medicine of its day. The claims were usually in fair and good taste, ranging from

Fleming's eight-year-old rye whiskey "for medicinal purposes, where a fine stimulant is required," to R. M. Rose's bolder suggestion that its rye whiskey was sold to "high-class families throughout the South" and R. M. Roses "counteracting against many ills promoted by sudden changes in temperature." Sure, some brands skirted the line, saying "your health demands that you exercise discrimination in selecting your whiskey. Old Braddock Maryland rye is a safe choice . . ."

Much of the bourbon being sold for medicinal usage between 1897 and 1906 was sold through drugstores, such as Bauman's drugstore in New York: "We buy all our liquors in bond and can guarantee their purity and excellence for medicinal purposes. Kentucky bourbon, seven years old, full quarts . . . $1."

After the passing of the Bottled-in-Bond Act, doctors and druggists could trust the whiskey they purchased from Kentucky or from wholesalers. If the stamp was on the bottle, there was verification of its authenticity. Most medicinal bourbon and rye was sold very tastefully, and the over-the-top claims that once dominated the whiskey market were disappearing. That is, except for one brand: Duffy's Pure Malt whiskey. The brand claimed to cure cancer, coughs, colds, consumption, grip, bronchitis, pneumonia, and "all diseases of the throat and lungs. It contains no fusel oil and is the only whiskey recognized by the government as medicine," a 1903 ad said. The brand boasted that seven thousand doctors and two thousand hospitals used Duffy's Pure Malt, though in reality the American Medical Association had boycotted the whiskey for its claims.

Owner Walter Duffy was also steadfast on calling it medicinal whiskey, which helped him evade the whiskey tax. The first FDA administrator, Dr. Harvey W. Wylie, said, "Duffy's Malt whiskey was one of the most gigantic frauds of the age and a flagrant violation of the law."

Duffy's lost a court case in the New York Supreme Court that declared it should pay liquor taxes. By this point, the medical community had grown tired of Duffy's claims and just wanted whiskey. And the temperance leaders were using medicinal whiskey as a talking point for legislation.

The National Congress of Mothers' Club and the Women's Christian Temperance Union were campaigning for pure food, drink, and drug legislation. The temperance leaders frequently opposed medicinal whiskey usage, but one of their arguments was based on the fact that you couldn't trust the whiskey's efficacy. "It is well known that most of the 'rectifier's' permits issued by the United States' officers are procured by wholesale liquor-dealers and others whose especial business is to mix, compound blend and 'cut' liquors," the *Cyclopedia of Temperance and Prohibition* concluded in the 1890s. Twenty years after this statement, the WCTU grew in numbers, as did other groups, all calling for a ban on alcohol. They were going after alcohol in every way they could. From a temperance perspective, supporting a pure food and drug bill would be a step toward eliminating their enemy.

Meanwhile, distillers and wholesalers continued to scuffle over legislation. In 1906, the legislative debate centered around assuring consumers that whiskey was "pure." The Bottled-in-Bond Act was nice, but there was no protection of purity in the blends or whiskeys that were not bottled-in-bond. The Pure Food Law, as it was initially called, was introduced in February 1906, and it required the blenders to submit their formulas. "This crusade against blended whiskies, exploited by certain distillers, while it was based on error and mercenary motives is unjust to the distillers and blenders of standard whiskey. These efforts exploit blended whiskey as an 'imitation' whiskey, 'spurious whiskey,' 'decoctions,' etc., cannot be verified by any data," the National Wholesale Liquor Dealers Association wrote. At the center of this bill was the definition of the word *blend* and other whiskey types. Distillers wanted the tags like *spurious, imitation, impure, or adulterated* applied to blended whiskey, which wholesalers called "a misnomer and a false statement. Opponents of blended whiskey assert that 95 percent of the whiskey used as beverage for years is and has been blended."

Congressmen intensely debated this bill, with Illinois congressman James Mann saying that fruit had been colored with poisonous red dye and liquor had received added chemical fillers. But the government's pure food commission was quick to not let this information get out of control. "The Commission on Purity of Food has never made any claim that neutral spirits is poisonous or injurious to health, but everyone connected with the business knows that spirits being perfectly neutral is deprived of some of the by-products of distillation, and does not improve with age." The Commission of Purity of Food observed that while 50 million gallons of Kentucky whiskey were sold, only 22 million gallons had actually been produced—arguing that this proved "cheap whiskey" or "neutral spirit" had been added.

Although the bill covered several types of drugs and foods, liquor brought the most heated debates. And there were obvious holes in the legislation, such as its failure to establish police jurisdiction for enforcing the laws, and, as the *Washington Post* pointed out, that it offered the layman no protection "at all in the purchase of pure drugs." But the public was often more concerned about the whiskey labeling.

Attorney General Charles Bonaparte submitted the legal definitions for whiskey labeling under the Pure Food Law to the Department of Justice, in which straight whiskey would be labeled as such; a mixture of two or more straight whiskeys would be labeled blended whiskey or whiskeys; a mixture of straight whiskey and ethyl alcohol, provided that there is sufficient amount of straight whiskey to make it genuinely a mixture, would be labeled as compound of, or compounded with, pure grain distillate; and imitation whiskey would be labeled as such. The bill passed with overwhelming support, even though the *New York Times* called the bill's debate "one of the wildest times that has been seen this session." President Theodore Roosevelt signed it into law June 30, 1906.

As the Pure Food & Drug Act was adopted by the states, there lacked an obvious definition. Nowhere in the act did it define bourbon whiskey.

By December 1906, the federal government had been inundated with queries regarding bourbon whiskey. Could neutral spirits or coloring be added? Secretary of Agriculture James Wilson:

> The question presented is whether neutral spirits may be added to bourbon whiskey in varying quantities, colored and flavored, and the resulting mixture be labeled "blended whiskies." To permit the use of the word whiskies in the described mixture is to admit that flavor and color can be added to neutral spirits and the resulting mixture to be labeled whiskey. The Department is of the opinion that the mixtures presented cannot legally be labeled either blended whiskies or blended whisky. The use of the plural of the word in the first case is evidently improper for the reason that there is only one whiskey in the mixture. . . .

In other words, there was a lot of wiggle room for a blender wanting to use the powerful brand word of "bourbon." There also lacked a true legal definition of *whiskey*. In all of the Pure Food & Drug Act's grandeur, it had failed to define whiskey. This allowed rectifiers the legal loophole of labeling some products whiskey that by today's standards would likely be considered a grain vodka blended with rye whiskey.

To counter this trend, bourbon distillers labeled the products "pure food" whiskey, and distillers advertised their bourbon as such. A February 1910 ad: "Old Crow. Old fashioned hand made sour mash. Straight Pure Rye. The standard of rye whiskey, guaranteed pure rye whiskey under national Pure Food Law Serial Number 2165. NOT BLENDED. NOT ADULTERATED."

Multiple distillers sued the revenue collectors for enforcing the Pure Food & Drug Act, and they were winning injunctions in Ohio and Illinois over the simple fact that their products were being forced to change names. The Pure Food & Drug legal debates also brought out the resentment toward Kentucky from the rest of the country. When fighting for their own interests, Illinois, Indiana, and Ohio distillers accused Kentucky of trying to create a monopoly. "This controversy over what is whiskey is more due to the unfair monopoly sought by extreme distillers of bourbon in Kentucky and a few distillers of rye in Pennsylvania than to any requirement of the pure food law," said George Dieterle, of the Union Distilling Company in Cincinnati. Dieterle, who also served as president of the National Whole Liquors Dealers, failed to realize—or at least appreciate—the fact that the words "rye" and "bourbon" carried no meaning under the Pure Food & Drug Act.

Of course, the Kentucky distillers were pursuing a definition of whiskey—their entire livelihood depended upon it. In fact, Kentucky bourbon distillers might have been damaged by the Pure Food & Drug Act. In 1908, the government seized products labeled as "Bourbon whiskey" that was actually made in New Orleans from black strap molasses treated with sulfuric acid and shipped to Baltimore. The government sued the Louisiana distillers for libel under the Pure Food Law, saying

After the passing of the Pure Food & Drug Act, bourbon did not have a proper definition, and blenders could mix neutral grain spirits with whiskey and still call it bourbon. While M. Cronan & Company labeled its J. B. Sefton brand a "blended bourbon whiskey," many less-scrupulous bottlers placed the good name of bourbon on any spirit.

PURE FOOD & DRUG ACT OF 1906

While whiskey and other liquors caused most of the public debate for the Pure Food & Drug Act, tainted meat and poor vaccines were also reasons for the bill's creation.

In 1898 and 1899, soldiers died from eating embalmed meat. It was meant to be preserved for soldiers during the Spanish-American War, but chemicals used to preserve the 327 tons of meat "caused great sickness in the American Army," testified Major General Grenville Dodge.

In 1901, tainted vaccines caused multiple child deaths. Thirteen children in St. Louis died of tetanus-contaminated diphtheria antitoxin. Nine children in Camden, New Jersey, died from bad smallpox vaccine.

The meat industry came under more scrutiny after a group calling itself the "poison squad" volunteered to test common preservatives of the day, including borax, sulfuric acid, saltpeter, and formaldehyde. Dr. Harvey Wiley, considered the father of the Pure Food & Drug Act, oversaw the poison squad tests.

But the meat's death knell came when Upton Sinclair published *The Jungle* in February 1906. The instant bestselling novel offered disgusting details about the meat-packing industry, including diseased cows going to slaughter, guts going into potted hams, and sausage-grinding machines catching dead rats.

Both the vaccine and meat industries received government legislation for their own specific issues, but consumers also received assurances in the Pure Food & Drug Act. It passed the House June 23, 1906, by a vote of 240 to 17. America wanted protections for the industries providing them food and medicine.

This political cartoon pays homage to Bureau of Chemistry Chief Chemist Harvey Wiley, who was considered the father of the Pure Food & Drug Act. *FDA Archives*

the goods were not bourbon whiskey but distilled molasses. The District Court of Maryland case brought important points into question: Was the molasses-based bourbon misbranded? Could bourbon be made outside of Kentucky?

The federal lawyers used previous cases and trade history to fill in the holes of the Pure Food & Drug Act. Before they went to deliberate, the jury was instructed:

> That if they shall find from the evidence that the phrase "bourbon whiskey," as understood by scientific men, the liquor trade, and the public generally is confined to distillate of grain made from the mixture of fermented grain of which mixture corn constituted the greater part, and shall find that the contents of the barrels libeled in this case are a distillate of molasses, and shall further find that the said barrels are branded "bourbon whiskey," then the said barrels are misbranded. . . .

The government also argued that bourbon whiskey, as understood in the trade, "is confined to a whiskey made in Kentucky."

If the jury said Louisiana distillers were not libellant, more distillers would label molasses spirit as bourbon, and Kentucky distillers would eventually lose their marketing power. The verdict was "for the libellant," and the liquor trade and government all sighed in relief.

But it was just one case, and others would surely follow if a stronger definition were not established. The blenders up north were also angling for the Kentucky bourbon consumer. Hiram Walker & Sons, Walkerville, Ontario, purchased ad space in Kentucky newspapers:

> Kentucky Straight Whiskey, when new, is rank with fusel oil, but the makers always assured consumers that this noxious impurity is transformed by age into delightful ethers, etc. A few years ago it was found that age makes no change in the fusel oil except to remove its vile odor. The Kentucky distillers knowing well the aversion to fusel oil, were in desperate straights; so they boldly declared that real whiskey new or old, must contain the fusel oil, and denounced all refined whiskey as a base imitation. And the bureau backed them up. Canadian Club whiskey was condemned solely because it contains practically no fusel oils. . . .

Shortly after President William Taft took office, he had to have seen this constant "what is whiskey?" exchange clogging up his court system and lawmaker chambers. In 1909, with the United States more than one hundred years old, distillers were constantly ranting their opinions about whiskey. Taft had enough. The president planned to learn "what is whiskey?"

Taft called a formal hearing and invited all interests to give their sides, as well as Dr. Wiley, the father of the Pure Food & Drug Act, and British chemists who had helped their governments reach a formal whiskey definition. He wanted to come to a final decision as to definitions of whiskey and imitation whiskey—a term used for the blends. In his decision, Taft wrote:

> That after an examination of all the evidence it seems overwhelmingly established for a hundred years the term "whiskey" in the trade and among the customers has included all potable liquors distilled from grain; that the straight whiskey is, as compared with the whiskey made by rectification, or distillation, and flavoring and coloring matter, a subsequent improvement and that therefore, it is a perversion of the Pure Food Act to attempt now to limit the meaning of the term "whiskey" to that which modern manufacturers and taste have made the most desirable variety. . . . I think the fundamental error in all conclusions differing from this is one of fact as to what the name of "whiskey" actually has included for the last hundred years, [Solicitor General Lloyd Wheaton Bowers] fell into what seems to be the error of making too nice a distinction in reference to the amount of congeneric substances or traces of fusel oil required to constitute whiskey for practical purposes when the flavor and color of all whiskey, but straight whiskey have been chiefly that of ethyl alcohol and burnt sugar.

In what has become known as the "Taft Decision," which landed the president in the Kentucky Bourbon Hall of Fame, Taft allowed the words "bourbon" or "rye" to accompany the term "straight whiskey." The president wrote:

> Some time during the Civil War it was discovered that if raw whiskey as it came from the still, unrectified and without distillation, and thus containing one-half to one-sixth of 1 percent of fusel oil, was kept in oak barrels, the inside of the staves of which were charred, the tannic acid of the charred oak which found its way from the wood into the distilled spirits would color the raw white whiskey to the conventional color of American whiskey, and after some years would eliminate altogether the raw taste and the bad odor given the liquor by the fusel oil and would leave a smooth, delicate aroma, making the whiskey exceedingly palatable without the use of any additional flavoring or coloring. The whiskey thus made by one distillation and by the aging in charred oak barrels came to be known as "straight whiskey," and to those who were good judges came to be regarded as the best and purest whiskey. . . .

Taft called the liquor trade "frauds" for trying to deceive consumers with "false labels" of bourbon. "The way to remedy this evil is not to attempt to change the meaning and scope of the term 'whiskey' accorded to it for one hundred years and narrow it to include only straight whiskey. . . . The way to do it is to require a

Kentucky is the epicenter for bourbon. Although bourbon can be distilled in other states, the Bluegrass State is its home, and Louisville is the largest city. These buildings were once a part of Whiskey Row, a thriving commerce section of Louisville that traded barrels of whiskey. Its demise began in the early 1900s amidst Prohibition talks and the internal disputes between distiller and wholesaler. As bourbon became cool again, the Main Street area has been revitalized.

branding connection with the use of the term 'whiskey,' which will indicate just what kind of whiskey the package contains." Taft then laid down the hammer, leaving zero wiggle room in the current legal framework; he even called out the blenders for their common complaining ways:

> Those who make whiskey of rectified, redistilled or neutral spirits cannot complain if, in order to prevent further frauds, they are required to use a brand which will show exactly the kind of whiskey they are selling. For that reason it seems to me fair to require them to brand their product as "whiskey made from rectified spirits," or whiskey made from redistilled spirits or whiskey made from neutral spirits. . . . Where straight whiskey and whiskey made from neutral spirits are mixed, it is proper to call them a blend of straight whiskey and whiskey made from neutral spirits. . . . [T]he public will be made to know exactly the kind of whiskey they buy and drink. If they desire straight whiskey, then they can secure it by purchasing what is branded

"straight whiskey." . . . The straight whiskey men are relieved from all future attempt to pass off neutral spirits whiskey as straight whiskey. More than this, if straight whiskey or any other kind of whiskey is aged in the wood, the fact may be branded on the package, and this claim to public favor may be truthfully be put forth. Thus, the purpose of the pure food law is fully accomplished in respect of misbranding and truthful branding.

Taft's cabinet retooled the Pure Food & Drug Act based on his definitions. It took him nearly seven months to determine "what is whiskey?" But the reasoning and research he used to make the points were leaps and bounds more thoughtful and meaningful than anybody before or since President Taft. He did for American whiskey what no distiller could: Taft gave consumers confidence.

Unfortunately, the alcohol industry was so busy fighting for tax reform, other types of alcohol, and fraud within their own ranks that the temperance groups simply outflanked them.

Going into the twentieth century, bourbon distillers mostly used column stills, but many used an easier-to-transport pot still like this one. Today, pot stills are making a slight comeback in bourbon. This one belongs to Tom's Foolery Distillery in Cleveland, Ohio.

When President William Taft (left) took office in 1909, the term *whiskey* was not clearly defined. Distillers attempted to blend neutral spirits into whiskey or labeled non-bourbon as bourbon. To rectify the situation, Taft underwent a seven-month study of "what is whiskey?" When he released the Taft Decision, distillers finally had government definitions of whiskey. *Library of Congress*

CHAPTER 4

"WHISKEY IS THE DEVIL'S OWN BREW"

The scene was all too familiar: a man lay near a tavern, dead and covered in mud. From the mid-1800s to the 1910s, there was little governmental effort to stop the drunken man stumbling home or drinking too much. The drinking-too-much stories were so common that newspapers only covered them when they became fantastic, perhaps to spread awareness of bad drinking habits. "An unknown man drank himself to death in Sacramento street groggery last night," the *Albany Daily Democrat* recorded in 1889. "He entered the place, and without any apparent bravado deliberately set to work to drink every thing in the house. He drank a half dozen bottles of various kinds of wine, and then tackled the whiskey, and finally wound up with six glasses of beer. Another glass was ordered and furnished, but before he could raise it to his lips he fell to the floor insensible."

Occasionally, as was the case in Sharon, Pennsylvania, in 1886, local governments charged the whiskey dealer when men drank themselves to death. Or as in a 1907 Watonga, Oklahoma, drinking death, they would investigate why a person would knowingly consume fifteen shots of whiskey in a span of thirty minutes. But there was almost no effort to educate an individual on the dangers of chugging whiskey. Instead, the people serving the liquor—and perhaps rightfully so—came under scrutiny.

Multiple temperance organizations attacked the taverns, sometimes literally, as in the case of Carrie Nation and her hatchet-wielding friends. Nation whacked taverns with her hatchet, while her more controlled temperance-minded friends pursued legislation at all levels of government and publicly attacked politicians who supported whiskey. After Taft's "what is whiskey?" debate, temperance-leaning newspaper *Wyoming Daily Tribune* suggested:

Although this photo shows Carrie Nation holding a Bible, she was best known for carrying a hatchet. She was arrested for bashing bars with hatchets and throwing rocks through tavern windows. A boisterous voice of temperance, Nation became the public face of the Women's Christian Temperance Union, but did not live to see federal Prohibition be enacted. *Library of Congress*

Whiskey is the devil's own brew. Whiskey is the greatest enemy of civilized nations. Whiskey robs women and children of their happiness and their patrimony. Whiskey makes measly, maudlin men at forty when they should be in the prime of vigor and usefulness. Whiskey is the poison that kills intellect and morality and makes of man a brute. Whiskey is the handmaiden of the penitentiary, the insane asylum and the poorhouse.

There was little temperance believers wouldn't blame on whiskey, but words did little harm to distillers.

Temperance political action is what caused fear to distillers.

City and state governments started with banning the selling of intoxicants in brothels, where thousands upon thousands of drinks were poured before the patron and prostitute performed their sexuals. They then pursued bans in taverns and saloons, and finally instituted dry legislation in towns, counties, and states.

BOURBON DRINKING DEATHS

In Kentucky, drinking deaths were so common that they made the funny pages:

Old Kentucky Reporter—What shall I say of this man who drank himself to death?

City Editor—Say that he died a natural death, of course.

—*Coffeyville Journal*, 1897

There were many voices for temperance. The broad-stroking national voices were the Women's Christian Temperance Union and the Anti-Saloon League. In whiskey-making country, the temperance opinions were constant and strong, and they hoped for an end to drinking. "The saloon. This is the devil's monster institution," said Dr. G. A. Lofton at a central Baptist Church gathering in Nashville. "The saloon is the force of far more than half the crimes and miseries of the country. It has not a single argument for its existence and every argument for its destruction." Of course the likes of Dr. Lofton, a roaming Baptist minister, did not see taxes earned from the saloon or distillery as positives for the community.

The benefits of whiskey and other alcohol were discredited with every opportunity. In 1909, the respected *Scientific Temperance Journal* declared whiskey to be an "unsatisfactory stimulant" after a study of sixty-two patients with acute infections. The study was not a smear campaign as previous efficacy claims had been. Rather, it showed the results of a controlled study finding that depression increases with every teaspoon of whiskey. These studies caught the attention of the American Medical Association, which offered a voice in the *Journal of the AMA* for temperance leaders from the Women's Christian Temperance Union: "This kind of temperance instruction is most hopeful, for when people learn that some of the most successful physicians of the world do not believe in the necessity or usefulness of alcoholic liquors in the treatment of disease they are much less likely to begin the use of these seductive drinks."

Distillers were losing the war of words. Temperance leaders were buying advertorials in hometown newspapers near distilleries, converting politicians into drys, and encouraging states to enact Prohibition. By 1901, 119 of 137 counties in Tennessee voted to go dry and nearly 50 percent of Kentucky's voted to go dry. The temperance leaders lauded these victories in whiskey-friendly states. "Kentucky, a state noted for fast horses, bourbon whiskey, and pretty women has 76 prohibition counties out of a total of 163," it was declared in the *National Advocate*, a National Temperance Society publication.

In 1909, Tennessee passed a statewide prohibition. As he was leaving office, Tennessee governor Malcolm R. Patterson said: "Prohibition has been almost as

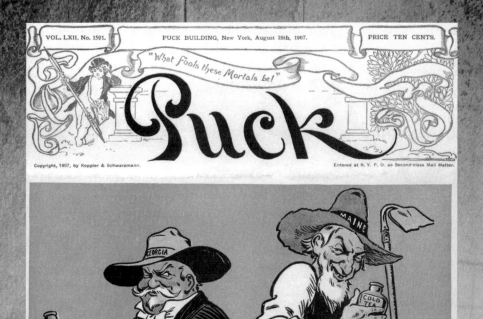

VOL. LXII. No. 1591.   PUCK BUILDING, New York, August 28th, 1907.   PRICE TEN CENTS.

"What Fools these Mortals be!"

Puck

Copyright, 1907, by Keppler & Schwarzmann.   Entered at N. Y. P. O. as Second-class Mail Matter.

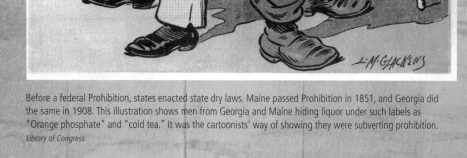

Before a federal Prohibition, states enacted state dry laws. Maine passed Prohibition in 1851, and Georgia did the same in 1908. This illustration shows men from Georgia and Maine hiding liquor under such labels as "Orange phosphate" and "cold tea." It was the cartoonists' way of showing they were subverting prohibition.
Library of Congress

disastrous to our state as the civil war itself. It has weakened our people, increased taxes, created factions, bred schisms, inflamed passions, caused fraud in elections and finally betrayed the Democratic Party to its enemies." Either before or almost immediately after, some Tennessee distillers established contracts with Kentucky companies to continue selling their whiskey.

After seeing the effects of Tennessee's prohibition on their communities, Kentucky temperance leaders changed their tune. Former congressman Henry Watterson tried to reason with the state's public on how to handle Kentucky's distilleries. "There are two ways of dealing with it," Watterson wrote in 1914. "We can enact such laws as they have enacted in Tennessee, practically confiscating the distilleries and the breweries. Or, we can make such police regulation as will regulate, and stop an agitation which alternates venality and strife."

When Watterson penned this, World War I had just begun. In addition to the fact that the United States was about to go to war, there were several factors at

TEMPERANCE LEAGUES

Singing the tune for temperance were nearly two dozen prohibition-minded organizations. They all had different agendas and some merely used temperance to achieve their ultimate goals—such as the Ku Klax Klan, which wanted segregation; and the Women's Christian Temperance Union, which wanted suffrage. The major groups either campaigning for temperance or the upholding of the Eighteenth Amendment included:

American Temperance Society
American Temperance Union
Anti-Saloon League
Board of Temperance Strategy
Cadets of Temperance
Catholic Abstinence Union of America
Church of Temperance Society
Congressional Temperance Society
Flying Squadron of America
Friends of Temperance
Intercollegiate Prohibition Association
Ku Klux Klan
Knights of Father Mathew
Lincoln-Lee Legion
Methodist Board of Temperance, Prohibition and Public Morals
National Temperance Council
National Temperance Society and Publishing House
Prohibition National Committee
Prohibition Party
Royal Templars of Temperance
Scientific Temperance Federation
Sons of Temperance
Templars of Honor and Temperance
Women's Christian Temperance Union
Woman's New York State Temperance Society
World League Against Alcoholism

Charles Nelson operated one of the most successful 1800s-era distilleries in the country. In Greenbrier, Tennessee, Nelson patented his own distillation technique and produced 380,000 gallons of Charles Nelson's Green Brier Tennessee Whiskey in comparison to Jack Daniel's 23,000 gallons made the same year. The distillery was "Old Number Five" because it was in the fifth tax district and produced more than thirty bourbon and Tennessee whiskey labels. Nelson passed away in 1891; his wife, Louisa, ran the distillery until 1909, when Tennessee enacted a statewide Prohibition. The Charles Nelson name resurfaced in the 2010s, when brothers Andy and Charles Nelson brought back their family's Nelson Green Brier Distillery (pictured) to Nashville.

play that would dictate the fate of the American distiller. One factor nobody could see coming: prohibitionists connected the enemy at war—the Germans—to alcohol, saying most American brewers were German, that you couldn't trust them, and thus you must support Prohibition. The second factor: the grains used for making whiskey were needed for the war effort. Some distilleries converted their stills to aid the government with industrial alcohol, and the Distillers Securities Corp. formed a subsidiary under the name of the United States Industrial Alcohol Company to facilitate the government's needs. And the War Trade Board made sure grains were used for food and for its allies, often sending up to fourteen thousand tons of cereal grains to suffering countries, such as Holland.

By June 1917, the government introduced a war tax bill that suspended production by distilleries and established that bonded whiskey aging would be subject to new tax. Medicinal whiskey and industrial alcohol production were not subject to the law. The tax included the existing $2.20 per gallon of liquor, plus a tax of $20 per bushel (from $3 to $9 a gallon) upon all grain, cereal, and other foodstuffs. The distillery community knew it could not recover from this, and there was doom and

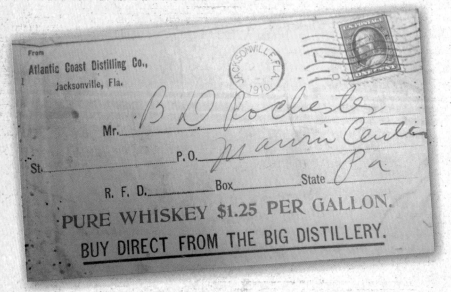

From

Atlantic Coast Distilling Co.,
Jacksonville, Fla.

Mr. *B D Rochester*

P. O. *Marrin Center*

Pa

St.

R. F. D. _____ Box _____ State

PURE WHISKEY $1.25 PER GALLON.
BUY DIRECT FROM THE BIG DISTILLERY.

Although the early 1900s had challenges for distilleries, the years also brought business perks. Consumers could buy directly from distilleries, though it was not a common practice.

gloom throughout the country. "The Peoria distilleries manufacture some alcohol for scientific and commercial purposes," W. E. Hull, general manager for Clarke Bros. & Co., told a newspaper after the ruling. "But whiskey is the main product. A distillery of large capacity cannot operate on a small scale at a profit. There haven't been enough war orders from the United States or the Allies to keep more than one of the distilleries busy, and no new ones are in prospect. Hence the distilleries must close."

From 1911 to 1917, Kentucky distillers paid $191 million into the Federal Treasury for bonded whiskey. After the new edict, only a handful of the 205 Kentucky distilleries were selected to continue operation for medicinal or industrial use. Even they had to know the writing was on the wall—the end was near.

Decades of fighting taxes, legislation, fraud, temperance and now war—bourbon distillers had finally thrown in the towel. But they were much smarter than anybody could have imagined; they were all about to become very rich.

Selling Stock

After the government's for-the-war prohibition took hold in 1917, the bourbon distillers had to know that they were about to lose everything, that the sweeping temperance arm would soon overpower them with untrue rhetoric and political action.

On October 28, 1919, Congress passed the Volstead Act (HR 6810) that banned alcoholic beverages, their production, and distribution. Despite numerous successful blocks of a national Prohibition, including an earlier President Woodrow Wilson veto, this time it stuck and convincingly passed the house with a vote of 287 to 100.

1917 DISTILLERS

In 1917, the government received requests from virtually all distillers to create industrial alcohol for munitions. Prior to the War Tax Bill, the government worked with distillers on denatured alcohol production, so many facilities were capable of handling the distillation output for the war. But unlike World War II, which had thousands of tanks, World War I had less need for industrial alcohol. In Kentucky, the government chose to work with a only a few distilleries for industrial alcohol production: Glenmore Distilleries Company, Owensboro; Peerless Distilling Company, Henderson; Midway Distillery, Midway; George T. Stagg Distillery, Frankfort; and James E. Pepper, Lexington.

Peerless Distilling Company was one of the few bourbon distillers licensed to distill industrial alcohol in World War I. It went defunct after Prohibition, but Corky Taylor has returned his family distillery, opening the Peerless Distilling Company in Louisville in 2015.

FAKE WHISKEY

As the Prohibition loomed, hints of what was to come filled the headlines. The country began to experience a rise in alcohol deaths in 1918. With Prohibition less than a month away, fifty-one people died from poisoned whiskey in a couple of days. No longer able to purchase whiskey from a legitimate seller, consumers bought whiskey from non-reputable people who were coloring wood alcohol and adding sugar with rye extract. On December 26, 1919, forty-five New Englanders died "terrible deaths" from the alcohol.

Before Prohibition passed, distillers and rectifiers used the export allowance in the Bottled-in-Bond Act to offload whiskey overseas to countries greatly in need of spirit. They sent whiskey to port towns in hopes of striking deals with nearby Cuba and the Bahamas, two countries with dealers who in turn planned to set up bootleg operations once America's Prohibition hit.

The Distillers' Securities Corporation struck one of the first deals and sold twenty-five thousand barrels of Kentucky whiskey to the British government in February 1918. This whiskey was planned for the "men at the front. . . . England has exhausted her supply of rum for soldiers. Therefore, she is buying as a substitute, pure American whiskey, buying as much as she can against the day when the supply in the United States will have been executed," Distillers Securities Corporation said. "After four years of warfare the Allies have come to realize the medicinal value of alcohol when rightly used. In the trenches, in hospitals applied internally and externally it is a Godsend to the boys who are giving their all to make the world safe for democracy."

Other distillers followed suit, with published reports saying that nearly twenty distillers became instant millionaires with the prices realized for whiskey after the war prohibition took effect. Analysts estimated that one unnamed distillery with twenty thousand barrels could realize a profit of $3.52 million; and another with fifty thousand could profit $5.88 million in 1918. The price increased from fifty to sixty cents per gallon in 1917 to $3.05 per gallon (not including tax) in 1918.

The demand for Kentucky straight bourbon was through the barrel, but the distillers were on the clock. They had until July 1, 1919, under an amendment in the Agriculture Bill to take whiskey out of bond. Lawsuits gained them an extension, but whiskey exports would no longer be allowed as of January 16, 1920, when Constitutional Prohibition went into effect.

Distillers shipped to the Bahamas through Triaca Company in Baltimore, Maryland. But they were consistently robbed, losing barrel after barrel, case after case, to bootleggers. The Cecil Distillery of Highlandtown, Maryland, claimed it had eight barrels of ten-year-old whiskey valued at $4,000 stolen from the port. Theft perhaps affected shipments, but the Lake Ellerslie steamboat was the first exclusive liquor ship to sail from Baltimore and would transport fifty thousand barrels of whiskey to the Bahamas. Other entrepreneurs such as Gertrude Lythgoe, "Queen of the Bootleggers," would wait to buy and later sell to American bootleggers.

Some Kentucky distillers believed the greater opportunity was in Cuba, because of its rum-making heritage. They planned to send 37 million gallons of bourbon whiskey to Charleston to ship, but while they were waiting on the legal workings to extend the deadline, Cubans realized they had the Kentuckians over a barrel and demanded $12.50 per barrel to store the bourbon. Some investigated shipping barrels to Mexico, but most found this to be impractical. The Dowling family, on the other hand, figured Mexico to be the best bet. They moved their still to Juarez, Mexico, and planned to make Mexican bourbon (see page 91).

As the shipment deadline loomed, temperance headline writers offered a victory headline to their people: "Pity the poor distillers—$60,000,000 worth of whiskey unable to ship." But there still was no legal loophole in the Prohibition legislation that allowed distillers to sell whiskey through medicinal channels, leading insurance companies to discontinue coverage to distillers. On December 19, 1919, some 35 million gallons of Kentucky bourbon sat in warehouses uninsured. "Kentucky distillers heard today a decision by the Connecticut Mutual Insurance Company branch office here that liability for whiskey could not further be provided . . . because no valuation can be placed on liquor now that it cannot be sold."

Distillers were chasing every avenue, making every call, and cashing in on every favor. Less than a week after they learned whiskey was no longer insurable, Kentucky's whiskey interests made arrangements to sell forty thousand barrels of young whiskey (1.4 million gallons) to the French. Brown-Forman's Owsley Brown spearheaded this effort and ensured the stocks arrived in war-torn France a year later. They also sold to Germany and some stocks to Cuba, despite the high barrel costs. But the bulk of the whiskey sat in bonded warehouses, and nothing in the Volstead Act gave instructions on what to do with the whiskey.

As the clock struck midnight on Prohibition day, medicinal whiskey rules were unclear.

CHAPTER 5
THE FIGHT FOR PROHIBITION'S MEDICINAL WHISKEY

S hortly before Prohibition passed, the United States saw one of the most horrific pandemics in history. The Spanish influenza killed between 20 million and 40 million people worldwide, and to no one's surprise whiskey was advertised as a treatment. Hospitals and clinics were so inundated with flu-sick patients that they didn't have time to take temperatures or blood pressures. According to navy nurse Josie Brown, who worked in the Navy Hospital in the Great Lakes in 1918, "We would give them a little hot whiskey toddy; that's about all we had time to do."

The Spanish flu outbreak played a pivotal role in the campaign for Prohibition-era medicinal whiskey. Physicians used whiskey as a treatment to the outbreak. In this 1918 photo, the American Red Cross prepares to gather influenza patients in St. Louis. *Library of Congress*

Whiskey, every form of whiskey, was once again called into medical service. But unlike previous national medical needs, whiskey's efficacy was called into question in the early 1900s and legitimate doctors requested other forms of medicine, such as quinine and Asprinol. The *Scientific Temperance Journal* told readers whiskey had "no value" for flu treatments. Nonetheless, medical directors were practically begging city commissioners and police chiefs to allow whiskey into their hospitals. In Georgia, the physicians sent urgent appeals for medicinal whiskey. Georgia had already enacted a statewide prohibition, and the physician's bid for more whiskey was unsuccessful. Legal whiskey simply did not exist in many regions. By the fall of 1919, many whiskey distillers had exported much of their stock, and the government was trying to figure out what to do during Prohibition. Whiskey's medicinal efficacy was hotly debated, and it was not just the temperance doctors who said whiskey did not work for influenza treatment. Several medical journals from 1900 to 1919 downplayed whiskey's efficacy for treatment and in fact began to discourage physicians from prescribing it. The Great Lakes Hospital commandant Capt. W. A. Moffett said whiskey had no effect, even in large quantities, on combatting influenza. On the other hand, it was a medicine that doctors knew. Dr. Charles Higgins, in Providence, Rhode Island, said he found whiskey to be a "valuable . . . treatment of my influenza cases. I find that it is a great aid to the assimilation of good. It tides the patient over the danger period of his illness. It counteracts the poison of the disease in the system. I think it is wise to use a fair amount mixed with milk. . . ."

In fact, most of the medical community still used whiskey for several treatments, from swollen joints to whooping cough. Thus, when Prohibition became law, medicinal whiskey was seen as a matter of national health, and bourbon distillers were on the front lines along with doctors and druggists—all with unique points of view—trying to save medicinal whiskey.

In 1919, national Prohibition officials estimated that 50 million gallons of whiskey sat in bonded warehouses. But there was considerable confusion as to what would happen to this whiskey once Prohibition became law. The initial Prohibition legislation allowed for medicinal whiskey and sacramental wine, but "as prescribed by the Commissioner of the Internal Revenue," who offered vague mandates about liquor-selling permits for pharmacies and wholesalers. As the deadline for Prohibition approached, the government held hearings to create a functional plan. All sides expected a pro-medicinal-whiskey voice from distillers, but it was the medical community that legislators really listened to.

There appeared to be a schism between the druggist community and the physicians. "Every national drug organization was represented by one or more of its officers, or counsel, or both, and a number of state and local pharmaceutical associations were also well represented," the *Northwest Druggist* reported of the December 2, 1919, hearings on the allowance of medicinal liquor. The druggist organizations made promises to Congress that it would dispel any who violated the law and said they were needed for controlling the intoxicating liquors. They preached urgency as the country fought the Spanish flu. And there were also business concerns for the distillery community. Said Ohio congressman William Gordon:

No provision is made for compensating those of our citizens who have large sums of money invested in the manufacture and production of spirituous, vinous or malt liquors. The enormous increase in the sale of the many different varieties of patent medicines containing large percentages of alcohol throughout prohibition territory in the United States, whereby the consumption of spirituous liquors has actually increased with the growth of dry territory, will probably prevent any loss and damage by the manufacturers of whisky and other hard liquors. The constantly increasing demand in dry territory of alcoholic liquors for "medicinal" purposes, although sold in the form of patent medicines, will no doubt continue to increase with the increase in so-called dry territory; but wine and beer containing a very small percentage of alcohol can not be thus mixed and sold, and their manufacture and sale would stop if this measure could be enforced. No provision is made in this joint resolution for supplying the deficiency of between three

Although the initial Prohibition law allowed for medicinal whiskey, it was unclear how the process would work. Because of this uncertainty, distillers sold whiskey to foreign governments. Many bourbon distillers attempted to store whiskey in Cuba, but this effort failed and they were forced to lobby for medicinal whiskey.

hundred and four hundred millions of dollars annually which will be lost to the public revenues of the United States by the adoption of this measure, to say nothing of the loss of revenue to the States and their different subdivisions. The consequences of this legislation have not been fully considered by its authors and proponents.

Unfortunately for distillers, Congress was more concerned with appeasing the dry consumer than with the $400 million lost in public revenues they provided.

As Congress took its chambers in early January 1920, it endured protests from the religious, medical, and alcohol communities, among others, all demanding certain alcohol allowances and questioning why one group was treated differently than the other.

Inside the medical community, the doctors were turning on the druggists.

The pharmacist community believed it had become the "goat" for the physicians who overprescribed whiskey; the defense from physicians was that they had no choice but to prescribe either whiskey or narcotics. The elimination or decrease in the use of medicinal whiskey did cause medical minds to pursue new forms of drugs. One that became a replacement for medicinal whiskey was often its complement—quinine, a drug from cinchona bark that is still used today. Drug companies capitalized on this trend as well: "Better than whiskey for colds and flu. New elixir called Asprinol, medicated with latest scientific remedies, used and endorsed by European and American Army Surgeons to cut short a cold and prevent complications. . . . Proclaimed by the common people as ten times as quick and effective as whiskey. . . ."

Despite the growth to come in medical treatments, 1920 was not the year to take medicinal whiskey away from the doctor as a treatment for the Spanish flu. Sacramento pharmacist F. J. Quirin said:

> During the influenza epidemic . . . whiskey was very freely prescribed by physicians for their patients, and, as a druggist, I have no hesitancy in saying that . . . it was the cause of saving many lives. There are many people who will agree with me in this. Liquor is being prescribed in cases of pneumonia and other diseases. Much more might be said against Prohibition of the kind proposed, but I believe the influenza epidemic alone is sufficient to convince most people of medicinal value in certain areas.

Congress passed a restrictive Prohibition enforcement act that allowed the use of medicinal whiskey. The number of hurdles put in place, however, made many people look for new occupations. Internal Revenue declared:

> Physicians may prescribe wines and liquor for internal use or alcohol for external use, but in every such case each prescription shall be in duplicate

MEXICAN BOURBON

Before Prohibition, John and Mary Dowling moved distillation equipment to Juárez, Mexico, to start the D&W Distillery. The Dowlings were co-owners of the Waterfill & Frazier Distillery in Kentucky, so they used this label along with the words "Mexican bourbon." (This author has tasted the so-called Mexican bourbon, and it's the worst bourbon that's ever touched his lips.) Because they could legally distill in Mexico and the US government allowed for small quantities of medicinal whiskey imports, the Mexican bourbon had a healthy following during Prohibition.

D&W paid $2.20 per gallon in taxes to Mexico and was also a leading employer in the area, recruiting El Paso residents. Distiller A. Beam needed twenty-five men annually for production, offering them $12,000 a year. The brand would become a thorn in the side of Kentucky distillers, as they sold their bourbon cheaply and sullied the brand name of the spirit.

Before Prohibition, well-known Kentucky bourbon families—the Beams and the Dowlings—pursued a distillery business in Juárez, Mexico, where they made Mexican bourbon up until 1964 under the name D. W. Distillery.

and both copies signed by physicians handwriting. The quantity prescribed for a single patient at a given time shall not exceed one quart. In no case shall a physician prescribe alcoholic liquors unless the patient is under his constant personal supervision.

All prescriptions shall indicate clearly the name and address of the patient including street and apartment number, if any, and date when written: the condition or illness for which prescribed and the name of the pharmacist to whom the prescription is to be presented for filling.

The physician shall keep a record in which a separate page or pages shall be allotted each patient for whom alcoholic liquors are prescribed, and shall enter therein, under patient's name and address, the date of each prescription, the amount of and kind of liquors dispensed by each prescription, and the name of the pharmacist filling the name.

These guidelines were considered so restrictive that many druggists chose to close shop rather than pursue a permit. "Before the Prohibition amendment went into effect we used to sell liquors upon a physicians prescriptions. The prescriptions were filled in the same manner as those for drugs. There were no precautions to be taken; no stringent rules to observe; no laws which might possible be evaded.

PROHIBITION CHRONOLOGY

Prohibition didn't just happen overnight. The temperance movement saw a steady rise from the moment settlers arrived in the New World.

1642   Colony of Maryland punishes drunkards through a fine of tobacco.

1664   Virginia passes law prohibiting clergymen from excess drinking.

1833   Georgia passes first legislation to allow a dry vote.

1851   Maine Law enforces Prohibition in the state.

1869   National Prohibition Party is formed in Chicago.

1890   The Reading Railroad fires all employees who frequent saloons and brothels.

1893   Anti Saloon League is founded in Oberlin, Ohio.

1917   Before the United States entered World War I, 60.7 percent of the country lived in dry territories via local and state governments.

1918   Wartime prohibition.

1920   Eighteenth Amendment, the Volstead Act, becomes effective in January.

The text of the Enforcement Act makes it impossible, however, for us to continue the sale of liquors," a source told the *New York Times*.

If the druggists thought they had a lot of red tape, it was nothing compared to what Brown-Forman and others went through in order to obtain medicinal permits.

On paper, distillers faced more than two dozen regulations that required reports on grains, buildings, and employees; and they were under the watchful eyes of the federal agents at all times, not to mention having to keep everything under lock and key. Even if the laws were a bit tedious, the country was under Prohibition, and bourbon distillers appreciated the medicinal whiskey option on the table. This one sentence had to feel like salvation to those sitting on thousands of gallons of whiskey: "Intoxicating liquor so procured by such persons may only be sold or furnished by them in wholesale quantities to other persons entitled to procure the same unless other provided by the terms of the permits." After receiving state and federal permits, distillers were instructed to label all containers with name of manufacturer, kind of spirit and proof, name of seller, date of sale, and name of purchaser. Initially, only two Pennsylvania distillers received distillation permits, while the Kentucky and Illinois distillers either converted their plants into industrial alcohol facilities or sold the whiskey sitting in warehouse through medicinal channels.

Of course, they faced opposition to medicinal sales.

Some states refused the health-care sale of whiskey. Indiana Prohibition commissioner Charles Orbinson said whiskey could not be sold in the state for medicinal purposes, because to do so conflicted with the state's Prohibition laws that passed prior to the federal Prohibition. "Regulations have been received from the bureau of internal revenue providing that permits may be issued by state prohibition directors to physicians for the prescription of booze and to druggists for the sale of booze on prescriptions. But the federal government will in no way intervene with the enforcement of state law," Orbinson said.

Indiana eventually allowed the use of medicinal whiskey toward the end of Prohibition, as most states did. The press called these medicinal whiskey prohibitive states "Bone Dry States."

So many people were so ill that the government had to cap the number of bottles of whiskey they could receive, eventually restricting a patient to one whiskey bottle each ten days. The initial law also dictated that distillers could not withdraw more than a combined 1.5 million gallons in a year. This put incredible constraint on the doctors and druggists attempting to genuinely treat patients. By 1922, the American Medical Association claimed it was unable to procure enough pure medicinal whiskey from licensed druggists and was forced to purchase from bootleggers.

FAST FACT

$400 million was the estimated value sitting in bourbon warehouses on January 16, 1920.

Distilleries were also under constant shakedown.

Starting in 1920, distillers received medicinal wholesale licenses and could acquire stocks under government watch and with the appropriate paperwork. But some bourbon distillers tried to skirt the regulations.

On January 18, 1920, only one day after national Prohibition became law, R. E. Wathen and W. F. Knebelkamp of Wathen & Co. Distillers were arrested for illegal removal of whiskey from warehouses. Interestingly, the federal government charged Wathen, a Louisville millionaire, with defrauding the government for the potential lost taxes of $140,000 in a beverage tax and $40,000 in medicinal tax. A year later, revenue agents seized a New York warehouse that allegedly received seven hundred cases from Brown-Forman, who argued that there were only five hundred cases shipped and that they were legally shipped with a verified permit and the name of the New York Prohibition director. But the revenue agents simply didn't trust distillers or people owning warehouses full of whiskey; they seized Brown-Forman's whiskey to "verify" its legitimacy.

Meanwhile, as legitimate whiskey salesmen were subject to legal shakedowns, bootleggers were forming strong syndicates that became trusted sources for medicinal liquor. Criminals even targeted bonded Kentucky bourbon distillers. In

PERMIT ISSUED UNDER THE NATIONAL PROHIBITION ACT AND REGULATIONS

To W.L. Weller & Sons Inc.
J.P. Van Winkle, Sec. & Treas.
1033 Story Ave., Louisville, Ky.

Application having been duly presented and approved, you are hereby authorized and permitted, subject to the further restrictions of your State Law, to sell intoxicating liquors in accordance with the provisions of Sections 951 and 952, Regulations 60.

This permit covers the sale of such spirits as have been produced by W. L. Weller & Sons, and the United Distillers Company when operating as duly registered distillers Nos. 17 and 6, respectively and are now stored or will be stored later in Concentration Bonded Warehouse No. 17, Free Department, at Louisville, Kentucky, operating under Permit No. Lou. Ky. P-15 Supplemental.

Dated Dec. 31, 1926
Wm. O. Mays
Prohibition Administrator

SPRING
1917

PROOF
100

CAUTION NOTICE

"This bottle has been filled and stamped under the provisions of an Act of Congress, approved March 3, 1897, entitled 'An Act to allow the bottling of distilled spirits in bond.' Any person who shall re-use this bottle for the purpose of containing distilled spirits, without removing and destroying the stamp affixed to this bottle will be liable for such offense to a fine of not less than $100.00, or more than $1,000.00, and to imprisonment for not more than two years."

Produced by Mary M. Dowling Distillery No. 59, 8th District of Ky., Bottled at Dist. Bonded Warehouse No. 17 District of Ky.

A. Ph. Stitzel, Incorporated
Permit No. Ky. P-15
Whiskey—½ Pint—100 Proof
Manufactured Prior to Jan. 17, 1920
For Medicinal purposes only. Sale or Use for other purposes will cause Heavy Penalties to be inflicted.

Whiskey distillers were required to label whiskey as "medicinal purposes only." This particular bottle holds unique historical meaning. It says it was produced by Mary M. Dowling Distilling Company through Pappy Van Winkle's A. Ph. Stitzel company. Mary Dowling, whose family owned Waterfill & Frazier, also started the Juárez distillery that made Mexican bourbon.

Lebanon, Kentucky, four masked men took guards hostage at the Mueller, Wathen, and Kobert Distillery. They bound one with wire inside a warehouse as the crew stole ninety-two cases of whiskey.

There was also the concern of counterfeiting by legitimate resellers.

Louisville druggist Hurley Pope was arrested for a statewide plot to sell $22,500 of fake whiskey. Agents followed resellers with close ties to distilleries, but did not foresee the massive and dangerous upstarts of George Remus, Bill McCoy, Al Capone, and numerous other bootleggers taking advantage of Prohibition.

After two years of medicinal whiskey sales, the distillers found themselves under constant government supervision, were harassed by the feds during shipments, and were competing with the bootlegger.

In July 1922, the leading US distillers called on the president and the Treasury to properly enforce Prohibition, claiming that Federal Prohibition Commissioner Roy A. Haynes allowed the "illegal and discretionary administration of the Volstead Act." The bourbon companies called themselves the "Custodians" of pure bonded medicinal whiskey and issued the president a stern letter arguing that their governmental instructions varied from agent to agent and that some agents gave "unwarranted verbal instructions." The commissioner, they said, was "hampering proper distribution of pure aged medicinal whiskey and pure grain alcohol for medicinal use to the wholesale and retail druggists of the United States and to the manufacturers of necessary medical products." The distillers called the enforcement policy:

> [the] official oppression of legal distribution . . . resulting in the substantial denial to the public of its right to secure medicinal whiskey and pure grain alcohol as provided in the Eighteenth Amendment and the Volstead Act. . . . It is common knowledge that production of illicit of poisonous character and smuggling of spurious liquors is substantially unchecked . . . While this policy is to deprive legal dealers and manufacturers of legitimate supplies, it also brings about subterfuges whereby every artifice to violate the law is encouraged on the part of moonshiners, smugglers and those who misuse denatured industrial alcohol with deadly consequences.

The distillers' protests did not fall on deaf ears. Secretary of the Treasury Andrew W. Mellon, who owned the Overholt Distillery in Pennsylvania, worked to increase the withdrawal of whiskey for medicinal uses and to strengthen enforcement of the act, including increasing the undercover dry agents to snuff out illegal liquor syndicates and limiting the harassment of the doctors and pharmacists who issued

NON-KENTUCKY DISTILLERIES

How distilleries handled their business to prepare for Prohibition would determine their respective area's distilling history. Peoria, Illinois, mostly converted their facilities to food plants, while Pennsylvania concentrated on exporting their stocks in 1918 and 1919. Kentucky, in a sense, got stuck with the bulk of their whiskey and were forced to lobby for and sell it as medicinal whiskey. The plus side to this strategy was it kept bourbon brands in front of the consumer, even if only as a medicinal whiskey. Of the major distilling areas, only Kentucky remains as strong as it once was, and the medicinal whiskey efforts certainly played a roll in this.

These barrels and demijohns are stored in Cognac, France, at the Pierre Ferrand estate. Brown-Forman's Owsley Brown received a special permit to sell the French thirty thousand barrels of bourbon in 1920.

whiskey prescriptions. But the Anti-Saloon League fought back, saying that every effort to aid the medicinal alcohol movement undermined the new amendment in the Constitution. "The next flank movement of the opposition is to ask for a scientific commission to determine what is intoxicating liquor," said Wayne B. Wheeler, the generalissimo of the Anti-Saloon League. Those speaking for the sick offered a sensationalized view: "Thousands among the sick are rendered helpless and possibly suffer death by the lack of 'liberal' interpretation of the already iron-clad law," according to a 1922 *Washington Times* story.

In addition to sick patients genuinely in need of a drink, bootleggers were stealing legitimate medicinal whiskey because it was of better quality and guaranteed to be

CUSTODIANS OF WHISKEY

In 1922, the US distillery industry formed an alliance to preserve their bonded whiskey, believing they were being treated unfairly. The group included the Chairman Owsley Brown, Louisville; H. W. Gaylord, New York; Henry Naylon, Baltimore; Edmund H. Taylor, Frankfort; George R. Landen, Cincinnati, R. E. Wathen, Louisville; and Roy Rosenfield, Chicago.

WHAT WAS WHISKEY IN PROHIBITION?

In 1925, the United States Pharmacopeia listed whiskey as "an alcoholic liquid obtained by distillation of fermented mash of wholly or partly malted cereal grains, and containing not less than 47 percent and not more than 53 percent by volume of ethyl alcohol. Must have been stored in charred wood containers for a period of not less than four years." In other words, a Prohibition-era whiskey could be less than 50 percent actual whiskey. Thus, both druggists and patients coveted straight bourbon whiskey.

pure. And who wouldn't want medicinal ten-year-old bourbon over made-in-the-woods whiskey?

Furthermore, Mellon forecasted a whiskey shortage. In 1922, he cut nationwide medicinal whiskey withdrawals from 10 million gallons to 2 million a year. The next year, after a Supreme Court ruling allowing foreign vessels containing medicinal liquor, Mellon gave the approval for foreign envoys containing medicinal whiskey. Officials closely inspected the foreign liquor ships and were granted the "widest latitude concerning medicinal whiskey." But Mellon knew the allotment of foreign whiskey was not sustainable and that whiskey evaporated 3 to 5 percent a year while in the barrel—he had to increase the amount of whiskey in warehouses to meet the medicinal demand. By June 1925, officials estimated there were only 26.8 million gallons of spirits in bonded warehouses, down from 50 million in 1919. That number was reduced to 15 million gallons of whiskey in 1926. America was in the middle of a medicinal whiskey crisis, since it was still used for treating every-thing from the cold to pneumonia. The government had to act fast.

In 1924, Treasury officials seized $11.2 million in alcohol. Confiscated whiskey would be tested for quality and introduced into the medicinal market. A total of 2,238 medicinal whiskey holders—druggists, doctors and distillers—violated the Volstead Act in 1925. The most common arrest was for aiding a bootlegger.

Mellon sought to cut the bootleggers' supplies and allow legitimate whiskey producers to expand without interference. "It is the policy of the department to concentrate its efforts against the organized traffic, and that this may be done effectively to encourage in every possible way local enforcement by the states and communities, releasing federal agencies from the necessity of doing local police work to the detriment of the main objective," Mellon said.

Mellon's plan to protect medicinal whiskey was soon enacted. Within months of ramping up enforcement efforts, undercover agents were seizing thousands of gallons of stolen medicinal whiskey. But these confiscations were only a drop in the bucket of the bootleg trafficking, and additional efforts were needed to improve medicinal whiskey supplies.

In January 1927, Mellon began campaigning for a dry reorganization bill that would increase Prohibition units and give them autonomy from the internal revenue bureau. He also wanted a medicinal whiskey bill that created a private corporation to take over all existing supplies of liquor. The new corporation— under government supervision, of course—would buy and sell all liquor stocks and take on distribution of medicinal whiskey. President Coolidge, who had vetoed a previous bill encouraging the distribution of medicinal whiskey stocks by the government, was in favor of Mellon's plan because it would prevent bootleggers from counterfeiting standard brands, according to the office of the Treasury.

Mellon recommended that Congress approve the manufacture of 3 million gallons of whiskey. At this point, only a few northeastern distilleries had received permission to distill small amounts. The Treasury Department believed that enforcement should be directed at the bootleggers and that the distilleries, who were legitimate and following the laws, should be allowed to meet the medicinal needs of America. But the early 1927 bill died, and one of its greatest opponents was from a state that could have greatly benefited from it. Kentucky Democrat Congressman Ben Johnson described the medicinal bill as an instrument to defeat Prohibition and said it empowered distribution under the guise of medicine. A committee was appointed to further investigate a medicinal whiskey bill.

But the crisis was urgent. Soon, poor sick children with eye infections and pregnant women suffering from toe swelling would be without whiskey. After Congress's failure to pass a medicinal whiskey bill, the Treasury planned to grant

DOWNSIZING AND DIVERSIFYING

In addition to selling medicinal whiskey, some bourbon makers downsized, selling corporate shares, assets, and real estate. Brown-Forman sold buildings, W. A. Gaines sold shares. And James Beam diversified into the quarry business. Beam also worked with Leslie Samuels, of the Maker's Mark Samuels line, to start a car dealership in Franklin.

But the most promising business ventures were related to what the bourbon makers already knew, and none were more successful than Owsley Brown, of Brown-Forman, in France. After thirty thousand barrels were shipped to France under special permit to the government prior to Prohibition, he went to the country a few months later to market the whiskey to French liquor dealers.

Government agents were consistently seizing stills that were supplying gin and whiskey to speakeasies and bootleggers. Illegal whiskey became medicinal whiskey's biggest competition. *Library of Congress*

permits to distilleries for medicinal whiskey production. The current law allowed them to grant two. Hearing of whispers of this, fifteen Kentucky and Pennsylvania distilleries applied for distilling permits, but no action was taken. Two weeks after the Treasury's bill died, Congress revised the legislation and introduced it to the House in a form that allowed issuances of whiskey distilling permits to not less than two and no more than six distilleries.

Suddenly, the political tides were turning, and former dry politicians were supporting medicinal whiskey. The medicinal whiskey bill passed Congress and went to the Senate, while Senator William E. Borah, a noted dry Republican, said the medical authority changed his mind about medicinal whiskey's benefits. Borah even supported an abolishment to its "one pint in ten days" rule. This change in the dry landscape signaled a possibility of the unthinkable—to distill again.

FAST FACT

In a 1921 American Medical Association survey, 51 percent of US physicians were in favor of prescribing whiskey.

Unlike today, the 1920s whiskey consumer did not prefer older whiskey. Thus, this seventeen-year-old Old Crow bottled in 1925 illustrates that distillers were willing to sell older, and often unwanted, medicinal whiskey due to the shortage.

New Make

As Congress considered the new medicinal whiskey bill, the arguments had not changed. What had changed, though, was the increase in violence now causing some dry-leaning perspectives to move toward legitimizing alcohol sales. But doctors also worried about the government dictating medical programs. After the Supreme Court upheld the medicinal liquor limitations in 1926, the American Medical Association's Dr. Wendell C. Phillips said:

> No one is able to foresee to what extremes of restrictive legislation Congress may be driven by uplifters, professional reformers, cultists and fanatics, once they gain the power, or what drug or therapeutic procedure, personal privilege or constitutional rights may fall under the ban. Not even the middle ages boast of a greater triumph of legislative imperialism over the methods and achievements of science.

At this point, the opinion of distillers appeared to not even matter. The Treasury did not even consult the distillery community when creating its medicinal whiskey plans. The distillers grew tired of this and demanded an audience with Congress.

During the next go-around at revamping regulations for distillation during Prohibition, members of Congress asked production-focused questions that would help them determine unit limits and help them sell a plan to fellow lawmakers. How much would it cost? How much should they distill? Do brands really matter?

In 1927, Congress called in distillers for a Ways and Means Committee hearing to discuss medicinal whiskey production.

Perhaps better than anybody before or since, the American Medicinal Company's Levi Cooke, a lobbyist for hire, outlined the production details of the distillery community over the previous ten years:

> At that time [1917], there were in the several hundred distillery bonded warehouses, 270,000,000 gallons of proof spirits, all of which were competent for use as beverage spirits. Of that quantity, a part, less than half, was alcohol, high-proof spirits. The rest was rye and bourbon whisky with some gins and some brandies. Prior to war-time prohibition, when it became effective, and prior to January 16, 1920, when national prohibition became effective, that quantity had been reduced until there were in some two hundred and sixty-odd distillery warehouses a total of about 70,000,000 proof gallons, as of the coming in of national prohibition. During the first year of national prohibition, and before the regulation by the Treasury had become settled with respect to medicinal spirits, there was a considerable withdrawal.
>
> Gradually, during 1921 and 1922, the withdrawal of the distilled spirits for medicinal use, whiskies principally, had settled to about 2,000,000 gallons a year, and it has persisted with fair regularity at that figure.
>
> Therefore, you can consider that the four or five years of national prohibition enforcement has resulted in a take by the country, 26 States permitting sale of medicinal spirits, of approximately 600,000 to 650,000 three-gallon cases, now packed in pint bottles, 24 pints to the case.
>
> The situation that existed immediately after prohibition, when the distilled spirits were in this large number of distillery bonded warehouses, many of them in country districts, with poor police protection; and an inability on the part of the Federal Government to guard all the warehouses well, there was some stealage and it was also a very expensive undertaking by the Government to man the warehouses with guards and storekeeper gauges. Each plant cost from $5,000 to $10,000 per annum of Government money for public service and care by storekeeper gauges and guards.
>
> It was that situation, both the matter of expense and the leakage of distilled spirits in violation of the law, out of those warehouses,

FAST FACT

For the first five years of Prohibition, only twenty-six states allowed the sale of medicinal spirits.

that brought about the principal special act affecting distilled spirits for medicinal use, after the national prohibition act. . . .

Cooke, a relatively small player in the grand history of bourbon, testified that 12 to 14 million merchantable bonded whiskey gallons could be safely maintained if the withdrawal rate remained 2 million gallons. Cook testified:

If the Congress of the United States conceives its duty under the national prohibition amendment and the laws in enforcement thereof, to maintain a pure, sound supply of medicinal whisky, the Congress must do something very shortly . . . Some of my clients say they will manufacture whisky, but when I have quizzed them on the economics and financing of it, they confess that they would go a little way, they would make one small crop, possibly, or a small crop spring and autumn when they first manufactured whisky, but not one of them—and I am compelled to speak frankly—will, I believe, manufacture five continuous crops of whisky, of 5,000 barrels apiece, because it means the laying down as of 1927, 1928, 1929, 1930, and 1931, of the cost of producing those whiskies, and allowing them to lie idle, evaporating, maturing, and then at the end of five years, they can begin to realize on what by that time will have become an enormous investment.

Cooke argued it would take 3 million gallons of whiskey to produce 2 million gallons to bottle after evaporation while in the cask, estimating that would require a $10 million investment from the distillery community. And this is where Cooke cast his fishing line into Congress to see if they would bite. He was trying to increase Congress's sense of scale for production. "I do not believe that any individuals will be willing, even if they could apportion shares, to finance over that period of five years that very large undertaking," he said.

Congressman Charles R. Crisp took Cooke's bait and asked if some distillers could manufacture twenty-five thousand barrels. And at that point Cooke set the hook and hammered home an opportunity to maximize revenue:

It would cost as much to put a distillery in condition to manufacture 5,000 barrels as it would to manufacture 60,000. Individuals might say, we will gamble—and you have got to use that word—we will gamble on the conditioning of a distillery, the purchase of grain, the financing of the crop, the securing of the barrels, being at high cost, and we will make a crop of whisky and see what happens.

Cooke argued that the reason why Large Distillery and Gwynnbrook ceased production in the early 1920s was the enormous investment without a guaranteed return.

It is absolutely uneconomic for individuals to undertake the manufacture of whisky in this limited field and under all of the restrictions that are bound to exist under prohibition. It is a topsy-turvy uncertainty that any man will shrink from if he is respectable in his financial thinking. It is a situation in which some gamblers might engage and hope for luck and hope that the conditions 5 or 6 years hence would result in great financial gain to them. They would take a large gambler's profit, and, in my judgment, be entitled to it if they won.

Of course, Cooke also spoke of the distillers' sacrifice and their importance in difficult times. "Distillers [have] been good citizens. My clients are ready, as public-spirited citizens, to surrender their independence, to surrender possibly enormous profits that no one could criticize them for taking if they have the

During the medicinal whiskey Congressional hearings, the distillery community educated the congressmen, saying that the investments required to produce five thousand barrels was the same as that required for twenty thousand barrels. This photo is of the former Wild Turkey Distillery.

opportunity to take them, and allow this thing to go forward, surrendering their great assets to the corporation."

The Reorganization Bill of 1927 gave druggists and physicians broader prescription power of medicinal whiskey, and it permitted greater distillation allowances. But at least one bourbon distiller did not agree with bill's minutia, fearing it would drastically increase price of bourbon from $30 per case to higher than $45. S. C. Miller, vice president of Frankfort Distilleries, testified that the new law did not limit the amount of whiskey permitted for prescriptions. Miller said, "There is not a line or a word in this measure which in any manner seeks to control the alcohol industry. It is my fixed conviction, from a careful study of this bill, that it would have no practical effect in strengthening the enforcement of the prohibition laws."

The drys challenged these latest medicinal attempts, offering to change the Republican Party's moniker from the Grand Old Party to the Grand Old Whiskey Party. The Women's Christian Temperance Union stood strong on its "science" and continued its march against medicinal whiskey. Ella Boole, president of the National Woman's Christian Temperance Union, said of the nation's 152,000 physicians, only 65,000 had received medicinal permits—as if this somehow indicated that other doctors were opposed to whiskey. Although it's more likely the other doctors simply wanted to avoid paperwork or practiced in bone-dry states, she was right in the fact that only thirty-three states allowed medicinal whiskey in 1927. But even the WCTU was changing its tune toward medicinal whiskey, essentially saying that if it was to be allowed, then let it be pure. "We believe that the supply of whiskey for purely medicinal purposes should be protected from adulteration, that doctors who use it conscientiously may have a dependable remedy," Boole testified.

The Anti-Saloon League appeared to just want checks and balances. "Experience in the states has shown that if you do not put some restrictions upon a doctor one or two doctors in a small community, a few others in larger ones, will transfer the beverage trade over through the prescription trade and prescribe tremendous amounts of whiskey," testified Wayne B. Wheeler, general counsel of the Anti-Saloon League.

Nonetheless, the government was working to squash the lowering dry tide. But nothing compared to the medicinal whiskey narrative of Emma Gilliom, the sister of Indiana attorney general Arthur Gilliom, who campaigned to allow medicinal whiskey in Indiana. Whiskey allegedly saved her life. Mr. Gilliom said:

> I was called to the bedside with the understanding that she was dying. Dr. CC Rayl of Decatur, the attending physician told me that a little whiskey would be helpful. I immediately started out to look for some whiskey. With

my sister dying it required more than seven hours to find any liquor, but finally I found it at the home of a friend in Fort Wayne. I took a pint of it back to the hospital and I am told it was instrumental in saving my sister's life. Do you suppose that I was going to sit idly by and watch my sister die when there was a chance to do something for her? There is not a normal human being in American who would see a loved one perish if whiskey would save the life. The case was identical to the case where the life of governor Ed Jackson's wife was saved by whiskey and where the lives of my two children also were saved by administering whiskey.

Gilliom's sensational claims were just a few of millions made as a thirsty country just needed a drink. Although Congress indicated the government would issue thirty-six distilling permits, published reports said the Internal Revenue commissioner planned to grant five distilling permits in 1927, out of fifteen applications. In fact, the publicly traded companies such as National Distillers enjoyed strong trading based "on the belief that the government would permit the manufacture of whiskey," an AP story said in June 1927.

But the increased interest in medicinal whiskey was not enough to get the still fired up in 1927. New leadership inside the Treasury killed the effort, saying "no emergency exists and no action will be taken on applications of a number of whiskey producers for licenses to resume distilling." The Treasury leadership felt no action was necessary until the country's supply was completely exhausted.

The former assistant secretary general, L. C. Andrews, who spearheaded the medicinal whiskey efforts, believed five-year-old whiskey was necessary for medicinal purposes. The new boss, Seymour Lowman, did not think age mattered when referring to medicinal products; thus, he did not see the same immediacy as Andrews.

For the distillers, this had to be a devastating blow amidst positive signs of encouragement. A change of the guard toward medicinal whiskey was certainly under way, and even some drys were softening their point of view. By November 1929, whiskey in storage was down to 10

Since medicinal whiskey was not permitted in all states, state interests pursued far-fetched campaigns about people being on their deathbeds until illegally transported whiskey saved their lives. An Indiana politician claimed whiskey procured in Illinois saved his family.

million gallons. With the government determining that four-fifths of all the remaining whiskey was bourbon, the Treasury finally allowed for the manufacturing of additional supplies. "Whiskey to be dispensed must be of the standard set out in the United States pharmacopeia, and that is the old bottled-in-bond standard, requiring ageing of not less than four years in the wood. So we will have to start manufacturing at a point where the supply has been reduced to four years, plus reasonable commercial quantity, which I would say would be about nine months or a year," said Prohibition Commissioner James Doran.

By the time Doran printed distiller applications to mail to the government's shortlist of candidates, the country was down to 9.5 million gallons of medicinal whiskey. But only three distillers initially applied for the medicinal distillery license, likely due to the fact that they didn't trust the system or think it would actually come to fruition. Fifteen had applied before but only five selected, so why waste the time only to be disappointed again?

But with his assurance that distillers would indeed be allowed to distill again, Doran resolicited for applications and by September 1929 he had received fourteen applications.

Two companies that initially could not apply were Overholt Distilling and Schenley, as they were under investigation for violations of Prohibition laws. But when the Justice Department threw the case out on the last day of 1929, they were allowed to distill and sell whiskey again starting January 1, 1930, because, as Doran said: "These companies are quasi-public institutions. Druggists and doctors all over the eastern section of the United States depend on them for medicinal whiskey."

Thus, in 1930, after years of debate and promises, the government granted distilling permits because the liquor stored in distilleries and bonded warehouses had been reduced to a quantity insufficient to supply the country's "non-beverage" needs. Permits were initially granted to A. Overholt & Co., of Bradford, Pennsylvania; Large Distilling Company; Schenley Distillery with facilities in Kentucky (George T. Stagg in Frankfort) and Pennsylvania; American Medicinal Spirits of Louisville; A. Phillip Stitzel Company; the G. Lee Redmon Company (Brown-Forman); Frankfort Distilling Company; and the Glenmore Distilling Company. Distilling permits were also granted to twenty brandy distilleries and two rum distilleries, but all were designated a certain allotment of distillation time. For example, American Medical Spirits was permitted to distill bourbon in Kentucky and Maryland rye at the former Mount Vernon Distillery and immediately began production of eighteen thousand barrels.

Permits were also granted to distillers so they could bottle specific brands: Overholt, Old Taylor, Old Crow, Golden Wedding, Old Hermitage, Greenbrier, Old McBrayer, Bond & Lillard, Mount Vernon, Spring Garden, OFC, and Old Grand-Dad. These initial permits allowed for companies of the respective brands to lease still time.

Within a month of the government announcing legitimate distilling contracts, Prohibition agents broke up a $50 million bootleg liquor ring that included former

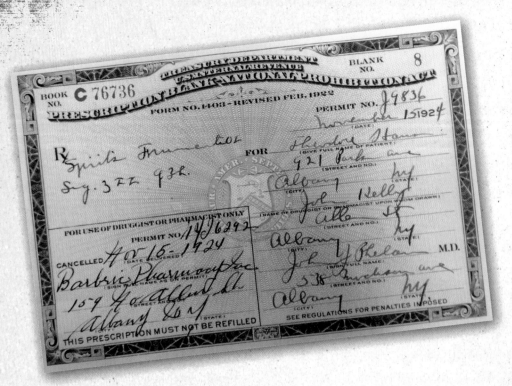

While medicinal whiskey was legal to prescribe, depending on the state, many doctors felt the prescription requirements were too steep.

legitimate distilling companies. Fleischman Yeast Company, Cor Products Refining Company, and Glenwood Distilling Company officials received indictments for connections in trafficking bottled-in-bond whiskey into speakeasies. "These companies were 'cover houses' used to cover diversion of alcohol secured on permits," officials said after the arrest.

In fact, as medicinal whiskey production kicked up, the government was putting a major dent in the bootlegger's supply. Those who said medicinal whiskey production would hurt the bootlegger were right. Whether by agent design or coincidence, bootleggers were forced to procure liquor from more at-risk moonshiners and thus they were more exposed. The year 1930 was a victorious one for bourbon distillers, as major bootlegger arrests went up and the dry politicians were losing office. And New York governor Franklin Roosevelt expressed his favor for repealing Prohibition, while President Herbert Hoover was discussing repeal, too.

As for the medicinal whiskey debate, it became less common than the debate on Prohibition in general. Drys changed their message from absolution and "whiskey evils" to one of education. "People must be taught not only to refrain from the sale of alcohol, but more important, to abstain from its use, not because they fear the law or the officials, but rather they know what alcohol is and what it will do to those who use it," said R. N. Holsapie, Michigan superintendent of the

Prohibition gave birth to criminal syndicates led by violent bootleggers. Al Capone (pictured) was thought to have pioneered the St. Valentine's Massacre in 1929, when six rival gang members were executed. However, Capone was in Florida at the time and investigators could not pin murder on him under 1920s-era laws. The actions of Capone and other violent gangs led to increased legal authority for investigators, and it gave Prohibition repeal proponents a strong argument that ending Prohibition would also end bootlegger-led violence. *US Department of Justice*

Anti-Saloon League, at the state's 1930 convention.

Meanwhile, the majority of Americans were leaning toward repeal. A *Literary Digest* poll had become the country's leading tally for the Prohibition mood. Its 1930 results showed 41 percent wanted repeal and nearly all wanted either modification or better enforcement of the law. *Literary Digest* also noticed a trend in the drys changing their votes: "An increasing number of our friends are claiming the modification vote as a legitimate part of their outfit. . . . They argue that many sincere Prohibitionists, disguised with their scandals of enforcement and anxious for reform, have marked the modification square as a compromise, rather than a vote either for repeal or for a continuation of present conditions."

But distillers had their sights set on the here and now. They were making whiskey again, and they were doing business as if nothing had ever happened. The Treasury Department allowed distillers to buy stocks from seized assets. And Brown-Forman and W. L. Weller & Sons were permitted to purchase two thousand barrels of pre–World War I whiskey from former "King of the Bootleggers" George Remus, via his secretary Miss Blanche Watson, for $250,000, or $125 a barrel. Brown-Forman received 1,500 barrels of the lot, and it was never explained how Remus, a convicted bootlegger, was permitted to sell whiskey.

The medicinal whiskey distilleries were also allowed to lease stills to approved companies. In 1931, George T. Stagg president Albert B. Blanton informed his district supervisor of Prohibition permits, "This company has been granted an additional allotment of medicinal whiskey to be made in the year 1931, and it is our desire that part of this allotment be manufactured in the name of 'The John T. Barbee Company,' and we hereby consent to issuance of permit for 18,500 gallons of medicinal whiskey to be made at Distillery No. 113, District of Kentucky, Frankfort, Ky. . . ."

The George T. Stagg Distillery transferred the distillery to the John T. Barbee Company, "in compliance with regulations for such cases provided that at 12:00

o'clock, midnight, on January 13, 1932, the mash and beer on hand and all the unfin-ished spirits outside of the Cistern Room of Distillery No. 113, located on Leestown Turnpike, 1½ miles North of Frankfort, Kentucky, be transferred from the George T. Stagg Company to the John T. Barbee Company," a company with Schenley Products Co. as the primary stockholder. Schenley also purchased the George T. Stagg Distillery in 1929, so the company was funneling distillery projects under various names through George T. Stagg's facility. Nonetheless, they still had to go through the paperwork process. In an April 14, 1930, letter from a Schenley executive:

> Please be advised that our company has signified its intention to the Prohibition Bureau to amend its permit to manufacture medicinal whiskey by reducing the quantity. This is done in order that we have 25,000 gallons manufactured by you, under the name of The John T. Barbee Company, a corporation of Maryland, the stock of which is entirely owned by our parent corporation, namely, The Schenley Products Company of New Jersey . . . In the event of the application being granted and a permit is issued, we hereby authorize you to manufacture this quantity for them.

These prearranged distilling agreements were appreciated by the government, as it helped them project medicinal whiskey quotas. If anything, the corporate familiarity allowed for a smoother approval process.

However the contracts came to be, the communities near distilleries could smell mash in the air and hear barrels rolling into the warehouses, while the medical community had a national guarantee for medicinal whiskey. By April 1932, the public no longer considered the legitimate distiller to be the creator of evil elixirs. Thanks to the bootlegger, most reasonable people saw the distillery as just another workplace that happened to manufacture alcohol.

That's why Dr. James M. Doran, now the commissioner of industrial alcohol, had the ability to peel back one more layer of restriction for medicinal whiskey when he testified that the patient limitation for medicinal whiskey was hurting the country. "That limitation was one of the irritating things in the law that might very well be made subject to regulation than to statuary control. With respect to the frequency of prescribing for any one patient, I believed that the statutory limi-tation should be withdrawn. I do not believe we should lose control of the number of prescriptions and the quantity that may be prescribed." Starting May 15, 1932, physicians could prescribe as much as they needed.

At the time, there were 5 million gallons of pre-Prohibition whiskey and 6 mil-lion of the newly distilled whiskey. All anticipated a prescription frenzy—cough, ache, ouch—for a nation that was suddenly and extremely sick. States still handled their own business, such as South Dakota limiting a physician to one whiskey pre-scription per day, and Indiana sought medicinal whiskey in drug stores at 50 cents

West Virginia was one of the last states to allow medicinal whiskey sales. Today, it's home to one of the most-successful smaller bourbon distillers in the country. Smooth Ambler Spirits is in Lewisburg, West Virginia, a dry beacon during Prohibition.

tax per pint. Even dry strongholds like West Virginia were relaxing their medicinal whiskey laws.

For the drys who predicted that medicinal whiskey would prove to be a way to break Prohibition, they had to know the inevitable was about to happen—that the prediction was right. The righteous temperance message just no longer held the same power. Now, people wanted work. And politicians wanted new roads. After West Virginia allowed medicinal whiskey at just four drugstores selling a total of 4,392 liquor tax stamps, they injected $2,196 of tax revenue into the state economy. This was not lost on New York governor Franklin Roosevelt as he ran for president. "Millions of people cherish the hope that their old standards of living have not gone forever. Those millions cannot and will not hope in vain," Roosevelt said at Chicago speech July 2, 1932. "I pledge you. I pledge myself to a new deal for the American people. Let all of us here assembled constitute ourselves prophets of a new order of confidence and courage."

People were depressed, and repealing Prohibition was a part of his platform for what he was marketing as a "new deal."

Continued on page 116

PROHIBITION DISTILLATIONS AND WAREHOUSING

From 1920 to 1923, the government allowed for small amounts of distillation from two distilleries in Pennsylvania and one in Maryland. On May 5, 1920, the Internal Revenue Bureau announced medicinal whiskey manufacturing contracts had been established with The Large Distilling Company, forty miles from Pittsburgh; Barrett Distilling Company, near Scranton; and Gwynnbrook Distillery in Maryland. They distilled until 1922. According to Congressional testimony from an industry spokesperson, their costs for distilling were too high and they merely stopped production.

After 1923, it took seven years for the government to issue permits again. It issued seven medicinal whiskey contracts in 1930 with a production goal of 2 million gallons.

Proof Gallons Distilled

1920	234,705 gallons	1927	None
1921	753,374 gallons	1928	None
1922	315,799 gallons	1929	None
1923	None	1930	2 million gallons
1924	None	1931	2.44 million gallons
1925	None	1932	1.71 million gallons
1926	None	1933	4.91 million gallons

Distillers also received annual permits to buy from warehouses and then sell into the medicinal whiskey trade. This has been a subject of great confusion over the years, because the companies often did business under several names, and the government permitted labeling under non-operating distillery names. But the number of US distilleries involved in the medicinal liquor trade was far greater than previously known.

In 1922, the Treasury Department reported medicinal liquor, mostly whiskey, was kept in three hundred warehouses around the country. Federal agents stood guard, while the Treasury planned to pare them down by five each year. That number escalated due to excessive withdrawals of liquor, thievery, poor planning, and evaporation. By 1929, there were only twenty-eight registered warehouses that could sell their contents to a permitted wholesaler. On the following pages are the warehouses federally permitted in 1929 for medicinal liquors.

California had several bonded warehouses during Prohibition for both whiskey and brandy. These barrels belong to

General bonded warehouse No. 2, the South End Warehouse Co. (Inc.), San Francisco;
special bonded warehouse No. 7, the Fresno Warehouse Co. (Inc.), Fresno; general
bonded warehouse No. 3, the Cook-McFarland Co. (Inc.), Los Angeles; distillery
warehouse No. 361, the California Products Co., Fresno

Illinois

General bonded warehouse No. 5, Sibley Warehouse & Storage Co. (Inc.), Chicago;
general bonded warehouse No. 6, the Railway Terminal & Warehouse Co. (Inc.),
Chicago; Distillery bonded warehouse No. 22, the Corning Distilling Co. (Inc.), Peoria;
Distillery warehouse No. 7, the American Distilling Company, Pekin

Kentucky

Distillery bonded warehouse No. 18, Hill & Hill Distilling Co. (Inc.), Owensboro;
distillery bonded warehouse No. 24, H. S. Barton, trading as Glenmore Distilleries Co.,
Owensboro; general bonded warehouse No. 1, the Louisville Public Warehouse Co.
(Inc.), Louisville; distillery bonded warehouse No. 5, Sunny Brook Distillery Co. (Inc.),
Louisville; distillery bonded warehouse No. 19, R. E. Wathern & Co. (Inc.), Louisville;
distillery bonded warehouse No. 368, Kentucky Distilleries & Warehouse Co.
(Inc.), Louisville; distillery bonded warehouse No. 414, G. Lee Redmon Co. (Inc.),
Louisville; Distillery bonded warehouse No. 35, F. S. Ashbrook Distillery Co. (Inc.),
Cynthiana; distillery bonded warehouse No. 5, Joseph Wolf, trading as James E.
Pepper & Co., Lexington; distillery bonded warehouse No. 33, the Frankfort Distillery
(Inc.), Frankfort; distillery bonded warehouse No. 53, E. H. Taylor Jr., & Sons (Inc.),
Frankfort; distillery bonded warehouse No. 113, George T. Stagg Co. (Inc.), Frankfort;
distillery warehouse No. 17, A. Ph. Stitzel, Louisville; distillery warehouse No. 106, W. A.
Gaines & Company, Frankfort

Maryland

Distillery bonded warehouse No. 27, the Baltimore Distilling Co. (Inc.), Warner, Wooster
and Alluvion Streets, Baltimore; distillery warehouse No. 3, the Hannis Distilling
Co., Baltimore

Massachusetts

General bonded warehouse No. 2, the Quincy Market Cold Storage & Warehouse Co.,
Charles River Stores, Boston; distillery warehouse No. 6, Everett Distilling Co., Everett

During Prohibition, whiskey was kept under lock and key, and federal agents maintained accurate records. To keep track of these warehouses, the government named the bonded warehouses by state, district and warehouse number.

Missouri

General bonded warehouse No. 2, the R. U. Leonori Auction Storage, St. Louis; general bonded warehouse No. 3, the Security Warehouse & Investment Co. (Inc.), St. Louis; general bonded warehouse No. 1, Adams Transfer & Storage Company, Kansas City; special bonded warehouse No. 1, Adams Transfer & Storage Co., Kansas City

New York

General bonded warehouse No. 2, the Keap Warehouses (Inc.), 181–207 Melrose Street, Brooklyn, New York City; general bonded warehouse No. 1, Cosmopolitan Warehouses (Inc.), 25–31 Rose Street, New York City; special bonded warehouse No. 2. the F. C. Linde Co. (Inc.), Beach and Varick Streets, New York City

Pennsylvania

No. 45, Sam Thompson Distilling Co., W. Brownsville; distillery Bonded Warehouse No. 5, the Large Distilling Co., West Elizabeth; distillery bonded warehouse No. 3, A. Overholt & Co. (Inc.), Broad Ford; distillery bonded warehouse No. 2, Dougherty Distillery Warehouse Co. (Inc.), 1121–1135 North Front Street, Philadelphia; distillery bonded warehouse No. 4, Joseph S. Finch & Co. (Inc.), 129 McKean Street, Pittsburgh

Louisiana

Distillery warehouse No. 2, Jefferson Distilling & Denaturing Co., New Orleans

Wisconsin

Distillery warehouse No. 3, National Distilling Company, Milwaukee

Continued from page 111

Even President Hoover campaigned under the promise that he would give states the rights to do as they wish with alcohol, adding that it was time to stamp out the speakeasies. "I cannot consent to a continuation of this present regime; I refuse to accept the return of the saloon with political and social corruption or to endure the bootlegger and speakeasy with their abuses and crime. Either is intolerable. Our objective must be the sane solution and not a blind leap back to the old evil days," he said as he accepted the Republican nomination.

Not long after Hoover's speech and Roosevelt's rise, Schenley visited Europe to reacquaint themselves with former distributors and distiller friends who might want to strike partnerships. The company informed its stockholders in 1932 that they anticipated a change in the country's liquor laws. "Unemployment in the United States has reached large proportions," a Schenley booklet said. "Various statutes have been passed by Congress and the state legislatures appropriating monies for feeding and clothing the distressed. This means increased governmental expenditures, inevitably resulting in more taxes."

PRICE INCREASE

Expecting the end of Prohibition, distillers raised their prices in September 1933. According to the Associated Press, all whiskey virtually doubled in price. Whiskeys that had sold for $30 for a twenty-four-bottle case were now selling for $30 to $72 at wholesale. Dr. James M. Doran, who oversaw medicinal whiskey, said the medicinal whiskey importers could match domestic prices even after paying a $5 per gallon tariff. Of course, distillers only enjoyed a couple of months of this price gouging. Prohibition was repealed December 5, 1933.

Because the country was falling into the Great Depression, economists began studying the loss of alcohol taxes. Prior to Prohibition, alcohol beverages had accounted for $500 million a year in tax revenue. Authors Raymond B. Fosdick and Albert L. Scott believed alcohol taxes would account for $700 million in 1933 on booze tax alone. So now, repeal proponents used the bootlegger, the economy, and states' rights as their chief arguments for repeal.

Dr. Howard Russell, founder of the Anti-Saloon League, argued the repeal sentiment came from "American multi-millionaires who want liquor to pay their income taxes." He was right.

The relentless efforts of bourbon distillers to maintain medicinal whiskey production slowly chipped away at the dry resolve. A few days after Prohibition's repeal, Schenley purchased full-page advertisements in several high-circulation newspapers, even though Prohibition still technically was in place. "After these 14 years of barred distillery

THE COOPERAGE INDUSTRY IN PROHIBITION

Prohibition not only damaged the distilling business, it hurt the cooperage industry that supplied barrels to brewers, wineries, and distilleries. The industry managed to survive through exportation. In 1929, the US Department of Commerce reported $9 million of tight barrels were exported—$1 million to Germany alone. They also exported white and red oak staves. Apparently, European brewers preferred American wood. "American white oak is favored because of its texture and durability," wrote W. K. Knox, chairman of the Rochester Cooperage, in 1933 in a correspondence to another New York businessman.

Coopers were no doubt savvy during Prohibition. They continued operation and managed to successfully lobby for a clause of "new charred oak" in bourbon's post-Prohibition definition. These 1930s coopers preserved an industry that is enjoying a revival right alongside bourbon.

doors, of rusting vats and stills, of grapes rotting on neglected vines, and empty warehouses, in which fine old whiskey should have been richly mellowing—after these 14 years of such discouraging inactivity, you must be inclined to wonder how really fine wines and spirits may be produced or bought," Schenley wrote.

Schenley championed its stalwart bourbons Old Stagg, OFC, James E. Pepper, Golden Wedding, and Albert Blanton as the "loyal president" of George T. Stagg.

According to Schenley's advertorial, all was hunky dory.

Perhaps not every bourbon company could afford to purchase lengthy advertisements like Schenley. But they were all just as jubilant. Little did they know that government interference was not yet over.

CHAPTER 6
BIG BUSINESS
Post-Prohibition Growth

Months before repeal, distillery states were preparing for the expected end of the Eighteenth Amendment, but at the discretion of state governments. Governors and attorneys general had to allow the incorporation of distilleries prior to the Volstead Act repeal.

In fact, after the Beer Bill signing in March 1933—the first legal step toward repeal—businessmen and distillers bought buildings and made plans to form the first distilleries in their respective areas. Whether this was done with the states' permission, well, that's subject to how you interpret an individual's intent. An entity could have purchased a building for a butcher shop, knowing it would become a distillery when the time was right.

President Franklin D. Roosevelt signs the Beer Bill with, left to right: Representatives Claude V. Parsons of Illinois and John W. McCormack of Massachusetts; Clerk of Committee, H. V. Hesselman, who brought the bill to the White House; and Representatives John J. O'Connor of New York and Thomas H. Cullen and Adolph J. Sabath of Illinois. It was an important step for repealing Prohibition. *Library of Congress*

Many businesses seemed to have the inside political track, giving them an advantage with investors and banks. The Hammond Distillery announced its plans the day after Indiana Attorney General Phillip Lutz Jr. ruled legal the incorporation of distilleries before Prohibition was officially repealed. Its owners included Julius P. Smientanka, a former Chicago-based internal revenue collector. Curtis B. Dall, the son-in-law of President Roosevelt, became the vice president and director of Peoria, Illinois's, Hiram Walker & Sons facility, while the plant manager was former congressman William E. Hull. In September 1933, Hiram Walker & Sons announced plans for the world's largest distillery in Peoria, Illinois, covering nineteen acres and with a capacity of twenty thousand bushels and twelve thousand barrels of whiskey weekly. Weeks before repeal day, December 5, 1933, Peoria was touting itself as the best American whiskey producer. "Located in the projected Illinois waterways, in the heart of the corn belt and near the coal fields. Peoria has the added advantage of a river whose water supply at certain depths is of excellent quality, and, what is more important, maintains an even temperature the year around," Hull told the *Evening Independent* November 22, 1933.

The promise of Prohibition's end led to distilleries touting their work opportunities. "Unemployment? Not around these parts," the Peoria newspaper wrote

BOURBON'S WORST GOVERNOR

When running for Kentucky governor in 1935, Albert Benjamin "Happy" Chandler Sr. assured distillers he would be a good leader for the state. But Chandler greatly penalized the bourbon industry with taxes.

He signed a nickel-a-gallon production tax on distilled spirits in 1935, meaning distillers paid both steep federal and state taxes. After his first term (December 10, 1935–October 9, 1939), Chandler served as a US senator until 1945 and then as the commissioner of Major League Baseball until 1951. He was reelected as governor in 1955, whereupon he increased the state spirits tax to ten cents per gallon. Chandler also added an annual ad valorem barrel tax, earning him the moniker of the "Anti-Liquor Governor."

Distillers were so outraged that they began moving barrels to other states to avoid the aging-barrel tax. Now when Kentucky elects a new governor, the bipartisan Kentucky Distillers' Association lobby hears from its membership: please, whatever happens, just make sure we don't get another Happy Chandler.

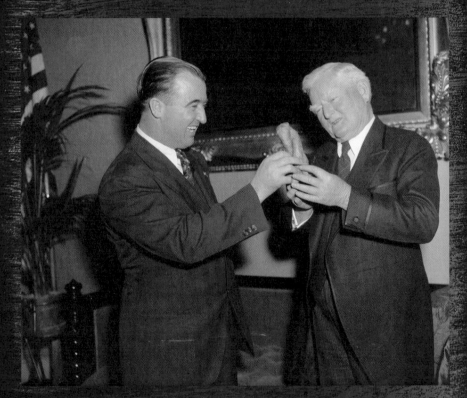

Then–US Senator "Happy" Chandler (Democrat) gifts Vice President John Nance Garner some Kentucky chewing tobacco. Chandler was much kinder to Kentucky's tobacco than its bourbon. *Library of Congress*

regarding the importance of the whiskey distillers. This sentiment was shared in all the major distilling regions. People were poor and needed work. Whether you were Baptist or Catholic, the distillery industry offered a welcomed job opportunity. But the morality issues that caused Prohibition weighed heavily on FDR, who wrote upon signing the Twenty-First Amendment on December 5, 1933:

> I asked the wholehearted cooperation of all our citizens to the end that this return of individual freedom shall not be accompanied by the repugnant conditions that obtained prior to the adoption of the Eighteenth amendment and those that have existed since its adoption. Failure to do this honestly and courageously will be a living reproach to us all. I ask especially that no state shall by law or otherwise authorize the return of the saloon either in its old form or in some modern guise. The policy of the government will be to see to it that the social and political evils that have existed in the pre-prohibition era shall not be revived nor permitted again to exist. We must remove forever from our midst the menace of the bootlegger and such others as would profit at the expense of good government and law and order.

The Whiskey Money Flowed

On that glorious day when bars could pour bourbon and most distillers filled barrels for the first time in thirteen years, an economic surge trickled down the alcohol industry in a time of great fiscal uncertainty. American investors sought distilling partners to once again produce bourbon. Every distiller boasted with what could only be described as excitement, all promoting their stills, bushels, and warehouses, and the big names associated with the brands. When the Fairfield Distillery sent a letter to investors, the company reiterated its powerful workforce and size of operation.

> The new plant, the home of Pride of Nelson and other popular brands, is equipped with a Horix bottling table, automatic bottle washer and filler and has a bottling capacity of forty barrels per day. Thirty girls were employed when the new plant was set in operation. The plant is steam heated with both sidewall heaters and the latest type unit overhead electric heaters. It has a spacious finished products room and a great deal of additional space for storage. It is also equipped with other modern conveniences for the health and comfort of employees. According to the chief distiller, Guy Beam, the new Fairfield plant will make its first run around January 15. The plant is equipped with a five story stillhouse, a new twenty-thousand-barrel warehouse, a new office building, a complete machine shop and the bottling line. There is not a second-hand piece of machinery at the plant . . .

Fairfield's letter is indicative of the language all distillers used to garner interest from potential investors, though the process varied from state to state.

With the Prohibition repeal, the federal government gave each state its alcohol rights back. In effect, each state became its own country in terms of the alcohol business, giving the counties and cities their own rights to govern alcohol as they pleased. This model exists even today and is the reason why dry counties and cities still exist. Before starting a distillery, potential businessmen still had to jump through government hoops.

With the help of investors, Frank J. Parker, of Titusville, Pennsylvania, optioned a former radiator plant for $10,000 shortly after Prohibition, with intentions of turning it into a distillery, but first faced a judicial hearing in order to begin operations. He claimed to have owned $250,000 worth of distillery equipment and offered work for more than one hundred people, but the distillery finances failed and Parker left the Titusville populace disappointed. The Titusville distillery was one of many spirits projects that just couldn't get off the ground. For every Hiram Walker, there were five projects like the Titusville distilleries that didn't make the headlines. Money was just too tight. The US unemployment rate was 24.9 percent in 1933, when consumers were victims of $140 billion disappearing from deposits. In the 1930s, more than nine thousand banks failed, which led many distilleries to seek non-bank streams of revenue.

Among sources for funding were outside businessmen from Chicago and New York. Many pursued outside-Kentucky partnerships, while smaller distilleries shoestringed family money together, some selling a few cattle here and there, and taking on non-distilling ventures to diversify revenues.

The larger distillers chose the publicly traded route. Hiram Walker, National Distillers, and Schenley were conglomerates that commanded healthy earnings for their investors. But going public was also an option for the midlevel distilleries one-sixteenth the size of Schenley.

On December 1, 1936, the Kentucky Valley Distilling Company filed registration with the US Securities and Exchange Commission for 120,000 shares of cumulative preferred stock at $5 a share. Kentucky Valley Distilling operated in Chapeze, Kentucky, and had connections to the time's highly coveted brand—Old Charter.

By 1937, there were more than 530 Kentucky bourbon brands, all competing for shelf space in packaged liquor stores and in taverns. In the Kentucky distilling industry, there's a saying that everybody gets along, especially the production people, but that the sales and marketing staffs can be a little cutthroat. The competitive nature of the 1930s marketer was quite apparent in the retail trade advertisements. They all claimed to be the best, some clinging to the tried-and-true claim of "much greater demand than anticipated," as K. Taylor Distillery told retailers in 1936.

With the incredible investment money pouring in, the 1930s were a time of opening and then quickly expanding. In 1936, Glencoe added four twenty-six-thousand-gallon

The Dant family's bourbon history runs deep in Kentucky. Joseph Washington Dant built a small distillery in 1836 in Marion County. He sired seven sons, including J. B., who introduced the world to his Yellowstone Bourbon. J. B.'s talent was cut short during Prohibition; but he joined the Taylor & Williams Distillery, and conglomerate Schenley Distillers Corporation purchased the right to the J. W. Dant Brand as a part of its expansion program after repeal of Prohibition.

fermenters to its eight twelve-thousand-gallon fermenters, Labrot & Graham added a bottling line to increase capacity to three thousand cases daily, National Distillers' W. A. Gaines revamped the E. H. Taylor & Sons plant, and the Cummins Distilleries planned to add equipment to increase to 175 barrels per day. And all distillers boasted their job opportunities.

In Pennsylvania, the Overholt Distillery, owned by National Distillers, said it was operating at capacity at around 337,800 gallons per day and employing 125 workers. This strength in work went a long way during economic downtimes, but that didn't stop the government from wanting its taxes.

Almost immediately after Prohibition's repeal, bourbon distillers were in the crosshairs of tax-hungry and temperance politicians who sought to tax bourbon as much as they could and to limit alcohol's advertising ability. Of course, the country needed revenue. Herbert Hoover's Revenue Act of 1932 reduced the share of federal tax revenues from personal and corporate income taxes while increasing excise taxes on merchandise and services, such as movies, gasoline, and radios. Few people knew that post-Prohibition, the bourbon industry was subject to much governmental scrutiny.

BUYING SOURCED WHISKEY

If you wanted to own a bourbon brand in the 1930s, all you needed was cash and the right connections to purchase whiskey from the distilleries, who were more than eager to sell you unwanted stocks. After you and the distillery agreed to terms, the facility would send you a certificate called a "warehouse receipt" that looked like an old stock bill.

Other distillers, distributors, and even upstart companies purchased sight-unseen bulk whiskey, set up contract distillation contracts or bought the warehouse receipts of select barrels. The Bernheim Distillery charged ten cents per barrel per month for aging. Should a distillery want to buy and bottle right away, that was within the law so long as the taxes were paid. After Waterfill & Frazier submitted its $333.34 for 150 barrels purchased from the Tom Moore distillery, the Revenue Department quickly encouraged the company to pay tax now instead of holding it over in bonded warehouses.

Due to the lack of well-aged whiskey, many distilleries were putting young bourbons onto the market, some as young as one year old. Others were turning to blends of bourbon, a style that mingles several bourbons from several different distilleries. However, those with capital still managed to procure leftover stocks made during Prohibition.

In the 1930s, whiskey traders worked with distilleries to broker bulk whiskey to bottlers and wholesalers across the country. The Lancaster-Bennet Company Blue Book was a reliable guide to whiskey prices. Old Belmont, Tom Moore, and Bonnie Bros. commanded premiums in 1937.

Distillery workers roll barrels to the scales, as a government gauger records each barrel's weight. After Prohibition, a government representative would be on active distillery premises until the 1980s.

1930s Governing

Alcohol tax represented more than a half-billion dollars or 13 percent of the total federal tax collections in 1936. Bourbon distillers didn't seem to mind the federal taxes, and they even welcomed taxations at the state and local levels, too, often perplexing some industry insiders. In an essay titled "Why Invite Burdensome Taxes," the Central Kentucky Liquor Dealers Association wrote in February 1936:

> Recent news dispatches appearing in the daily press carried the thought that the distilling and retail liquor industry in Kentucky were eager for the General Assembly to place both production and consumer taxes on their products. Knowing that no group can survive excessive taxation under any form or name, it is doubtful that these taxes are as eagerly sought for as we are led to believe. . . . The average distillery in Kentucky would pay about twenty-five hundred dollars per year for the privilege of operating in this state . . .

The distilleries may have welcomed any form of taxation just because it provided an opportunity to operate again. And the taxman must have known that

In addition to the growth the repeal created for distilleries, it increased jobs and revenue for several other industries, including still makers, coopers, retailers, and wholesalers. In this 1930s-era photo, the workers of Vendome Copper & Brass Works appear eager to start making stills again. To this day, Vendome manufactures the majority of the US distillation equipment. *Vendome Copper & Brass*

the distilleries and their investors were desperate to do business and would pay inordinate taxes just to stay in compliance. After all, the distillers appeared to have no problems with a government that watched their every move.

Through the National Firearms Act of 1934, the IRS's Alcohol Tax Unit deployed some 1,400 agents throughout the United States to collect federal taxes. Distillers who were legally operating prior to 1920 had to be scratching their heads at some of these laws. The federal government required agents on the premises at all times. The federal gauger protected the still and warehouses under lock and key. The states also had their own restrictions.

Distillers in states without strong interest groups faced steeper taxes than those with fruitful distilling industries. State distilling licenses varied and were as low as $100 and as high as New York's $5,000. New York's steep distilling costs and governmental restrictions are likely why the state did not regain its distilling culture until the twenty-first century.

New York required its distillers to take an oath and prohibited them from owning any other businesses. New York also did not allow convicted felons, especially those who contributed to "prostitution," and seemingly banned women from distilling;

New York's law made a point to discuss the hiring of "each male person by such distiller." The state's chairman of the Alcoholic Beverage Control Board believed these rules added to the "temperate use of spirituous liquors. . . . State board has approached the liquor problem with a spirit of liberality, and has adopted rules and regulations which it believes feasible, capable of enforcement and will reasonably serve the needs and customs of our people," wrote New York ABC chairman Edward P. Mulrooney, the former New York City police commissioner, to New York governor Herbert H. Lehman.

Mulrooney's general indictment of liquors being a "problem" for social settings and the need for "temperate use" shows how some people in power felt about alcohol. They still viewed it as a problem, but less severe than the problem of the bootlegger. The consumer population didn't seem to care about the taxes; they were more concerned about whiskey supply. Essayists urged whiskey distillers to store liquor in bonded warehouses and "be ready to supply the American demand with good American whiskey."

Protecting Bourbon

It had been nearly thirty years since legislators discussed "what is whiskey?" Now that the distilleries were sending tax revenue up the pipeline, there were new efforts at play regarding production. Shortly after the Pure Food & Drug Act, the United States questioned whether bourbon could be made with molasses. They also considered banning foreign grains for use in distillation. In a 1936 Judiciary Subcommittee hearing regarding a bill that would ban unlawful use of molasses for blending whiskeys, the sugar lobby protested that anything not labeled "straight" was fair game for blending use, arguing that distilled molasses is no different than distilled grain if used for a blend. In its argument for American-made molasses spirit in blending, the sugar lobby said foreign grains should be restricted. C. J. Bourg, vice president of of American Sugar Cane League, testified: "As between the American grain farmer and Cuban or Puerto Rican grower, we certainly favor the American grain farmer; and if it were possible within the law to make a restriction against foreign articles or buy expensive domestic molasses produced in Louisiana and Florida, we could not object." Bourg defended US molasses as being better for America than foreign grains, such as Argentinean corn and Danish rye.

The greatest legislative threat came from the effort to revise the Bottled-in-Bond Act. Canadian distillers and wholesalers once again attacked Kentucky bourbon producers, as if Prohibition had never happened. Now that their common dry enemy was nullified, they could attack the "monopoly of the market," testified Hugh J. McMackin, of the National Wholesale Wine & Liquor Dealers' Association

> **FAST FACT**
>
> A total of 467 million gallons of whiskey were stored in bonded warehouses in 1938, and there were 108 US distilleries in 1939.

on July 26, 1935. McMackin was in favor of the reintroduction of "bulk sales" of whiskey, a revision that was on the floor, but the new Federal Alcohol administrator favored the larger distillers. McMackin berated the bottled-in-bond distillers, who:

> . . . are bottling approximately 90 percent of the distilled spirits today. There are a number of other independent distillers, who, before prohibition, sold in bulk to wholesalers who were permitted to bottle and market their private brands for which they created local demand by newspaper advertising and marketed successfully in competition with nationally advertised products. When Mr. Choate issued his arbitrary ruling in May 1934, which denied other than the afore-mentioned favored six distillers and rectifiers the right to bottle, he established the monopoly which controls the marketing of legal liquor in this country today. The competition which

In addition to new regulations, post-Prohibition distilleries faced the elements. Kentucky's river towns frequently found themselves underwater. In 1936 and 1937, the Ohio River flooded Louisville and washed out several distilleries. Bottles and barrels were destroyed after the flood, and vast amounts of history and paperwork were lost. The City of Paducah received eighteen inches of rainfall in sixteen days. In response, the US Army Corps of Engineers built flood walls and dams to protect against future floods. *Library of Congress, US Farm Security Administration*

the liquor monopoly, fostered by Mr. Choate as F. A. C. A. Administrator and the Bureau of Internal Revenue of the Treasury Department[,] is composed of approximately 2,500 wholesale wine and liquor dealers who have been deprived of their right to bottle and market good legal liquor at moderate prices. This is competition which is feared as much by the bootlegger as by the liquor monopoly.

Numerous wholesalers, including the Kansas City Hirsch family that owned shares in Kentucky distilleries, encouraged Congress to grant wholesalers their right to buy and sell in bulk and bottle under government supervision. They called the post-Prohibition regulations an injustice.

Foreign distillers followed the wholesalers' attack, requesting a liberalization of the Alcohol Administration's regulations. They wanted blended whiskey to be allowed as bottled-in-bond, but the Americans argued that the bottled-in-bond act was not intended for foreign spirits. Congress later proposed a decree that no imported whiskey could be labeled "Bottled in bond. Under government supervision." It also imposed an embargo on any foreign distiller who refused the jurisdiction of the American courts. The Canadian government was not happy with this decision. "This bill . . . appears to me to attempt by an indirect method to obtain jurisdiction over Canadian nationals domiciled in Canada," declared Hon. C. H. Cahan, Canada's former secretary of state and someone who was considered a friend of the American trade. Canada warned that this attempt to protect America's Bottled-in-Bond Act would greatly jeopardize trade between the two countries, which had recently entered the US–Canada Trade Agreement of 1935. William Daum Euler, Canada's minister of trade and commerce, said, "What is illustrated here is an old story. The story of the difficulty of getting a trade agreement with the United States possessing the quality of performance. . . . For our neighbors—and this is said without intention to give offense—have a habit of giving with one hand, of taking away with the other."

The trade agreement reduced the tariffs on Canadian whiskey from $5 to $2.50, leading to decreased prices on Canadian bourbon (yes, they sold Canadian bourbon), blends, straight whiskeys, and bottled-in-bond whiskeys. Seagram's even advertised the tariff reduction: "Every penny of tariff saving is passed on to you. And in addition, substantial further reductions in price have been made to place these finer whiskies . . . Seagram's V.O. 6-years-old Bottled-in-Bond under Canadian Gov't Supervision, $2.09 a pint." Hiram Walker bragged after the trade agreement about its Canadian bourbon product: "A six-year-old straight bourbon whiskey, brought into a price class where you can enjoy it every day, by bringing bourbon stock in bulk from Canada, and bottling in Peoria. The tariff saving we pass on to you, 90 proof." For the American distillers whose fathers had fought off Canadian interests in the 1890s to create the Bottled-in-Bond Act, these labels had to feel like a slap in the face. They had to fight back legally or face losing the brand awareness they had built. There was nothing they could do to stop Canadian bourbon labels; although an early 1900s libel court case had defined bourbon as a product made in Kentucky, nothing legislatively protected them from foreign bourbon in 1937. They could, however, fight for bottled-in-bond—a sound piece of legislation signed by President Cleveland.

In 1938, Canadian whiskey imports dropped significantly because both Hiram Walker and Seagram began shipping barrels to the United States to age in US bonded warehouses. During Congressional testimony, Federal Alcohol Administrator Phillip E. Buck said Canadians received the "most-favored-national principle applied to whiskey." But he said tariffs on bonded whiskey—four years and older—was $5 per gallon; thus, Canadians were financially encouraged to produce blends instead of bottled-in-bond. The Americans held strong toward the one label they believed was as indicative of quality as the best Scotches and cognacs. They clung to this simple phrase: "stored in bonded warehouses under the US government supervision for no less than 4 years."

After Prohibition's repeal, bottled-in-bond came under attack with a brief attempt from Canadian interests to repeal the act and then attempt to label Canadian whiskey as bottled-in-bond. But the bourbon distillers staved off the fight. Government permits allowed whiskey to be in bond for eight years from the date of entry into a bonded warehouse. After eight years, it was forced out of bond for tax payment.

THE FEDERAL ALCOHOL ADMINISTRATION ACT

With repeal came new governing methods for alcohol. Immediately after Prohibition, the government relied on its former legislation, such as the Pure Food & Drug Act and the Bottled-in-Bond Act. President Roosevelt also created the Federal Alcohol Control Administration under title I of the National Industrial Recovery Act of June 16, 1933. The alcohol administrator became the chief authority for all things alcohol, but this policy was nullified after the Supreme Court ruled in *Schechter Poultry Corporation v. United States*, which struck down a part of FDR's New Deal legislation. In its judgment, the court said Congress could not regulate local community activity and that the Industrial Recovery Act gave a broad mandate of "fair competition." Thus, on May 27, 1935, the federal government had to go back to the drawing board on policy for regulating the alcohol industry.

The seventy-fourth Congress acted quickly, introducing HB 8870, the Federal Alcohol Administration Act. The legislation's goal was to "protect the revenue" and to regulate interstate and foreign commerce. When debating how to regulate alcohol, the whiskey trust and bulk whiskey sales were chiefly discussed. Congress made very clear in these hearings they were interested in ending the pricing monopoly and reintroducing the bulk whiskey sales market, which was thought to be a way of decreasing the bootlegger's value.

This early legislation still stands in parts but has been amended over time. The labeling standards were narrowly tailored to give consumers as much information as possible, an advantage modern consumers still appreciate. For example, amendment number ninety-eight: "The House bill provided that the regulations of the enforcement agency as to informative labeling should provide the consumer with adequate information as to the manufacturer or bottler or importer of the particular product. The Senate amendment provides that in case of domestically bottled goods the regulation shall require the label to show the name of the manufacturer or bottler or distributor, and, in the case of imported products, show the name of the foreign manufacturer and the domestic importer."

On June 8, 1938, regulators added the "state of distillation" for whiskey products, largely because some companies owned distilleries in multiple states. This clause would later be simplified, but the gist remained the same—bottlers are to list the state of distillation. This became the subject of several class-action lawsuits between 2013 and 2015.

The Canadian distillers likely realized that the bottled-in-bond fight was not worth it, and their government likely didn't want to battle a Congress they had already gone around and around with. Up to 1941, Canadian products listed as bottled-in-bond under Canadian government supervision were established under the fair-trade contracts to be allowable for sale to liquor licenses in the United States. Bonded whiskey was not Canada's strong suit anyway. They were brilliant blenders.

Instead of making bourbon its center-piece product, Seagram heavily promoted its blends. In 1937, Seagram's Five Crown Blended Whiskey was made up of 25 percent straight whiskey and 75 percent neutral spirits distilled from "American grains." Of course, the so-called neutral spirit was not aged and therefore lowered their production costs. This allowed Seagram Distillers to distribute its flagship products more cheaply than Schenley's and National's premium products and also did not make them as dependent upon the aged whiskey. This strategic move was based on the fact founder Sam Bronfman simply preferred the blended style over straight bourbons, not seeing the need to pay a premium at the barrel level. But Seagram did not ignore Kentucky, and in fact, it embraced the state's distilling heritage. Shortly after repeal, it purchased the Henry McKenna Distillery, Calvert Distillery, and the Old Prentice Distiller. After World War II, Seagram's purchased even more Kentucky distilleries and would later take its Four Roses Bourbon off the US market.

Of course, almost as soon as the distillery industry got off the ground and the parent companies were affirmed with their respective styles, the US government investigated the flow of whiskey. A familiar word was used—"monopoly."

Coming out of Prohibition, all distilleries were eager to get products on the shelf. One of them was Kentucky River Distillery's Old Settler. Located on the north bank of the Kentucky River in Jessamine County, the distillery had access to an unlimited supply of fine water and was considered good bourbon. But it could not compete against the larger brands. The distillery sold to Norton Simon in the 1960s. *Oscar Getz Museum of Whiskey*

BOURBON IN THE 1930s

In the 1930s, the government issued several regulatory standards for bourbon and other spirits, but there was confusion about the mashbill and the types of corn used. In Irving Hirsch's 1931 book *Manufacture of Whiskey, Brandy and Cordials*, the distiller wrote: "To make a straight bourbon use a sour mash made up from 50 percent Indian corn, 30 percent rye, and 20 percent barley malt."

Federal law only confused the matter. Despite the law changing after Hirsch's book, people still confused bourbon's corn percentages and types when reciting the regulation. This definition was in place in 1935:Despite the law changing after Hirsch's book, people still confused bourbon's corn percentages and types when reciting the regulation. These laws were in place in 1935:

> (d) Straight bourbon whiskey and Straight corn whiskey are straight whiskey distilled from a fermented mash of grain of which not less than 51% is corn grain. The designation of the product shall be straight corn whiskey only if it is without added color derived from charred oak or otherwise.

The immediately foregoing provisions were the result of an earlier amendment on March 15, 1935. Prior to this first amendment, and as it read in the Standards of Identity as originally issued, the definition of straight bourbon whiskey was: "Straight bourbon whiskey is straight whiskey distilled from a fermented mash of grain of which not less than 51% and not more than 80% is corn grain." (Bourbon is no longer required to be from at least 80% corn.)

In 1938, acting treasury secretary Roswell Magill approved "new charred oak container" language to bourbon's definition. The Federal Alcohol Administration Act would later say that bourbon produced on or after March 1, 1933, had to have been stored in charred new oak containers, likely to prevent late Prohibition-era used cooperage from entering the market. Bourbon had to be withdrawn from the cistern room of the distillery at not more than 110 barrel-entry proof and not less than 80 proof. Today, the barrel-entry proof is 125.

Due to the shortage of available stocks, the government permitted bourbon to be aged for not less than twelve calendar months if bottled on or after July 1, 1936, and before July 1, 1937; or aged for not less than eighteen calendar months if bottled on or after July 1, 1937, and before July 1, 1938; or aged for not less than twenty-four calendar months if bottled on or after July 1, 1938. During this era, bourbon was not a distinct product of the United States, and other countries actively produced and labeled products as "bourbon."

Seagram's vice president and treasurer James E. Friel, testifying before the US Congress monopoly committee. The distillery industry was continuously under investigation after Prohibition for price fixing. *Library of Congress*

Whiskey Power

Before Enron, Big Tobacco, and Major League Baseball captivated Congressional hearings, whiskey companies practically became D.C. residents. From 1919 and 1960, government officials discussed bourbon hundreds of times in public sessions. But none may have been more important than when the federal government looked into the whiskey business in 1939.

The Federal Trade Commission's Willis J. Ballinger opened the hearing presenting a study of a "monopoly and monopolistic conditions in the liquor industry." The FTC claimed it wanted a "glance" at the industry's growth from 1933 to 1938, to study its "extraordinary development," price structure, advertising activities, and merchandizing.

> This is an unequaled opportunity for economic study. The industry is large, touching both production and distribution in a highly integrated manner. . . . The prohibition interlude enables interesting comparison between new and old forms of industry. The price mechanisms involved cover the range of regulation and private control. The methods of distribution range equally wide.

On the surface, this could have appeared as simply the government's keen interest in its largest tax earner. But of course the distillers did not trust the US government, just as their ancestors in America, Scotland, or Ireland hadn't.

THE KENTUCKY DERBY CHASE

After Prohibition, horse racing, baseball, and boxing were the United States' top sports. And since horse racing's crown jewel—the Kentucky Derby—was in the Kentucky bourbon distiller's backyard, each major brand found itself in a race to own the publicity rights to the Kentucky Derby. From the end of Prohibition to 1942, dozens of bourbon advertisements filled the pages of Kentucky Derby programs, and the leaders of the pack were Brown-Forman's Old Forester, Paul Jones, and National Distillers. Like the horses in the race, each ad was strong, making a case for its bourbon to be the beloved spirit of the Kentucky Derby patron. Brown-Forman held true to the fact that Old Forester is a one-distillery bourbon, National plugged the mixability of its Old Grand-Dad and Old Taylor, and Paul Jones's Four Roses spoke of virtue in its blends.

May 4, 1935, Old Forester Bottled-in-Bond: "For 65 years Acknowledged by connoisseurs to be the finest of Kentucky whiskies. Old Forester, with its famous full-bodied flavor, mellow richness and glowing satisfaction, is produced by us only, and from our own famous formula, treasured since 1870. The famous Old Forester plain label appears only on whisky made by ourselves, in our own distillery, by our own methods. A limited quantity is now available."

In 1938, National Distillers: "And for a julep at its supreme best, ask to have it made with Old Taylor or Old Grand-Dad—two bottled-in-bond bourbons in which fifty Derby winners have been toasted—two magnificent whiskies that have spread Kentucky's fame for hospitality and genial living the wide world round."

In 1942, Four Roses, a Blend of Straight Whiskies: "Four Roses, you see, is more than a single straight whiskey—it's a superb combination of several selected whiskies. Even the youngest of these whiskies is 4 years old! All of them are old enough to be bottled in bond, and would be, if we thought they were be as good, sold separately that way. But instead, we prefer to bring these distinguished whiskies together—to unite all their virtues in one whiskey that is finer still. Four Roses is ALL whiskey—purposely reduced to 90 proof to make it lighter and milder."

Brown-Forman won the race and to this day is the premier bourbon sponsor of Churchill Downs and the Kentucky Derby. They won for more reasons than just spending more money: the Brown family had a passion for the race. In 1940, they created a special bottling for the sixty-sixth Kentucky Derby. It was only available to those in attendance and is this author's great white whale in bourbon collecting.

Stitzel-Weller was started by Charles Farnsley and Pappy Van Winkle on Kentucky Derby Day 1935.

At this point, forty-six of the forty-eight states had allowed the sale and manufacturing of intoxicating beverages. Oklahoma and Mississippi chose to remain dry under state laws. Since the taxation and enforcement of alcohol was still fairly new to the contemporary federal government, the FTC claimed that under the Federal Alcohol Administration Act, effective August 29, 1935, administrators should be granted more power, and that this hearing was just a part of the government's desire to quell any "unfair competition and unlawful practices."

The companies targeted were National Distillers, Seagram, Schenley, and Hiram Walker & Sons—otherwise known as the Big Four. According to the government, these four companies produced 60 percent of the total US whiskey. It also submitted as evidence that there were 126 distilleries in 1937 and only 108 in 1938, implying that the Big Four were squeezing out the little guy. But in their testimony, the distillers attempted to illustrate their importance to the country, especially to the farmers. At the core of the government's concern was pricing. When Phillip E. Buck, general counsel of the Federal Alcohol Administration, asked Setou Porter, president of National Distillers, about pricing, Buck made reference to a bottled-in-bond Kentucky bourbon costing the same amount to produce as a two-year-old Illinois bourbon. Yet it cost consumers twice as much. Porter snapped back, informing the counsel that corn farmers once commanded 90 cents to a dollar per bushel, but were only receiving 46 cents per bushel in 1939.

As for the cost differences between a $3.79 Bottled-in-Bond E. H. Taylor and $1.89 two-year-old Ten High Bourbon, Porter had to be smiling from ear to ear when he said: "It is generally recognized that bourbon whiskey made in Kentucky has a higher value than it has in any other bourbon state."

But Buck would get the last laugh. Three years after this hearing, the government announced that a federal grand jury had indicted nineteen major distilling companies and fifty-four individuals for fixing wholesale and retail prices. This started a multi-decade affair on Capitol Hill and in the courts. But when these allegations first publicly surfaced in 1939, the bourbon distillers had a greater problem. World War II loomed, and its bourbon production came to a screeching halt.

Master distiller Will McGill (pictured) was the master distiller for Stitzel-Weller, one of the few independent distillers capable of competing against the conglomerates. *Personal collection of Norman Hayden*

CHAPTER 7

DISTILLERS VS. NAZIS AND US GOVERNMENT

As the US military fought the Germans and Japanese in Europe, Africa, and the Pacific Islands, the distillery industry was asked to make a great sacrifice during World War II. In 1942, the War Production Board, the US government agency charged with production and procuring war materials, ordered the distilleries to create industrial alcohol for the war effort. The alcohol would be used to manufacture smokeless powder, chemical warfare materials, rubber, and medicinal supplies.

The Maryland and Pennsylvania distilleries were the first to receive this order, followed by fifteen Louisville, Kentucky, distilleries. By October 1942, the government said it needed 240 million gallons and ordered all distilleries to produce industrial alcohol, but an anonymous source at the time told the *Louisville Courier-Journal* that government would allow two thirty-day vacations each year for distillers to produce drinkable and sellable liquor. A distillery industry less than a decade removed from Prohibition did not appreciate the government forcing them to stop business operations, even if it was for the country's greater good. "The W.F.B. is not interested in establishing prohibition," the anonymous source said in October 1942.

But the distillery community was clearly remembering Prohibition. In a company newsletter, Brown-Forman told its employees in February 1942: "Many people connected with the liquor industry . . . are thinking of the impact of the war on our industry, in terms of what happened during the last war, which brought with it nationwide Prohibition." Brown-Forman's Owsley Brown saw the country's eventual need for industrial alcohol and built a $75,000 industrial still add-on in 1941.

The manufacturing of so-called war alcohol required rectifying collar columns that would distill spirit at 190 proof, but most bourbon stills achieved highs of only 140 to 160 proof, and possibly up to 175 proof. Stills required special outfitting to produce the industrial spirit, and there appeared to be no government assistance

The War Production Board produced multiple posters to garner support for at-home efforts during World War II and create a sense of urgency for battling Germany. *Library of Congress*

Every drop of mash was distilled for the war effort starting in 1942. The former Rossville Distillery owned by Seagram in Lawrenceburg, Indiana, was one of the many facilities making war alcohol.

in the conversion costs. "I talked to Henry Sherman of Vendome Copper and Brass Work regarding the cost of converting the Belle of Anderson distillery into a plant to produce alcohol," wrote Creel Brown Jr., president of J. T. S. Brown, to Taylor Hay, December 10, 1941. "Their firm has just recently completed installation of the necessary equipment at Old Lewis Hunter distillery at Cynthiana to make it into an alcohol plant. The total cost of that installation was $12,000. The size of the column was 42 inches. The Old Lewis Hunter distillery mashes approximately 1,000 bushels per day." In addition to still reconfiguration, sealed mash tuns were encouraged to "produce a bigger yield per bushel."

In fact, of all Kentucky distilleries that received the notice on April 1, 1942, only two—Brown-Forman and Joseph E. Seagram & Sons' Cynthiana plant—initially possessed the equipment to create industrial alcohol. Thus, the Kentucky facilities shipped their high wines ranging between 120 and 140 proof to an industrial plant in Terre Haute, Indiana, for redistillation. The Maryland and Pennsylvania Distilleries shipped their distillate to whiskey to Yonkers, New York, for redistillation.

The War Production Board's early plans diverted sugar and grains for industrial alcohol production, while choosing to redistill the spirits at specialized plants instead of outfitting bourbon stills with special rectifying columns. This method saved copper and other scarce metals for direct use on the war front. Canadian distilleries also made industrial alcohol for the Canadian Munitions and Supply Department, so effectively most North American distilleries were producing war alcohol. The War Production Board initially said it wanted 90 percent of the distillery capacity, leaving hope that whiskey production could continue in the time of war. But 90 percent eventually became 100 percent as it became clear the government needed all hands on deck for manufacturing. "The adequate production of industrial alcohol

WAR ON SLOP

Slop is distiller slang for the grains left over from distillation. The grains used to make the rudimentary beer that is distilled fall to the bottom and are sold or given to farmers.

During the war's alcohol-production phase, bourbon distillers were stuck with more slop or spent mash than ever before, and they needed to dispose of the spent grains in order to produce more rapidly. Traditionally, the leftover grains were sold or given to cattle and hog feeders. But the feeders complained about the higher percentages of wheat in the leftover mash, so they rejected much of the early war alcohol slop. Instead of being stuck with large piles of dried grain, some distillers dumped the distiller's grain into the stream. This led protestors to claim the slop killed fish, and eventually caused Circuit Court Judge William B. Ardery of Frankfort to fine several distilleries. Ardery accused the distilleries of being more concerned with profits than with a desire to comply with the country's war alcohol needs.

During the war alcohol production phase, distillers were forced to distill at higher proof levels and with higher amounts of wheat. This led to a farmer boycott; they did not want to feed the waste to their hogs and cattle. In turn, some distillers dumped the spent grains into the river, which killed fish.

As a solution to the slop problem, cattlemen and hog farmers began to accept the slop and give their animals a supplement to compensate for the lack of corn in the feed. Kentucky was asked to lower its stream pollution standards, and the War Production Board requested that distillers receive priority for steel to construct better facilities for the leftover grains.

INDUSTRIAL ALCOHOL COMMITTEE

The War Production Board created committees of industry to advise the government on how to best handle their respective fields. The industrial alcohol group included government presiding officer Dr. Walter G. Whitman, assistant chief of the chemicals branch; and various distilling industry members, including James McLaughlin, Carbide Carbon Chemicals Corporation, New York, New York; Dr. Lewis H. Marks, Publicker Commercial Alcohol Co., Philadelphia, Pennsylvania; Glen Haskell, US Industrial Chemicals Inc., New York, New York; H. F. Willkie, Jos. E. Seagram & Sons, Inc., Louisville, Kentucky; W. H. Venneman, Frankfort Distilleries, Inc., Louisville, Kentucky; Owsley Brown, Brown-Forman Distilling Co., Louisville, Kentucky; Julian P. Van Winkle, Stitzel-Weller Distillery, Louisville, Kentucky; I. Strouse, Baltimore Pure Dye Distilling Co., Baltimore, Maryland; J. B. Celia, Roma Wine Co. Inc., Fresno, California; and Carl J. Kiefer, Schenley Distillers Corporation, New York.

The George T. Stagg Distillery, now Buffalo Trace, is the only distillery still in operation that distilled industrial alcohol in both World War I and World War II. *Schenley Archives, Sazerac*

for use in the manufacture of munitions and other essential war materials is a matter of critical necessity," wrote Congressman Robert L. Doughton, the chairman of the Ways and Means committee, in 1942.

How the bourbon industry chose to operate fundamentally changed their relationship with the government.

Publicly, bourbon distillers presented a unified American stance, saying Kentucky distilleries would produce industrial alcohol "until the war is won." They hung signs in buildings encouraging patriotism, and Brown-Forman held contests among its three distilleries to encourage each plant to vie for the greatest production of alcohol.

According to a Kentucky Distillers' Association public address, "Kentuckians well may be proud that the entire production facilities of a leading industry of the Bluegrass State now are devoted to our Nation's War Effort." Distillers advised the War Production Board, and their trade group, the Distilled Spirits Institute, told the public, "Modern wars cannot be waged successfully without [industrial alcohol]. War alcohol is essential in the manufacture of smokeless powder, chemical warfare materials, synthetic rubber and medical supplies which alleviate pain, combat infection and save human lives. . . ."

In reality, even if the distilleries had not converted to industrial war alcohol facilities, they would have not been able to procure enough grains to distill. Nearly every bushel of corn, rye, and wheat was earmarked for the war. In fact, the war movement created slogans such as "Food will win the war," and Secretary of Agriculture Claude R. Wickard argued that American farmers needed to feed more than their own country and soldiers, saying they were responsible for 10 million in Great Britain. Whiskey production was not the government's main concern when it came to grains, but they genuinely needed the industrial alcohol production.

The distillers also reassured the government committees that the process was easy. "You don't even have to use any copper in distillers which make 190-degree proof alcohol for the manufacturing of war products and butadiene synthetic rubber. You can use any kind of metal—silver, steel, even wood or sewer pipe if necessary. Any chemist who sets up glass tubing in his laboratory can make 100-degree proof alcohol and there is no sense to statements that we can't enlarge our alcohol-producing facilities because copper is needed in the distilleries and copper can't be obtained because of its scarcity," H. Fred Willkie, vice president of production for Seagram, told the committee at the hearing.

On October 8, 1942, all American whiskey production officially halted. The whiskey companies still owned plenty of stocks aging in warehouses, but when would they be able to distill again? Despite promises, they were not granted whiskey production time until 1945.

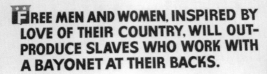

THIS IS ONE OF FOURTEEN SCHENLEY DISTILLERIES WORKING DAY AND NIGHT, TO FURTHER THE WAR EFFORT BY PRODUCING ALCOHOL FOR MILITARY USE.

FREE MEN AND WOMEN, INSPIRED BY LOVE OF THEIR COUNTRY, WILL OUTPRODUCE SLAVES WHO WORK WITH A BAYONET AT THEIR BACKS.

Schenley considered itself a fairly patriotic facility, hanging signs throughout the George T. Stagg facility and promoting the fact that many of its workers (pictured) made war alcohol for both big wars. *Schenley Archives, Sazerac*

Kentucky Distilleries

DEVOTE PRODUCTION FACILITIES
TO ESSENTIAL WAR MATERIALS

UNTIL the War is won the production facilities of Kentucky's distilleries will be devoted to making high-proof grain alcohol so vital to the manufacture of smokeless powder, ammunition, synthetic rubber and other materials of war.

- For months, plants of various members of the Kentucky Distillers Association have operated on a twenty-four, seven-day week basis producing war-time industrial alcohol. Through the pooling of equipment all Kentucky distilleries now are participating one-hundred per cent in our War Program.

- At the beginning of 1942 the distilleries of the nation were producing grain alcohol at the rate of 60,000,000 gallons per year. By September the annual rate had been upped to 135,000,000 gallons and the close of 1942 saw an annual production rate of 240,000,000 gallons. Of this latter amount Kentucky Distilleries will produce 90,000,000 gallons which is 37½ per cent of the national total or one and one-half the total annual production rate for the entire distilling industry in the first months of 1942.

- Close proximity to large smokeless powder and synthetic rubber plants enables Kentucky distilleries to provide this essential material of war with a minimum of transportation. Kentuckians well may be proud that the entire production facilities of a leading industry of the Bluegrass State now are devoted to our Nation's War Effort.

MEMBERS OF KENTUCKY DISTILLERS ASSOCIATION

Bardstown Distillery	General Distilleries Corpn. of Ky.	Old Heaven Hill Springs Dist. Co.	Taylor & Williams Distilleries
Bernheim Distilling Co.	Glencoe Distillery Co.	Old Joe Distilling Co.	The Blue Grass Distillery Co.
Blair Distilling Co.	Glenmore Distilleries Co., Inc.	Old Kentucky Distillery	The Dant Distillery Co.
Blue Ribbon Distilleries Co.	Hoffman Distilling Co.	Old Times Distillery	The Fleischmann Distilling Corpn.
Bonds Mill Distilling Co., Inc.	Jas. B. Beam Dist. Co.	Park & Tilford Distillers, Inc.	The Geo. T. Stagg Co.
Brown-Forman Distillery Co.	James E. Pepper Co.	R. E. Pogue Distillery Co.	The Hermitage Jistillery Co.
Buffalo Springs Distilling Co.	John A. Wathen Distilling Co.	Ripy Bros. Distillers, Inc.	The Old Crow Distillery Co.
Cave Springs Distillery Corpn.	Labrot & Graham	Schenley Distillers Products Corpn.	The Old Grand Dad Distillery Co.
Churchill Distilling Co.	H. McKenna, Inc.	Jos. E. Seagram & Sons, Inc.	The Old Taylor Distillery Co.
Dowling Bros. Distilling Co.	Medley Distilling Co.	Shawhan Distillery Co., Inc.	The Willett Distilling Co.
Elkhorn Branch of National Distillers	National Distillers Products Corpn.	Stitzel-Weller Distillery	Tom Moore Distillery
Fairfield Distillery, Inc.	Oldetyme Distillers	Sunny Brook Distillery Co.	Waterfill & Frazier Distillery Co.
Frankfort Distilleries, Inc.			Wathen Bros. Distillers

The Kentucky Distillers' Association actively promoted the fact its distilleries were engaged in war alcohol production.

The larger distilleries were making moves. Schenely's George T. Stagg Company made an agreement with a descendent of the Old Charter family, Elizabeth Chapaze, for land in Bullitt County; and its Franklin County Distillers purchased McKesson & Robbins in Nelson County, increasing their property and their access to water and equipment, and amassing significant facility expense. Glenmore Distilleries purchased the Taylor & Williams Distilleries, as well as Dant family assets, for more than $5 million. In 1943, the Joseph E. Seagram & Sons company spent $43 million to purchase Frankfort Distilleries Inc., whose property value plummeted during the war, according to newspaper accounts. The dwindling of independent distilleries caught the attention of the *Courier-Journal*, October 22, 1943: "Acquisition of Frankfort by one of the 'Big Four' would be an important step in the move long under way to concentrate the distillery business in hand of a few companies. Absorption of Frankfort by Seagram would remove one of the largest independents from the field."

The larger companies also used their distributor connections and marketing powers to squeeze the smaller distillers out of individual markets. "The big companies usually have extensive lines of cheap credit with which to finance the cost of labor and materials to carry whiskey while it is aging," wrote Donald McWain, the financial editor for the *Courier Journal*. "Small companies find that their loans for the same purposes usually command a higher rate of interest for proportionate amounts of credit."

Thus, it was easier for the little guy to just sell rather than try to stay in business. But the federal government grew concerned with the number of acquisitions. After Seagram acquired Frankfort's two hundred thousand barrels of aged whiskey, the Big Four accounted for some 73 percent of the total whiskey stocks. Suddenly, the distilling business was becoming a monopoly due to government-enforced distillation. This put the government in an odd situation. It needed the distiller support to produce war alcohol but could not allow the remaining whiskey stocks to be absolutely controlled in price and volume by a handful of companies. A senate resolution was passed to investigate the alcoholic beverage industry.

The Liquor Monopoly

Prior to the war, there were more than 500 million gallons of whiskey aging in bonded warehouses, but by December 1943 this amount had dwindled to a mere 203 million gallons, leaving distillers no choice but to advertise the "whiskey shortage" in more than two hundred newspapers across the country. Just as they were getting back in the distilling groove, they were now setting low ceiling prices, agreed upon with the government, to keep the consumer happy. They also feared poor-quality whiskey entering the market, as they painfully experienced in 1934 when distillers were putting out barely aged bourbon just to meet the thirsty post-Prohibition demand. To quell the national negativity toward whiskey distillers, the Distilled Spirits Institute purchased full-page Q&A advertisements:

It must be made clear that the only reason there isn't any legal whiskey at all, is because whiskey must be aged before it is suitable for consumption.

It cannot be made today and sold tomorrow like most other products. If it could, the country would have been bone-dry months ago because there would have been no reason for a stock. Never was the old adage more applicable—"you can't have your cake and eat it, too."

In a 1943 Glenmore Distilleries advertisement, the creators of Kentucky Tavern, Glenmore said, "Since October 1942, Glenmore has made no whiskey—we've made war alcohol for the government instead! It's our duty and we're cooperating 100%. If, then, our products are not always on the shelves, we hope you'll cheerfully understand. We are trying to speed the day when we can again lay away new whiskey and again freely distribute the pre-war bourbons that the situation has forced to allot in moderation today."

There was consumer concern and confusion over the whiskey shortage. People wanted to drink good bourbon but didn't necessarily grasp the fact that distilleries were making industrial alcohol. They also saw a growing trend of so-called whiskey blends being offered under bourbon brand names. Distributors and distilleries pumped marketing dollars into promoting blended whiskey, often at the

LIQUOR STORES IN WORLD WAR II

In recent years, US consumers and this author have complained about a shortage of premium bourbon. But when compared to the 1940s, the contemporary whiskey shortage doesn't hold a candle. And despite whatever the distillers of the time were telling Congress, liquor stores were receiving vast requests for 100-proof bourbon. When ordering from distributors, liquor stores requested bottled-in-bond bourbon but instead received only blends—a noticeable downgrade in quality for their consumer base. As one newspaper reporter noticed: "The distillers' system of distribution or voluntary rationing or compulsory forcing of blends, or whatever the trade may choose to call it, was having the effect of driving the home consumer into the saloons . . ."

If they had the stock, liquor stores advertised their supply as "pre-war bourbon." In Bloomington, Illinois, National Wine Liquors advertised 2,500 bottles in a "whiskey galore" prewar bourbon sale. Full quarts of Walker's Deluxe Illinois Straight Bourbon Whiskey sold for $4.20, while a full fifth of Old Quaker five-year-old Straight Bourbon went for $3.49. But like most of these mid-1940s everything-must-go sales, the bulk of the deals were in the blends, such as Seagram's 5 Crown Blended whiskey for $3.50 for a full fifth. Though they didn't know it, liquor stores contributed to rise of blends.

INDUSTRIAL ALCOHOL PLANTS

Not all distilleries converted their stills to become industrial alcohol facilities, per a July 31, 1943, government report. These whiskey distilleries converted into industrial alcohol facilities, while others were either not operational or sent distillate to be redistilled by one of these facilities. Stitzel-Weller converted its still in 1944.

Illinois

American Distilling Co., Pekin
Hiram Walker & Sons, Peoria, Illinois

Indiana

Clifton Springs Distilling, Greendale
Schenley Distilleries, Lawrenceburg
Joseph E. Seagram & Sons, Lawrenceburg

Kentucky

Brown-Forman, Louisville
Glenmore, Owensboro
Green River Distilling, Stamping Ground
National Distillers with locations in Forks
    of Elkhorn, Bardstown, Gethsemane,
    Lawrenceburg, and Louisville
New England Distilling Company, Covington

James E. Pepper, Lexington
Joseph E. Seagram & Sons, Louisville
George T. Stagg, Frankfort

Maryland

The Calvert Distilling, Relay
Monticello Distillery, Cedarhurst

New York

Fleischman Distilling, Charles Point

Pennsylvania

Continental Distilling, Philadelphia
Jos. S. Finch, Schenley
Kinney Distilling, Linfield
Koppers United, Kobuts
Overholt & Co., Broad Ford

peril of bourbon. In a 1940s-era Q&A advertisement for Seagram's Calvert blended whiskey, the distiller argued blends were the product of the future. "After Repeal, only 10% of all whiskey sold was blended whiskey. By 1942, before the whiskey shortage, the tend to blends was so great that the figure was 50%. Today, 80% of all whiskey sold is blended whiskey . . . and undoubtedly many distillers who are making blended whiskey for the first time will continue to produce it to meet popular demand."

Of course, blended whiskey was much cheaper to produce, because it could use grain neutral spirit and did not require aging. This fact was not lost on Congressman A. J. May of Kentucky, who protested both the trend of the larger distilleries purchasing independents and the trend toward blends. "They take one gallon of T. W. Samuels whiskey and blend it with spirits or new whiskey and make four or five gallons, or even more, for this one gallon. Then they put it on the market under a

Distilleries also saw a large portion of their workforce drafted. This World War II pilot painted an Old Schenley cocktail on his plane and sent a photo back to his colleagues. *Schenley Archives, Sazerac*

MEDICINAL WHISKEY

Although it was still prescribed in the 1940s, medicinal whiskey no longer dominated the prescriptions of the time. Pharmaceutical historians call this the era of antibiotics.

In this era, researchers maximized penicillin's potential, and purified actinomycin became a tool against diseases such as typhoid, dysentery, cholera, and undulant fever. In 1944, Merck discovered streptomycin as a treatment to tuberculosis. Four years later, University of Wisconsin professor Benjamin M. Duggar isolated chlortetracycline from *Streptomyces aureofaciens*, called aureomycin. Bacitracin and methotrexate, one of the earliest anticancer agents, were created in the 1940s, along with other drugs, leading companies like Brown-Forman and Schenley to diversify their portfolios with drug research and assistance.

By 1950, medicinal whiskey was still prescribed, but it became more of a home remedy than a professionally prescribed drug. Today, medicinal alcohol is still prescribed in severe cases in alcohol withdrawals, where it is administered as a diluted intravenous drip to help wean the patient.

new brand name and sell it, in some instances, higher than the old brand originally sold for," May said. "Kentucky, the home of good liquor, has been hit hard under the belt by this monopoly."

May brought these charges in a session of Congress focusing on National Distillers and McKesson & Robbins:

> About April 1, 1943, the National Distillery and McKesson & Robbins bought out the Glencoe Distillery of Louisville for which they paid approximately $3,500,000. This distillery cost approximately $270,000 to build. The buyer paid for 30,000 barrels of whiskey at the price of $2.25 per gallon, although the O.P.A. ceiling on old whisky is $1.21 per gallon. About 5,000 barrels of 1942 distillation was figured at $2 per gallon, while the ceiling fixed by the O.P.A. is 89 cents per gallon. So the sale of this 5,000 gallons was $1.11 in excess of the ceiling price. How can these concerns do this sort of thing in violation of the OPA ceiling price?

May also suggested that the larger companies were making backdoor deals with wholesalers, who were once their legislative enemies.

Frank Ludwick, the chief of the distilled spirits and wine section of the War Food Administration, investigated another side of the problem: distilleries were buying wineries. By 1942, distillery companies purchased 14 of 439 Californian wineries that represented some 22 percent of the state's total capacity, furthering the government's claim of a monopoly. With 90 percent of the country's wine production occurring in California, the government was deeply concerned that distillers were setting grape prices and using wine for distillate instead of selling as wine. The regulators seemed to have a general distrust for most in the alcohol business, and they were especially concerned with price fixing. The distilling industry did not like the term "price fixing"; distillers preferred to call it rationing because they had not been allowed to make whiskey during World War II. Senator Homer S. Ferguson (Republican, Michigan) found the rationing argument to be absurd:

> Then why have not the other industries that have quit making products— let us take the automobile industry for they rationed those—they did not say to the automobile manufacturers, "you form a monopoly and do the rationing," did they? Has there been any other industry where they have quit manufacturing where the government has said to them "you do the rationing yourselves." Has there been any other and if there has not, why do you apply to the liquor business?

Ferguson declared that allowing the distillers to ration or price fix served only corporate interests, and not the public's, as required under the Emergency Price Control Act of 1942. The regulation set forth by the beverage division of the Price Control allowed for 25 percent markup on wine to wholesale and 50 percent at retail; but spirits was 33.5 percent at wholesale markup and 15 percent at retail. Therein lied the crux for whiskey. The trend for whiskey on the shelf was not for pure, but for blended whiskey, and Ferguson called this a "workable rule" that could lead to greater profits for blended whiskey vs. bonded bourbon. There was also concern that distillers were changing labels, slapping better-known brands on cheaper liquid to drive up the price to higher than the government's ceiling. The investigators had found examples of bourbon priced over the maximum price.

Senators were also concerned that distillers were choosing the markets to serve. the manager of the Cleveland-Allerton Hotel wrote to the majority of the major distillers, practically begging for whiskey: "Our stock of whiskey is practically exhausted and our need is urgent. Our policy and practice is to comply with all laws and regulations and therefore we are not receiving whiskey that others who are willing to violate the law are privileged to have. We have made diligent and extensive efforts to buy the whiskey we need, but we have been unable to do so because we are unwilling to deal in the black market. . . ."

But as the Senate investigated this manner, they realized this was a state matter, for liquor makers could not sell to Ohio in the same way they would to Illinois. Hiram Walker's Ohio manager replied to the Cleveland note: "While we would like very much to accommodate you, nevertheless I regret to advise that Hiram Walker has no whiskey of any type available for sale . . . Whatever quota we receive for Ohio must be sold direct to the state for general distribution."

WHISKEY PRICES

Under the Emergency Price Control Act of 1942, whiskey prices received ceilings and were strictly enforced. The maximum price varied by state and month. The early price settings had a legal loophole that led to distillers placing brand names on inferior products. For example, a long-time straight bourbon now had a blend. This allowed to distillers to earn greater profits based on the cost of production. They were also hoarding stocks, making barrels stretch for as long as they could. This led to several Senate hearings, including an attempt to change the price ceiling.

TYPE	PROCESSORS' MAXIMUM PRICE PER CASE OF FIFTHS	AVERAGE RETAIL PRICE PER FIFTH-GALLON BOTTLE
100 proof "Bottled in Bond"	$22.99	$3.30
85 proof Straight Whiskey	$18.14	$2.65
90 proof blend of straight whiskeys, average age of 3½ years old	$20.40	$2.95
85 proof blended (27½ percent neutral spirits; average percent whiskey, 72½ age of whiskey three years)	$19.29	$2.80

The fact is, the government was looking into every angle to improve the current system that based pricing off of proof and rewarded blends by making them a cheaper product to produce than bottled-in-bond. They were also concerned that distillers were releasing new brands of inferior quality at the prices of premium brands. This action was possible under loopholes in the price administration that allowed ceiling prices to be based upon pre-existing dates when there was no original ceiling price, according to the Senate committee:

> Manipulations resulted in the public paying exorbitant prices for poor quality liquor. After much damage had been done this way, the office of price administration modified its regulations to provide that ceiling prices on new brands would be based upon the quality of liquor sold, rather than upon any pre-existing sales. In view of the recent action of the war production board, allowing the distillers to produce beverage spirits for a 30-day period, it is incumbent upon the distillers to show their good faith by releasing more

whiskey from their bonded warehouses to help alleviate a condition which has been occasioned at least as much by the "hoarding" of the distillers rather than by any "hoarding" which may be chargeable to the American public.

The committee believes that the present arrangement whereby the liquor industry has placed itself under a plan of severe self-imposed rationing is contrary to the best interests of the public and is unjustified by the present conditions. Such an arrangement, if by tacit agreement between the distillers is a violation of the spirit, if not the letter of the Sherman anti-Trust act.

In addition to these Senate hearings, the liquor industry was facing antitrust allegations on many fronts.

The Department of Justice indicted Schenley Distillers Corporation, Bayonne Wholesale Liquor firm in New York, and ten people with conspiracy to violate price ceilings. The Department of Justice alleged that Schenley kept false records, but the company steadfastly denied these allegations. Around the same time, Seagram Distillers, All State Distributors, McKesson & Robins, and Stickney Cigar Company lost an antitrust suit and were forced to pay $42,500 in fines for fixing wholesale and retail prices in the St. Louis and Kansas City markets.

Attorney General Francis Biddle had subpoenaed Schenley, Hiram Walker, National Distillers, and Joseph E. Seagram and Sons, as well as eighty-five smaller distillers, vintners, processors, and wholesalers, to make a case for illegal monopolistic practices. He required records of virtually the entire liquor industry. "The ramifications of the industry are so complex," said Assistant Attorney General Wendell Berge, who was in charge of the investigation, "that it is impossible to get an accurate picture of the interlocking ownership and interests by studying only a few of the leading companies. There is a substantial public interest involved in the operations of this industry, and we have decided to make our investigation as complete and as detailed as possible."

There were continuous allegations and a lot of indictments, investigations, and the occasional murder—a Kansas City distributor was thought to have been killed by a competing Schenley distributor. Distillers won some rounds, with Colorado allowing in-state price collusion in an appellate courts (this would be overturned in the Supreme Court), and Indiana permitting Schenley to instruct a retailer to sell below the minimum price.

In November 1948 the Department of Justice completed its investigation, and US Attorney Ernest L. Branham was prepared to present the evidence before a grand jury to determine whether the Big Four were acting in unison in their advertising and acquisitions, and if they were controlling grain prices, trying to destroy small independent liquor distillers, and violating fair trade. But Branham's net was a little wider than just the Big Four; he included Continental Distilleries and Brown-Forman in his allegations, saying the six companies owned 94 percent of the whiskey cooperages. Branham wanted the bourbon cooperage industry separated from the distillery, forcing the barrel industry to be independent again, and wanted injunctions against further acquisitions in the liquor business.

Julian P. "Pappy" Van Winkle was considered one of the great distillery men of his time. Truthfully, he was not a distiller, but an iconic salesman, who once convinced Conrad Hilton to carry private labels of Old Fitzgerald. As one of the lone independent owners, Pappy was called to testify about the Big Four for alleged monopolistic actions.

In some respects, Branham's allegations made the Big Four (perhaps Big Six) sound more like the Prohibition-era mobsters than tax-paying US citizens. "It has been charged that the independents have had to pay these six companies liquor bonuses for the privilege of buying barrels during the recent shortage," Branham said. "In the state of Illinois, we have just received a complaint that a dealer cannot buy well-known brands unless the dealer purchases other brands of other companies where there are interlocking directors."

The investigation charged that Seagram "invaded the American market," acquiring Rossville Distilleries in Lawrenceburg, Indiana, as well as twenty-three other facilities. It pointed to National Distillers having acquiring thirty-two distilleries since repeal. Branham alleged that Hiram Walker had also invaded the American market, acquiring eighteen distilleries between 1934 and 1948. Schenley acquired forty companies during the same period. Branham estimated the Big Four purchased more than $152 million in distilleries from 1938 to 1943.

The Department of Justice also questioned whether the advertising was unlawful. The DOJ's report created a narrative of an unfair competition:

> Since production far exceeds demand, the industry believes that limited sales at good prices are preferable to increased sales at lower prices. A

well-advertised name at a good price is preferred to obscure names at uncertain prices and skilled advertising has been done to establish and maintain this policy through the medium of brand names. Hiram Walker's Canadian Club, Schenley's Three Feathers, Seagram's Four Roses and National's Old Overholt are synonymous for good whisky to countless people everywhere. In magazines, newspapers, billboards, manuals, menus, cookbooks, on the streetcars and street corners, the magic of the celebrated names is brought to the attention of the public. In many minds, the brand names of the Big Four are associated with such diverse things as duels, dreams, financial acumen, roosters, roses, mistletoe, and history.

According to the advertisements, they "fortify decision," "sharpen perception," "inspire history." They intrigue the fancy with such declarations as "Who has not tasted a mint julep has lived in vain"; "The bourbon and mint are lovers"; "The honey of Hymethus can bring no such solace to the soul." For the association of these ideas with the various brand names in the mind of the consumer, staggering sums of money have been expended. From 1934 to 1938 the Big Four expended about $50,000,000 in advertising, and it has been estimated that for that period an average of 1,350 advertisements of alcoholic beverages appeared weekly in sixty dailies and thirty magazines. It is advertising which makes a consumer willing and anxious to pay a good price for his particular brand. This does not mean that he cannot buy an equally good product at a cheaper price, but if he has the money he takes it for granted that the best advertised is the best brand. The newcomers to the field and the small independents cannot boost their brands in this fashion.

BUYING FAIRFIELD

The Big Four went on a buying spree after Prohibition and during World War II, a piece of evidence used against them. One of the stealthier buys was Schenley purchasing the Fairfield Distiller from McKesson & Robbins for $550,000 in 1945. McKesson & Robbins produced the Chapin & Gore label, but also underwent a federal investigation of its own. In 1938, the Securities and Exchange Commission determined that $20 million of the $87 million on the books were phony, leading to requirements that public companies must have outside auditors look at the books. McKesson & Robins became the McKesson Corporation, the eleventh-highest revenue-generating company in the United States.

Amidst the bourbon controversy of the 1940s, an important brand was born. In the early 1940s, the Austin Nichols president, Thomas McCarthy, would draw whiskey from premium barrels in the Anderson County Distillery or Old Ripy warehouses and take them with him on his wild turkey hunts. His friends would say, "Hey, when are you going to get more of that wild turkey bourbon?" The name stuck, and Wild Turkey was born. "We've made Wild Turkey the exact same way and ain't changed a thing," master distiller Jimmy Russell said. When Austin Nichols purchased the Old Ripy Distillery in 1971, Russell came with the facility and the two became synonymous with Kentucky bourbon.

But nothing stuck better than the act of uniformly fixing resale prices. "A good example of price fixing is the fact that the Big Four have acted uniformly in attempts to have their products fair-traded in different parts of the United States, including the District of Columbia, where there is no fair-trade law, and some have withdrawn their products because the retailers do not adhere to suggested resale prices," the report said.

The DOJ had a case and strong evidence, as well as legal precedent in a 1942 Colorado case that went to the Supreme Court.

But Department of Justice dropped its anti-trust investigation. Senators demanded answers. The senate subcommittee for the DOJ held hearings to learn why they dropped the investigation too soon.

Stitzel-Weller's Pappy Van Winkle, who said he was "very friendly" with Schenley, testified that Stitzel-Weller was not allowed to insure twelve warehouses of surplus stock because the Schenley Corporation already had them insured up to the limit under a blanket policy. This left Van Winkle's whiskey vulnerable. "If [Schenley] blanketed them, that meant $500,000 on 12 warehouses. . . . If you put a blanket on our distillery warehouses for say, $1 million on each warehouse, unless warehouse A is specified, it will blanket all of them. So you will have $1 million on each of them which multiplies 12 times," Van Winkle testified. "Insurance policies are usually written with a 90-percent coinsurance clause, and we could not even collect what we had. We became a co-insurer."

An independent, Stitzel-Weller had longstanding cooperage relationships, namely with Motor Wheel cooperage and Louisville Cooperage, both of which had been acquired by competitors. After Stitzel-Weller used up its forty thousand barrels, Van Winkle went to Motor Wheel Cooperage for a repurchase. Motor Wheel officials told Van Winkle that they were negotiating with National Distillers, and "they told us very frankly that they were not in a position to make any contracts because they were in the process of making the sale," Van Winkle testified.

Van Winkle, a devout Republican, also testified that the four distilling firms gave $230,000 to the Democrats in the 1948 campaigns. This was partly confirmed by James E. Friel, vice president of Seagram, who admitted to giving $30,000 to the Democrats as well as $20,000 to Republicans shortly after the Justice Department made antitrust inquiries.

The 1951–1952 DOJ senate hearings wrapped up with the testimony of Louis Mann, the president of 1,150-bushels-a-day Sherwood Distilling Company in Westminster, Maryland, which sold bulk whiskey to the Big Four as well as bottled whiskey to wholesalers. Mann offered a different perspective. Mann's warehouses held whiskey for Hiram Walker and Seagram, but he also competed against them in liquor stores.

OREGON AND WASHINGTON BUY DISTILLERIES

While the government was making a case against the Big Four distilleries buying all the little guys, two state governments purchased their own distilleries. In what might be the most unique distillery sale in American history, the states of Oregon and Washington purchased Kentucky's Shawhan Distillery and Waterfill & Frazier in 1943. The states purchased the seventy-eighty thousand barrels of whiskey for $6.65 million to provide their state-owned liquor stores. George P. Lilley, then-chairman of the Oregon Liquor Commission, said the states then resold the distilleries to their original owners.

When Brown-Forman began purchasing cooperages, they were lumped in with the larger companies. The government investigated Brown-Forman and others for monopolistic practices.

Through his New York representative, Sherwood entered a thousand-case-a-month agreement with Brooklyn's Standard Food & Products to sell the company blended whiskey under a special label in the fall of 1949. The deal was worth $250,000 a year, a sizeable revenue stream for the small distiller. The distillery lost the business, though, because Standard Foods made an agreement with Seagram that it would not sell other blends unless Seagram approved it.

The Sherwood Distilling Company was a highly touted 1800s-era rye distiller, and its post-Prohibition rise was negatively impacted by Seagram's agreement with Standard Foods. The Senate could do nothing about it. When the Senate completed its probe, investigators criticized the Department of Justice, saying political contributions influenced the DOJ's decision to drop the case. In November 1952, the government increased the excise tax to $10.50 per gallon, an increase of 854 percent, and eleven months later, the Justice Department announced another probe into the liquor business.

The distilling industry was also battling an attempted ban on alcohol advertising, as well as hundreds of municipalities, counties, and states who wanted Prohibition in their small pockets of the world. The DOJ's attempt to break up the Big Four was unsuccessful, and the conglomerates had now been battle-tested in the courts, Senate, and Congress, while surviving Prohibition and enduring the industrial alcohol production of World War II. They had to ask themselves: Can we finally make whiskey without government inference?

STATEWIDE MONOPOLIES

In the 1930s, states were in charge of regulating the sale of alcohol. Many chose to retain control of the sales in what was known as a state-run liquor monopoly. They sold the liquor to the consumer. The other system was considered an open wholesale system, in which states issued licenses to private wholesalers.

Both systems still exist and both sides continue to hotly debate the topic.

One thing has not changed: pro-liquor-monopoly politicians sing the high revenue praises, while those who oppose it say it disrupts free enterprise.

Pennsylvania, a liquor control state, reported more than $31 million in profits in 1942—the same year Texas and Kentucky considered the motions to convert their states into liquor monopolies.

As their whiskey distillers were converting their facilities to produce industrial alcohol, Kentucky legislators proposed state control of wholesale and retail distribution in a fashion similar to that in other states. A liquor monopoly council chaired by Lieutenant Governor Rodes K. Myers said the move would give Kentucky an additional $3.75 million annually and fix the "liquor problem" that had "arisen somewhat out of rather indiscreet sales, such as sales on Sunday, to minors and drunks and after Midnight," the Associated Press reported. At the time, 69 of Kentucky's 120 counties were dry, and the measure was voted down. Texas would not even study the matter.

James Haswell, a *Detroit Free Press* journalist, captured the post-Prohibition distribution situation: "Every state is having troubles over liquor. Headaches differ, but every state has them."

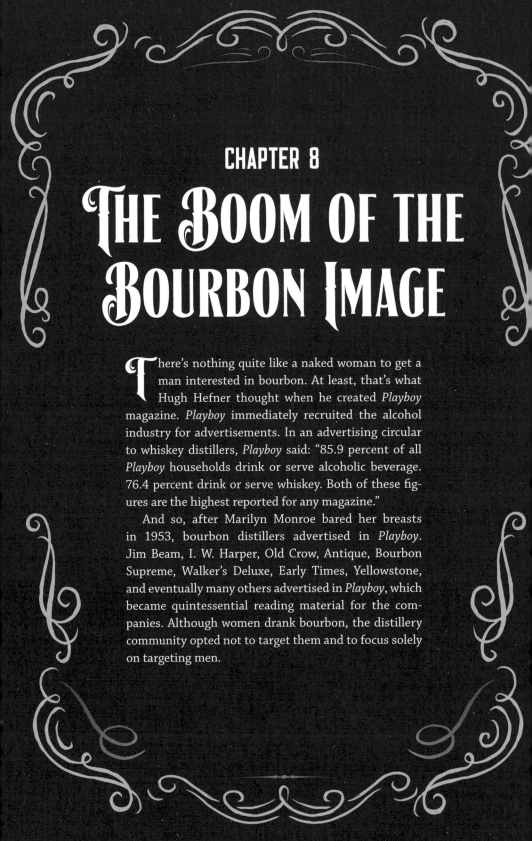

CHAPTER 8

THE BOOM OF THE BOURBON IMAGE

There's nothing quite like a naked woman to get a man interested in bourbon. At least, that's what Hugh Hefner thought when he created *Playboy* magazine. *Playboy* immediately recruited the alcohol industry for advertisements. In an advertising circular to whiskey distillers, *Playboy* said: "85.9 percent of all *Playboy* households drink or serve alcoholic beverage. 76.4 percent drink or serve whiskey. Both of these figures are the highest reported for any magazine."

And so, after Marilyn Monroe bared her breasts in 1953, bourbon distillers advertised in *Playboy*. Jim Beam, I. W. Harper, Old Crow, Antique, Bourbon Supreme, Walker's Deluxe, Early Times, Yellowstone, and eventually many others advertised in *Playboy*, which became quintessential reading material for the companies. Although women drank bourbon, the distillery community opted not to target them and to focus solely on targeting men.

In fact, a 1957 liquor-focused Fawcett Publications study offered this wifely statement: "My husband is the absolute King in this department. He pays for it and decides what to get, and the price." The study pointed toward wives making less than 5 percent of the liquor purchases for the home and quoted another woman from the study: "It's a funny thing, but I never took a drink before I was married. I guess I learned to drink from my husband."

This desire to target only men with advertising coincided with a rising tide of temperance leaders attempting to ban alcohol advertising. The brewers, distillers, and winemakers fought these attempts in congressional hearings, saying such bans represented just another form of prohibition. The Federal Trade Commission entered the picture and regulated alcohol advertising, but did not impose a total ban, just restrictions. And the distilling community opted to enact its own set of self-imposed guidelines that did not allow advertising on radio, television, in the comic pages of newspapers or newspapers, in publications owned by retail liquor dealers, religious publications, or anything related to a school or university. "No advertisement of distilled spirits shall contain an illustration of a woman unless such illustration is dignified, modest and in good taste, and no such advertisement shall depict a woman in provocative dress or situation," according to the Distilled Spirits Institute's "Code of Good Practice." Despite this edict, distillers still used scantily clothed women for their advertisements, and they also decided to target only men. Race did not matter.

However, Schenley memos from the 1960s indicate bourbon marketers pursued African American markets when other spirits would not. The country was in the middle of the civil rights movement, and black consumers refused to support products that ignored them. "We should discuss the merits of a mixed drink program for the Negro consumer. He is not as a general rule, a mixed drinker. We might find that it is better to promote Ancient Age on the rocks or Ancient Age and soda, etc., rather than a Double A Royale. The main idea is to have Ancient Age a permanent rather than short duration beverage—gimmick drinks—they die out," an Ancient Age memo concluded. Schenley then executed several campaigns with African American models drinking Ancient Age on the rocks.

These campaigns were successful and so were the dozens of other bourbon brands targeting men. Bourbon companies ignored women, despite the fact that they represented close to half of their workforce and were among the first distillers in this country. Bourbon makers simply did not view women as a viable market, and they also did not want to go round and round with the Women's Christian Temperance Union, which never took its foot off the pedal advocating prohibition and temperance at all levels of government. However, the most important new brand launched was greatly influenced by a woman. Marjorie Samuels came up with the name "Maker's Mark," the handtorn label, and the patented red wax that dripped down the bottleneck.

And there were developments outside domestic markets. After World War II, distillers were eager to compete with Scotch and Canadian whiskey for the modern

ADVERTISING POLICE

The 1950s were a time of bloody legislative battle as the temperance groups were trying to ban alcohol advertising. Several bills were introduced to the House and Senate to effectively ban liquor advertising. In 1958, the Langer Bill sought to ban advertisement and limit interstate commerce. The distillers argued these efforts were just another form of Prohibition, but advocates of the bans said it was merely a "temperance," not a prohibition. "It does not deny anyone who has a thirst for alcoholic beverage access to his favorite drink. It closes no distillery, brewery, tavern, cocktail lounge, or nightclub. It does not forbid the shipment of such beverages in interstate commerce. Its aim is what people now call 'temperance,'" testified Dr. John Coleman, a professor emeritus of political science at Geneva College in Beaver Falls, Pennsylvania.

In the end, Congress did not agree with Coleman's sentiment or others like his. The bills never made it out of committees, likely because alcohol companies were already facing great advertising scrutiny under the purview of the Alcohol & Tobacco Tax Division, which assigned agents to audit advertisements to ensure they were not misleading consumers and contained the proper class and type, among other things.

In 1958, the George T. Stagg Distillery received a letter from the director Dwight E. Avis, in which the government took issue with Old Stagg Kentucky Straight Bourbon's ad campaign "Great as a Warm-Up." In the ads, as is sometimes the case now, bourbon was referred to as a warm-up during the cold. But Avis said this misleads the consumer. "Since it seems clearly to convey the misleading impression that the advertised product will chase that chill and is therefore conducive to physical well-being in a contravention of Section 64 (d). There would be no objection to claims that certain hot drinks such as a 'Tom & Jerry' or 'Hot Toddies' made from your product are warming, if it is made quite clear that the statement or implication applies to the mixed drink, rather than to the distilled spirits used in its preparation."

Stagg's parent company, Schenley, and its legal offices, Cooke & Beneman in Washington, D.C., considered this claim questionable. "I think it can be argued that a product that warms you up doesn't necessarily give you any therapeutic result," wrote George Beneman in a letter obtained for this book.

Schenley's general counsel agreed with Beneman, but the company had no wish to square off with the government's assessment. "There is no desire to continue with this advertisement so there is no harm in graciously acceding to the ATTD's request," Schenley attorney Stanley Casden confirmed. The ad never appeared again. Alcohol advertisers of the time knew the ATTD was always watching.

man's palate in foreign lands. But the patriotic bourbon industry faced unexpectedly steep hurdles from a strong ally.

After World War II, British tafiffs limited bourbon imports to about $1,200 a year. At the time, distillers were fighting price-fixing battles in the Senate and didn't have the whiskey stocks to compete overseas. But when these battles were settled and they had the barrels in the warehouse, the distillers wanted the right to export, just as Great Britain was enjoying $60 million a year in Scotch exports. The Kentucky Distillers' Association and the newly formed Bourbon Institute said it wasn't fair that Americans couldn't drink bourbon while in the United Kingdom.

The industry hired retired navy admiral William J. Marshall to lead the Bourbon Institute, a nonprofit corporation promoting bourbon nationally and internationally. The Bourbon Institute spoke only for bourbon distillers and not just those in Kentucky—it also represented Illinois, Maryland, and Pennsylvania distillers making bourbon. Representing their views in Washington during the 1960 Department

Despite the industry efforts to not target women, bourbon makers still used women in advertisements. Jim Beam opted for Bette Davis holding a cigarette; Ancient Age featured a model holding a whiskey sour. *Beam Suntory*

WOMEN AND WHISKEY

Women have always been involved with whiskey. More so in Ireland and Scotland than in America, but early American women distilled whiskey, made stills, created barrels, and helped make bourbon the iconic spirit it is today. Women were most valued in the bottling line. When whiskey companies began bottling whiskey in the late 1800s, they realized men were not dexterous enough. With their fat fingers and calloused palms, men simply could not place a label on a bottle as well as a woman, whose hand muscles and hand-and-eye coordination were developed after years of knitting. Women bottlers formed their own unions and at one point demanded men not be allowed roles as full-time bottlers.

Today, women are the CEOs, distillers, marketers, key decision makers, and most importantly, the fastest-growing segment of whiskey drinkers. For more information on women and whiskey, read my book *Whiskey Women: The Untold Story of How Women Saved Bourbon, Scotch & Irish Whiskey.*

For good or bad, after Prohibition bourbon distillers sought only male drinkers. If women came along, then fine, but they were not the marketer's objective.

Ancient Age commissioned actress and model Sophia Loren in 1967. This in-store cardboard pop-up was in liquor stores briefly.
Schenley Archives, Sazerac

When Maker's Mark hit stores in 1958, the bottle stood out and sold for $6 at a time when most bourbon whiskey cost $2. The red dripping wax changed liquor-packaging design. Since its inception, Maker's Mark has sent more than one hundred cease-and-desist letters to competing brands for using wax to seal their bottles. The brand won a major lawsuit against Jose Cuervo, protecting its red wax seal as a trademark.

of Commerce's Special Conference with Food Processing and Tobacco Manufactures, Marshall testified that the industry desired a position in the foreign market after recovering from Prohibition and being forced to distill in the service the country. Marshall argued bourbon distillers lost significant ground to Scotch producers who made the word *whiskey* "in many countries is synonymous with Scotch and where bourbon is almost unknown."

During 1959, distilled spirits paid $4.3 billion in taxes. And despite all regulatory measures, taxes, and furloughed distilleries, bourbon distillers still sold 70 million gallons. But only 1 percent went to export.

THE BOURBON INSTITUTE

In 1958, the Bourbon Institute was formed, based not in Kentucky but in New York, with the mission of developing industry standards for bourbon and protecting the bourbon name. Lewis S. Rosenstiel, chairman of Schenley, sponsored the institute that planned to solidify bourbon's heritage. For ten years, it was the voice of the bourbon industry. It merged with other national spirits lobbies to form the Distilled Spirits Industry Council in 1973.

The Bourbon Institute was formed in 1958 and quickly began circulating various information packets, including this, "The Bourbon Story." They were the pioneers behind the Elijah Craig legend. *Oscar Getz Museum of Whiskey*

In the late 1950s, Italy and France removed trade barriers on American alcohol beverages and permitted unrestricted bourbon imports; but France forbade bourbon advertising, and other nations enforced either restrictive licensing or prohibitive tariffs. Perhaps the most damning situation was the European Free Trade Association, known as the "outer seven." The nations entered into an agreement to reduce tariffs on each other's products by 20 percent during 1960, and by 10 percent per annum until January 1, 1970, when tariffs would be completely removed. This gave Scotch producers absolute market control over bourbon, which was charged a 100 percent tariff on controlled amounts of exports. "It is impossible for American distillers to create new markets for their product with typical American salesmanship," Marshall said.

Bourbon distillers, many of whom were veterans of World War II, were perplexed with the United Kingdom's absolute dismissal of American whiskey. The two countries were close allies, but apparently not in whiskey circles. "American bourbon exports will be forced to compete with the exports of the United Kingdom on an even more inequitable basis, rather than moving towards any correction of current situations which are discriminatory against American whiskey," Marshall said.

Outside of the United Kingdom, it was just as bad. Brazil permitted two hundred thousand gallons of Scotch whiskey a year at a value of nearly $2 million, while limiting bourbon imports to just one hundred gallons a year. Brazil also imposed a 150 percent ad valorem duty, making bourbon nearly an upside-down business proposition in the South American country. Argentina imposed a 200 percent tariff on American whiskey.

Spain exported some one hundred thousand gallons of brandy and seventy-five thousand gallons of wine into the United States, but established a $15,000 American whiskey quota in 1960. At the time, the United States did not restrict alcohol beverage imports from any nation. Canadian whiskey and Scotch import rates were the exact same. The distillers tried to play catch up but couldn't get past the hurdles of the tariffs. It was in this Department of Commerce testimony the bourbon industry divulged its plan and hinted that they sought more than just reduced tariffs. "The Bourbon Institute is in favor of the liberal trade policy followed by the United States Government and recommends it as a model for all other nations, so that people the world over may come to know and appreciate one of America's great native products, fine old bourbon whiskey," Marshall testified.

In addition to the financial hurdles of exporting, bourbon distillers found that foreign consumers didn't understand bourbon, thinking it was another kind of Scotch. The Bourbon Institute recognized this problem and attempted to have the Department of Commerce educate other countries of this fact during trade negotiations. But the institute was also after something greater: they wanted to inform the public that bourbon was a distinctive whiskey type, that it was a traditional United States production, and that it deserved to rank with the greatest Scotches and cognacs of the world. "The bourbon industry feels that its product is a distinctively unique American product and that the sale of this product plays its part

MAKER'S MARK STARTS

As conglomerate brands were seemingly muscling out the little guy, Bill Samuels started Maker's Mark in 1953 but did not bottle until 1958. The name "Maker's Mark" was outside the box in a time of more traditional Southern names adorning labels, and it was capped with a red dripping wax. It sold for $6 a bottle at retail, immediately making it the most expensive bourbon on the market. The brand faced steep competition in every market, but allowed for an unusual ad campaign in 1966:

> It tastes expensive . . . and is. Maker's Mark is made expensively; by hand; in small amounts and flavored with homegrown wheat to make it softer. It's the softest spoken of the bourbons; you can stay with its easy taste. Bill Samuels, a fourth generation distiller, makes it on his farm near Loretto, Kentucky. Unless you really care how your whisky tastes, don't pay the price for a bourbon as a good as Maker's Mark.

> The brand became one of the fastest-growing brands in bourbon history and certainly changed the advertising game.

BROWN-FORMAN BUYS JACK DANIEL'S

In 1931, Schenley attempted to buy a popular distillery in Lynchburg, Tennessee, but the Motlow family refused and the spirits conglomerate instead purchased Tennessee whiskey rival George Dickel two years later.

Fast forward to 1956. Brown-Forman purchased the Jack Daniel's Distillery for $20 million. The distillery produced Tennessee whiskey, but it was often called bourbon, and Tennessee had only recently come up with its own "Tennessee whiskey" definition. This Jack Daniel's deal was a thumb in the eye to Schenley and put Brown-Forman on a level playing field with the former Big Four.

in the broader program of having American ways and products known throughout the world," Marshall said.

After this hearing, in a move likely planned beforehand, the Bourbon Institute and its membership focused on promoting the bourbon industry and improving its international standing. Domestically, in the 1950s and 1960s each distillery was following the individual path it chose. Stitzel-Weller was becoming known as an antichemist, hands-on distillery, with private labels popping up all over the country, ranging from Berghoff's to Macy's. Heaven Hill, a post-Prohibition family upstart that was barely a blip on the radar, introduced Evan Williams onto the market and was becoming a growing force in the business. Brown-Forman took a giant leap when in 1956 it purchased Jack Daniel's, in Lynchburg, Tennessee. Schenley and Seagram were innovating, experimenting, and creating new yeast strains, while National Distillers ventured into a series of decanters with its Old Crow bourbon that would send collectable ripples across the universe for years to come. But there was limit to domestic sales opportunity. And no matter how much Schenley marketed its Old Stagg bourbon or how much Pappy Van Winkle established private labeling contracts, they would never reach the same market potential as Scotch unless trade barriers were lifted. In 1962, Canadian whiskey exported 14 million gallons compared to bourbon's eighteen thousand gallons. Tariff cuts were essential to protecting bourbon's future.

Before his assassination, President John F. Kennedy had also been involved in reducing tariffs on American products, although bourbon at the time was not an American-only product. Although the majority of it was produced in the United States, some Mexican and Canadian bourbon labels had adorned American liquor-store shelves. Even the Kentucky distillers sold bulk bourbon to Mexican distilleries. Their marketing strategy, though, was to sell bourbon as an American story.

From 1958 to 1964, the Bourbon Institute brought to life the Elijah Craig charring barrel legend, and it was at this point they started talking about bourbon being

Prior to 1964, bourbon could be made anywhere in the world and labeled as such. This 1930s-era Canadian bourbon existed only briefly, but the Mexican distilleries continued to produce bourbon into the 1960s. Nothing could legally stop them. *Schenley Archives, Sazerac.*

special to America. "On April 30, 1789, George Washington was inaugurated as the country's first president in Federal Hall, in lower Manhattan. Members of Congress dined in Fraunces Tavern, a short distance away, that day. On approximately that date the Rev. Elijah Craig, a Baptist minister, distilled the first bourbon whiskey in his home still in Kentucky. The Bourbon Institute has proclaimed April 30 as the birthday of bourbon whiskey."

This press release was picked up in part by the HTNS News Service, which syndicated it to newspapers throughout the country in 1959. And so, people who read this subtle publicity stunt likely thought Elijah Craig invented bourbon on the same day George Washington was inaugurated. In the late 1950s, the only way the Bourbon Institute could have made bourbon sound more American was if they claimed the first barrel was used to squash a time-traveling KGB operative.

AUSTRALIA, THE BOURBON ALLY

While other countries were tariffing bourbon to high heavens, Australians couldn't get enough of it and represented the majority of the spirit's exports in 1961, when it jumped from two thousand cases a year to a hundred thousand. Distillers were able to market bourbon in Australia, a country that today remains an important export market.

The publicity strategy was to connect red-meat-loving Americans to bourbon's American heritage. The Bourbon Institute doubled down on patriotism, recalling its World War II war alcohol production (conveniently leaving out the price-fixing scandals), mentioning the jobs the industry created, and explaining how tariff removals would add another $150 million a year.

In 1962, bourbon eclipsed blended whiskey as the number-one-selling whiskey in the American market. Even the great cookbook author James Beard wrote in *House & Garden,* "Americans are obviously becoming more conscious of flavor of the whiskies they are drinking." Beard, the godfather of modern American cooking, said home ownership had a direct impact on bourbon sales, because people were entertaining in the home.

So, the Bourbon Institute had a connection to George Washington, created jobs, was allegedly invented by a God-fearing Baptist minister, and was adored by America's top chef. All it needed was a congressional favor and the institute's ultimate goal would be achieved.

Through its efforts to reduce tariffs and to protect bourbon abroad, the Bourbon Institute successfully lobbied to the Fédération Internationale des Vins et Spiritueux, the authority in world trade of wine and spirits, to grant "Bourbon whiskey" status as a product of US origin in November 1960. But the International Federation could not enforce this law unless the United States itself adopted a regulation that stated bourbon was a distinctive US product. Within two years, Congressman John C. Watts (Democrat, Kentucky) introduced a resolution that no whiskey could be imported into the United States labeled as bourbon. The resolution passed without a recorded vote, and foreign countries under the International Federation's purview could no longer label their whiskey as bourbon. But the legislation did not grant the distinctive product language the industry was looking for.

In February 1963, Thruston B. Morton (Republican, Kentucky) introduced a Senate resolution declaring bourbon a distinctive product of the United States. It passed the Senate in September and moved to the House's Ways and Means Committee the following year, which referred to bourbon as "our own native whiskey." The committee moved it to the House floor, where it was met with opposition.

The Mexican distillery producing bourbon had ties to New York Congressman John V. Lindsay, who said he could get no assurance that the Mexican-distilled bourbon would not be barred from the United States drinkers. The New Yorker wanted assurances that the executive branch would go easy on the distillery, which Lindsay said was run by "nice old ladies." Watts, who was the leading bourbon voice in Congress, offered to meet with Lindsay but refused to negotiate terms of the US designation. Lindsay's objection was enough to keep Congress from voting on April 30, 1964, which would have been the 175th anniversary of the imaginary date on which Elijah Craig invented bourbon. Lindsay blocked bourbon interests and clearly did not want the resolution to pass.

Congressman John V. Lindsay (Democrat, New York) opposed bourbon's US distinction. Lindsay was attempting to protect the interests of the Mexican distillery in Juarez that had been making bourbon since Prohibition. *Library of Congress*

It's not known if Lindsay and Watts met, but from the reports of Lindsay's demeanor May 4, 1964, it seems highly unlikely that he came to an agreement with Watts. After Watts reintroduced the bourbon resolution, Lindsay stood up and asked, "This Resolution does not intend to hurt someone who derives his income from the importation of a little tiny bit of bourbon whiskey?" Watts shook is head no, but the wording of Lindsay's question made it sound as if his constituent were the importer and not the distiller. Whoever's interest Lindsay was attempting to protect, he closed with poem before Congress:

> Is there a man with soul so dead,
> Who never to himself has said,
> This is my own, my native bourbon?

The House then reportedly shouted approval for the bill. Lindsay did not voice "no." Bourbon distillers had to feel as though they were on top of the world. The year was 1964, and bourbon was America's spirit, the dominant drink for the true man who liked two fingers, neat or maybe with a cube of ice or two. If he was a man, by God, give him bourbon. Little did the Bourbon Institute or its founders know that while they were focusing on legislative matters, the fickle consumer was turning his attention elsewhere.

WHO WAS NUMBER ONE?

When taking distillery tours, there's a lot of talk about who is the number-one-selling product from a historical standpoint. In the 1950s, Four Roses, Ten High, Old Crow, Old Hickory, Early Times, and Old Stagg all made this claim. Even Windsor Straight Bourbon advertised it was one of America's best-selling bourbons. Until now, it's remained a mystery as to who was really the number-one-selling bourbon of the 1950s. Sales data for this time is scarce, and the public information was not very good.

But Schenley and Brown-Forman memos obtained in the research of this book indicate that Schenely's Old Stagg and Brown-Forman's Early Times were neck and neck.

The controversy over identifying the best-selling bourbon begins in 1953 with Old Stagg Kentucky Straight Bourbon advertising itself as "America's Largest Selling Kentucky Bourbon." Brown-Forman then complained to the Alcohol and Tobacco Tax Division that *it* was the top bourbon. The government saw the Old Stagg ad and demanded to view sales of Old Stagg to verify the claim. The Grey Advertising agency had made this claim after reviewing the monopoly state liquor-store figures submitted to the US government. This federal inquiry about the advertisement came as Grey prepared to execute a national outdoor metal sign campaign with the slogan "America's Largest Selling Kentucky Bourbon."

Within months of the Old Stagg campaign, Brown-Forman ran a *Washington Post* advertisement that claimed it was "America's Top Selling Straight Whiskey." The two claims required an ATTD ruling about who could claim the use of best-selling bourbon, according to correspondence about the issue.

Schenley responded by providing the sales figures of seventeen monopoly and thirteen open states with a comparison of brands for the three months ending November 30, 1953. The figures showed Old Stagg led the pack, selling 155,250 wine gallons in the thirty-one states, while Early Times was second with 144,039 wine gallons. Brown-Forman offered national case sales data that indicated Early Times outsold Old Stagg three to two. But Early Times' numbers could not dispute the monopoly and open consumption figures Schenley provided, even if they were only for a three-month period.

But the government was not buying either claim, saying it needed "more specific figures." It also admitted that the standard for the best-selling spirit has always been established through public monopoly figures, and a federal representative told Schenley's legal counsel that he "could hardly believe that either one of you had not furnished truthful figures of sales."

The two companies were expected to provide more complete sales figures. Old Stagg showed figures from December 1952 to November 1953 that supported the claim it was the largest-selling straight Kentucky bourbon, as it showed its sales leadership in thirty out of forty-six states. However, Brown-Forman submitted private information of billings and depletions figures that showed Early Times indeed outsold Old Stagg three to two.

"Warm-up" time
is OLD STAGG time

Every mellow drop
TOP KENTUCKY BOURBON
that's why it's America's Top-Selling Bourbon

Ask for it today
at your favorite
bar and
package store

FULLY AGED FOUR YEARS

OLD STAGG

KENTUCKY
STRAIGHT
BOURBON
WHISKEY

BOTTLED BY
THE STAGG DISTILLING CO.,
FRANKFORT, KENTUCKY

OLD STAGG
FULLY AGED KENTUCKY BOURBON

BIGGER THAN EVER
VALUE, STILL ONLY $0.00 PINT
$0.00 4/5 QT.

KENTUCKY STRAIGHT BOURBON WHISKEY•FULLY AGED 4 YEARS•86 PROOF•©1952, THE STAGG DISTILLING CO.,FRANKFORT, KY.

Old Stagg was under government scrutiny for claiming to be the top-selling bourbon. In closed meetings, the government heard claims from Schenley, which owned Old Stagg, and Early Times owner Brown-Forman to determine who could rightfully claim the bestselling status. *Schenley Archives, Sazerac*

Schenley argued that standards for the best-selling bourbon should not be set simply because an industry member complained, and that Early Times' sales were largely from a few isolated markets. "It would be misleading to the American public for Early Times therefore to be permitted to say that it is America's top selling bourbon. We certainly would be more entitled to that statement than Early Times inasmuch as Old Stagg outsells Early Times in more states than Early Times outsells Old Stagg," a Schenley rep wrote.

The government ruled in favor of Early Times.

"It seems to me that if we are not to be permitted to make the statement that Old Stagg is 'America's Largest Selling Kentucky Bourbon,' then Early Times should be similarly being prohibited from making that statement. Clearly, figures based upon sales in 30 out of 46 states are entitled to more weight," wrote Schenley attorney H. L. Fein in 1954.

Despite the Early Times ruling, Old Stagg's claim continued to appear in advertisements in 1955. Perhaps the agencies were trying to test the ATTD's resolve or the ads fell through the cracks in select markets. They confessed to the mistake, and the ATTD director wrote to Schenley representatives, "In view of the steps taken to discontinue the dissemination of this sign and all others containing the actual representation, the file in this matter is being closed." And so, without a press release or fanfare, thanks to the US government, Early Times was crowned the country's number-one bourbon, knocking the reigning Old Stagg off its pedestal.

For the Schenley advertising team, the matter clearly was not closed.

In 1959, they proceeded with making claims about Old Stagg's best-selling nature:

Q: Why is Old Stagg Kentucky's Top Bourbon?

A: Because in all 2,652,638 barrels sold, its fine quality has never varied.

Schenley's legal team said the ATTD took "violent issue" with this particular ad for its misleading nature. By now, Schenley had begun putting more efforts elsewhere and Old Stagg had dropped to the fifth leading seller in Kentucky. The Doyle, Dane, and Berndach Inc. Advertising firm argued that the phrase "top bourbon of Kentucky" appearing on the label is a claim of taste, not a sales indicator. But the firm volunteered to discontinue the campaign to avoid "any legal objections."

Starting in 1960, Old Crow advertised itself as "the best-selling bourbon by far." These ads were quickly discontinued. National Distillers, Old Crow's parent company, likely received government correspondence prohibiting the language.

In the late 1960s, Echo Springs and Yellowstone made claims as "Kentucky's bestselling bourbon," while Old Heaven Hill advertised the same and then some— "take a tip from the bourbon country . . . $1,000,000 can't buy a better bottle of bourbon (neither can seven or eight dollars)."

Ten High came back to the best-selling ranks in 1975 when it claimed its "value has made it America's third best-selling bourbon." Jim Beam eclipsed them all in 1970 and never looked back. Today, only Jack Daniel's, a Tennessee whiskey, outsells Jim Beam bourbon.

As for Early Times and Old Stagg, the once disputed number-one-selling bourbon brands, Early Times is no longer bourbon. Brown-Forman converted the brands to a Kentucky whiskey rather than bourbon to allow for used cooperage in its creation. Old Stagg fell off the cliff until Sazerac's Buffalo Trace reinvigorated the brand, which is now a part of the Buffalo Trace Antique Collection and competes for best bourbon every year at most competitions.

EARLY TIMES
IS NOW AMERICA'S TOP SELLING STRAIGHT WHISKY

Nation pays its greatest tribute to premium quality as Kentucky's favorite Bourbon becomes the leading straight whisky in *all* America . . . *regardless of price.*

The rise of Early Times to its present position as America's top selling straight whisky is one of the most dramatic stories to come out of the whisky business since the war. In a few short years, Early Times has risen from a relatively obscure local brand to become the largest selling straight whisky in *all* America . . . *regardless of price.*

We are grateful for such an honor and pledge to continue making Early Times as you like it — bottled only at the peak of perfection. *The superior uniform quality of Early Times has never changed . . . and will never change. Early Times will always come to you at its full peak of flavor.*

THIS IS THE WHISKY THAT MADE KENTUCKY WHISKIES FAMOUS

EARLY TIMES

Kentucky Straight Bourbon Whisky

ESTABLISHED

BOTTLED BY EARLY TIMES DISTILLERY COMPANY LOUISVILLE, KENTUCKY

$4.89 FIFTH

Every Ounce a Man's Whisky

KENTUCKY STRAIGHT BOURBON WHISKY

EARLY TIMES DISTILLERY COMPANY
LOUISVILLE 1, KENTUCKY • 86 PROOF

When Early Times began advertising it was the top-selling bourbon, Brown-Forman complained to the federal authorities that Schenley no longer could claim a similar tagline. The government sided with Brown-Forman on the matter.

CHAPTER 9

RISE OF WHITE SPIRITS

It caught all the distilleries off guard—white spirits, specifically vodka.

The rise in white goods coincides with the fictional character James Bond making a simple request: he wanted a martini "shaken, not stirred." The phrase first appears in the novel *Diamonds Are Forever* in 1956, Bond says it in the novel *Dr. No* in 1958, and Sean Connery playing Bond orders the drink with the famous catch phrase in 1964—the same year bourbon received its designation and distillers were heavily investing into new facilities, advertising campaigns, and legislative efforts. It's also the same year the Vodka Information Bureau was loosely formed, taking a page out of the bourbon distillers' Bourbon Institute playbook.

In 1939, vodka only represented 35,370 gallons consumed in the United States, and it grew at a snail's pace until 1961, when it showed a 50 percent spike in eighteen- to forty-four-year-old men. Still, the category only accounted for a blip of the total spirits volume. According to advertising circulars for the spirits industry, vodka sold 19.5 million gallons in 1961 compared to 178.4 million gallons of total whiskey. But vodka was showing signs of growth, while bonded whiskey was losing momentum. In 1961, bonded whiskey dropped 7.1 percent in sales, while Scotch was flat. Vodka, rum, gin, and miscellaneous spirits were rising quickly.

Initially, culturists could not understand why vodka was taking off. After all, it was connected to Russia, the United States' enemy. "Whatever the Russians can do, we can do better. We must have developed a new breed of vodka drinker who can toss it off with any Russian and stay on his feet until the Communist is under the table," wrote Ellis L. Spackman, a syndicated columnist.

One theory was that vodka's popularity was growing because nobody could smell the spirit on your breath. Another was that youth thought it was cool and, well, James Bond enjoyed it. The Salvation Army took issue with young people drinking vodka, calling it "poison" and saying it contributed to the "amorality" of kids.

The American media mocked the Russians for their incessant vodka love, labeling the country's vodka drinkers "Ivan, the Russian Vodka lover." Some Americans even considered it treason to clink glasses of vodka with a Russian. When Secretary of State Dean Rusk and his wife toasted Soviet ambassador Anatoly Fyodorovich Dobrynin with vodka, a letter to the editor at the *Indianapolis Star* asked, "Is this diplomacy or just plain treason?"

Meanwhile, distillery companies were watching vodka sales outpace Scotch, become more profitable than bourbon, and win over American youth. Former Seagram's distiller Bill Friel remembers vodka's rise as devastating. "We could see what was happening, that vodka was increasing its presence and people, particularly women, were ordering all kinds of vodka drinks," Friel says.

How each bourbon-centric company chose to deal with the vodka trends would determine bourbon's future.

At Seagram, Friel, then a young production employee, and his colleagues wrote corporate executives to encourage them to create a vodka label because the market was changing so rapidly. "And we got a letter back to mind our own business. We were informed that Seagram would never put its name on a vodka," he says.

In some markets, vodka cost $3.69 compared to ten-year-old bourbon at $3.39 a bottle, showing that retailers saw vodka's potential profits as early as 1963. Mr. Boston and Smirnoff were brand favorites, but the bourbon companies also launched vodka brands. Glenmore and Schenley converted stills and offered significant still time to vodka production in order to diversify production.

The executives without an emotional attachment to whiskey had to love the rise of vodka. It could be made from anything and didn't require aging. Interestingly, most Americans didn't even know precisely what vodka was.

During the 1930s congressional liquor hearings, Senator Alben W. Barkley (Democrat, Kentucky) demonstrated the ignorance toward vodka held by most Americans. He mistook vodka for the liquor illegally made from Irish potatoes—which was *poteen*, not vodka. But this lack of awareness was also demonstrated in the government's initial alcohol laws.

The 1943 Federal Alcohol Administration Act listed vodka as a "generic" spirit along with aquavit, arrack, and kirschwasser. In 1959, the Alcohol & Tobacco Tax Division of the Treasury informed agents that vodka was essentially neutral

One of the early methods of competing with vodka was to simply do what vodka was doing—mix it with orange juice. *Schenley Archives, Sazerac*

spirit. By 1961, vodka was finally added to the class and type of intoxicating liquors, where it was referred to as a neutral spirit distilled from any material at or above 190 proof, reduced to not more than 110 proof. This was not a generous definition, as the off-the-still proof point was the same as for industrial alcohol. Both Polish and Russian regulations allowed for much lower off-the-still proof points, which would have allowed more nuance and ingredient-based flavor to come through in the spirit. Former spirits executives have said that this regulation lowered the quality of the spirit so it would not take market share from the bourbon and blended whiskey category. That explains how foreign brands were able to dominate the vodka market—their regulations simply offered better quality.

On the American side, bourbon distillers began adding vodka collars to their column stills and attempting to make vodka. Norm Hayden, a former Old Fitzgerald Distillery and Stitzel-Weller executive, said the government should have never allowed the term *vodka* in the first place. "One of the worst things that happened to bourbon was the government ultimately permitting the term vodka to be used in place of grain-neutral spirits, as long as grain-neutral spirits was denoted for alcohol, which, that's what vodka is. It had no real appeal," Hayden said.

Hayden recalls a private label client in California visiting the Stitzel-Weller Distillery in the 1950s. California was the ultimate win for distillers seeking to capture Hollywood and the Golden State's youth. Schenley even used a celebrity, former L.A. Rams tight end and Pro Football Hall of Famer Tom Fears, as a salesman, making this California firm a little ahead of the curve in marketing of vodka. The California firm met with Stitzel-Weller's Pappy Van Winkle and poured one of their best-selling drinks, a vodka and ginger ale. Pappy did not care for it and said: "That will never sell."

But, of course, vodka did sell.

One area that vodka really hurt was the private label business, especially for the Stitzel-Weller Distillery. Stitzel-Weller created private labels for dozens of companies, such as Macy's and the Drake Hotel. With vodka's popularity, the private label business was moving toward white goods.

By the mid-1960s, bourbon distillers were forced to compete with vodka on the white spirit's terms, taking bourbon outside of its comfort zone. Terms like "rare" and "old" and "straight" no longer carried the same weight, and an eight–year-old bourbon just wasn't as hip to the "groovy" James Bond–loving crowds. Younger consumers wanted to add juice to drinks now. Although bourbon marketers were accustomed to promoting highballs and old-fashioneds, the *crème de la crème* category had always promoted savoring whiskey neat or by adding ice or water. Ancient Age executed an "add orange juice" campaign. Glenmore pursued the premixed cocktail route, while Brown-Forman attempted to extract the color of bourbon for a product it called Frost 8-80, a whiskey that could compete with vodka; the company acquired eight-year-old Pennsylvania bourbon and filtered the whiskey until the color was removed. When it launched in the late 1960s, Brown-Forman said the product had sold remarkably well in test markets. Unlike bourbon, it could be used for martinis, daiquiris, bloody Marys, and numerous other drinks. The company spent $4 million in advertising, but despite early success, the product sat on shelves. Brown-Forman said consumers didn't understand the product, since there was nothing like it on the market, and soon initiated a national recall. "We told all of our retailers and wholesalers, you will not be stuck with Frost," said Chris Morris, a Brown-Forman master distiller.

Brown-Forman recovered tens of thousands of cases, cracked open every unsold bottle of eight-year-old Pennsylvania bourbon stripped of color, and poured them all into the distillery beer well to be redistilled. Employees then dug a landfill on Brown-Forman acreage, placed every bottle in the pit, bulldozed the glass until it was compacted in the earth, and piled the dirt over the glass. The failed product launch was such a failure that the word "Frost" was forbidden in Brown-Forman hallways. Some years later, an adolescent Morris, whose father worked at Brown-Forman, planned to wear a Frost T-shirt to a Brown-Forman company picnic. His father accosted him and said he'd be fired for wearing the shirt. "For a generation, you were not allowed to talk about Frost," Morris recalls.

For what it's worth to those white-whiskey pioneers, the concept was a last-ditch effort to compete with vodka.

In 1969, the industry successfully lobbied for a new whiskey type called "light whiskey," which had to be taken off the still at between 160 and 190 proof and aged in used cooperage. This provided blenders a cheaper-to-produce American whiskey to mix into their final blends, and it gave distillers a product to bottle that offered a lower flavor-profile standard that appealed to vodka drinkers.

Nonetheless, despite vodka chipping away at bourbon shares, bourbon was still the number-one-selling spirit in the United States. "We are pleased by the many clear indications that Bourbon producers are enjoying good economic health," testified Robert W. Coyne, president of the Distilled Spirits Institute. While that was true, the statement didn't present a full picture, because the distilleries with multiple spirits interests were either increasing vodka efforts or channeling the light whiskey movement.

Listen:
You've tried some whiskeys that growl.
Now try a new kind of whiskey.
Crow Light. It whispers.

Take a sip of Crow Light. We think you'll agree that other whiskeys—even the lightest Scotch, smoothest Canadian or mildest Blend—taste heavier by comparison.

And that's the way it should be. Crow Light is an entirely new and different kind of whiskey created to be the lightest whiskey ever made in America.

Lighter than Scotch, smoother than Canadian

Crow Light is light...lighter than Scotch. (That's true in color, taste, and strength). And if you think Canadian is the smoothest whiskey you'll ever taste, try Crow Light. "Crow Light is smoother," say the Canadian whiskey drinkers we've talked to.

Mixing whiskey

Try a Crow Light Sour. Or even a Bloody Mary...or Screwdriver...or anything else mixed. Crow Light's light whiskey flavor mixes unusually well.

Real whiskey down to its toes

Crow Light is real, 4-year-old whiskey, all right. But it's distilled and aged a very special way. Result: The gentlest suggestion of whiskey flavor—and lightness no other kind of whiskey can touch.

Some whiskeys growl. But Crow Light Whiskey whispers. And you can get a lot farther with a whisper than a growl.

Crow Light. The whiskey that whispers.

When National Distillers committed so much time and energy to Crow Light, there was a ripple effect down to the bourbon in the company. They essentially chose the new light whiskey category over bourbon and their distilleries suffered for it.

When Old Taylor closed in 1972, there was no announcement or press release. Three years later, National Distillers told workers of plans to renovate the facility, but nothing happened. When it was sold to Jim Beam in the 1980s, the historic, 1800s-era distillery was left for ruins. In 2014, a group purchased the Old Taylor Distillery and hired Marianne Barnes, a Brown-Forman master taster, to be the master distiller, making her the first female Kentucky bourbon master distiller.

Distillers now suddenly wanted to appeal to women, saying that the light whiskey effort was a commitment to them as well as the young drinkers. Kentucky distilleries accustomed to making bourbon were committed to make 170 million gallons of light whiskey in 1972. National Distillers said all of its light whiskey would come from Kentucky. Barton Distillery invested $4 million to promote its QT brand after early success, while Seagram's Four Roses Premium Light whiskey was doing "quite well." Heaven Hill's Don Colman told the *Louisville Courier-Journal* that they didn't aggressively pursue other spirits categories that showed import successes. "We decided not to miss the boat on light whiskey," Colman said.

The one major bourbon company that chose to gamble on bourbon instead of light whiskey was Jim Beam. Instead of following the trend, Jim Beam bragged of its American roots and attempted to distance itself—at least from a marketing perspective—from Russian vodka. "Word from the Kremlin today startled the Bourbon making world," a Beam ad began. "Unreliable sources from Moscow state that Bourbon is not an American spirit but, in fact, a Russian one. Bourbon, of course, is considered the only true American spirit.... [Russians] insist that bourbon was actually discovered earlier [in 1785] by Ivan Chekkakoff in a little town called Vladivostok. They further state that the famous Beam formula is nothing more than a copy of the Chekkakoff stuff." Beam pounded the newspaper pages with these half-page and full-page advertorials offering this comedic (for the time) Russian story and "Bourbon IQ Tests" that promoted the Beam name.

From 1972 to 1975, bourbon distillers, especially National Distillers, pumped a lot of resources into light whiskey only to find sales to be "quite disappointing." During this same time frame, Stitzel-Weller was sold, Old Taylor closed, and vodka surpassed bourbon as the number-one-selling spirit in the country. J. Richard Grieb, president of Smirnoff, made this announcement ten years after bourbon had become a distinct product of the United States: "Vodka has had such a dramatic growth in the last ten years is because it mixes with a whole lot of flavors people like. Vodka doesn't interfere with the flavor."

While many bourbon distillers focused on competing with vodka, Jim Beam focused on bourbon.

When learning of the sales eclipse, an anonymous bourbon distiller told a UPI reporter that the vodka trend was "like the Prohibition-era bathtub gin and orange juice." By this time, the distillery companies started looking at the next hot trend—tequila. But some bourbon brands—Jim Beam, Maker's Mark, Ancient Age, and Wild Turkey—continued to grow And there were signs that the consumers still loved bourbon. In 1979, Heaven Hill's bourbon business was up 8 to 10 percent.

Vodka's growth also came in a time of massive inflation and high energy costs. It made more business sense for a distillery company to diversify operations than to

Continued on page 186

If one were to identify the single worst year in bourbon history, it would be 1972. Vodka was closing in on the whiskey to become the top-selling spirit in the United States, and bourbon distillers were attempting to produce light whiskey to compete with vodka.

Stitzel-Weller was sold in 1972 to Norton Simon, which owned Somerset Importers and marketed Hunt-Wesson Foods, Canada Dry, and McCall publishing. The Van Winkle family did not want to sell, but the other stockholders voted to sell the distillery and its whiskey stocks for $20 million. Stitzel-Weller had produced Old Fitzgerald, Rebel Yell, W. L. Weller, and Cabin Still, which the *Associated Press* estimated was 3 percent of the 31 million cases of bourbon sold annually. "Several of us, along with Julian, we were trying to raise money and we had some pretty big rollers in the game, but it was just a little more than we really could put together," remembers Norm Hayden, who worked at the facility under the Van Winkles, Norton Simon, and United Distillers from 1946 to 1989. Julian Van Winkle II, the son of Pappy and a World War II tank commander, dusted himself off and started making bourbon with his own son, Julian Van Winkle III. "With money selling at 12 percent, labor unions hammering, costs rising daily, well, maybe it was a good time to get out. That's what I told myself," Van Winkle said in an interview in 1974.

Of course, the Van Winkles would continue their quest with a simple principle—less is more. "The key to succeeding in this market is producing in limited quantities. If you think you can sell 3,500, put out 3,000. If you think you can sell 10,000, put out 8,000," Van Winkle said during the launch of his new whiskey company—Old Rip Van Winkle.

In 1972, National Distillers also decided to go all-in on light whiskey, opening a bottling plant in Cincinnati. But it also discontinued operations at the beautiful Old Taylor Distillery near Frankfort. The plant would later be sold to Jim Beam and then sold again. It was salvaged for distilling parts until it was purchased in 2014, and the plant is once again aging spirit.

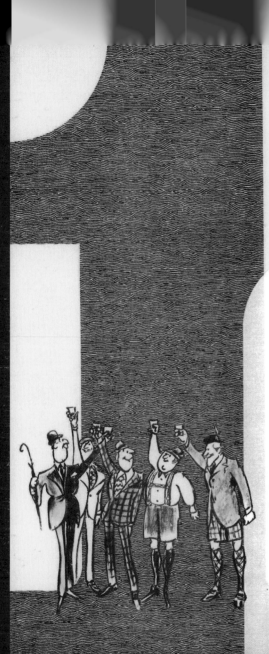

★

1971
1970
1969
1968
1967
1966
1965
1964
1963
1962...
...for
ten
years

BOURBON
has
been

NUMBER ONE
in total
whiskey sales
around the world

The Bourbon Institute
277 Park Avenue
New York 10017

In 1972, in one of its final public displays, the Bourbon Institute advertised bourbon's ten-year reign as the number-one-selling whiskey. But 1972 was really a year of loss for bourbon. Vodka was knocking it off its pedestal and distilleries were closing.

OPPOSITE: From the 1970s to mid-2000s, back bars shifted from carrying mostly whiskeys to more like this—

Continued from page 183

SHIVELY TAXES

On October 16, 1965, police raided Brown-Forman and Stitzel-Weller distilleries for alleged delinquent taxes.

A Louisville suburb, Shively, had raised its property tax rate from 40 cents to 75 cents and five distilleries in the area claimed the tax hike was illegal. The city then contended that Brown-Forman, Stitzel-Weller, Seagram & Sons, Yellowstone, and National Distiller's Products owed $51,000.

The raiders took one thousand cases of whiskey and furniture. But their warrant would not allow confiscation of bonded whiskey, either in barrel or bottle, the city's attorney said.

City officials continued raids, but a restraining order was placed on them prohibiting them from seizing office furniture. A month later, the Jefferson County Circuit Court Judge Charles M. Allen approved a settlement of $36,144 for Shively's whiskey storage tax for National, Seagram, Stitzel-Weller, and Glenmore's Yellowstone. Brown-Forman contested the $15,100 tax bill and later settled for $8,500 in 1966.

back bourbon's legacy. CEOs wanted diverse portfolios, but bulk whiskey sales broker R. L. Buse disagreed with this approach. In 1977, Buse told the *Louisville Courier-Journal* that bourbon distillers were spending $9 per case of tequila on promotions and only $1 per case to promote bourbon.

Buse was right. What if, instead of developing light whiskey brands, distillers had followed Beam's promotional lead? It's likely bourbon would never have lost its sales advantage. "We're not striking the general market like we used to," said Thompson Willett, president of the Willett Distilling Company, to the *Louisville Courier-Journal* in 1979. "We're concentrating on Kentucky and people who like fine whiskey."

Moving into the 1980s, independent distillers, Beam, National Distillers, and Schenley were all optimistic about bourbon. Heaven Hill reported that domestic whiskey had increased 6.4 percent in the first eight months of 1978, although those numbers were skewed because Jack Daniel's was consistently sold out and leading all American whiskey sales. Beam's Booker Noe said, "Bourbon in general is coming up." For Beam, and a handful of smaller distilleries, that was true, but for the rest of the distilling industry, it was all about vodka and other white goods.

After Double Springs Distillery purchased sixteen thousand barrels of Waterfill & Frazier ranging from light whiskey to twelve-year-old bourbon at auction, Robert P. Schecter captured the mood of bourbon distillers in the 1970s: "It's no longer a question of which bourbon. It's a question of which type of drink—vodka, gin, scotch, and so on. There's just no room in the marketplace."

By 1984, nearly four hundred vodka brands littered the liquor stores. Then came flavored vodka, leading to thousands upon thousands of vodkas covering every possible fruit, the occasional whipped cream, and peanut butter and jelly.

The blow vodka struck to bourbon companies was in some ways self imposed. Bourbon parent companies often made decisions that conflicted with their bourbon interests. It should be pointed out that bourbon held its position as the number-one-selling spirit only so long as the Bourbon Institute was active. Around the time it merged with the Licensed Beverage Industries and the Distilled Spirits Institute to form the Distilled Spirits Council, vodka leapfrogged bourbon. Vodka's surge didn't happen overnight, but bourbon's problems were certainly exaggerated by the fact it no longer had a national organization protecting its industry interests. Compared to the Bourbon Institute, the 1970s-era Kentucky Distillers' Association was little more than a drinking club.

In 1981, only Early Times and Jim Beam cracked into the top thirty *Beverage Impact* best-selling spirits brands. That same year, as bourbon seemed down and out, the brand with the dripping wax got a phone call.

LOWERING PROOFS

In the 1970s, brands were drastically lowering proofs to minimize losses due to inflation.

In 1974, Jim Beam's white label went from 86 proof to 80 proof. Kentucky Gentleman dropped its proof the same year, while other brands simply raised the price. Jim Beam attributed the proof lowering to increases in costs: grains had increased in price 300 percent in a 1.5 year period, and glass had gone up 20 percent. National Distillers stuck with 86 proof for Old Grand-Dad, Old Taylor, and Old Crow, but experimented with 80-proofers.

Jim Beam White Label remained 80 proof.

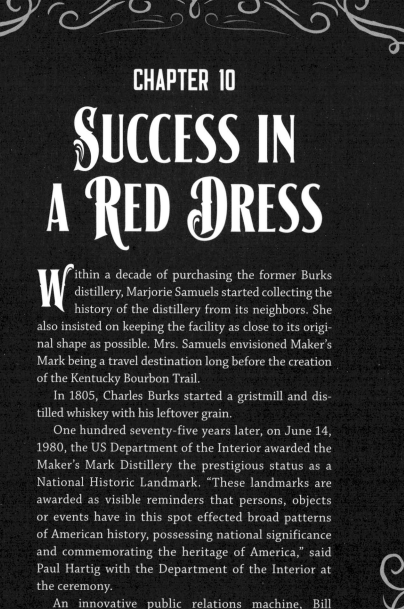

CHAPTER 10

SUCCESS IN A RED DRESS

Within a decade of purchasing the former Burks distillery, Marjorie Samuels started collecting the history of the distillery from its neighbors. She also insisted on keeping the facility as close to its original shape as possible. Mrs. Samuels envisioned Maker's Mark being a travel destination long before the creation of the Kentucky Bourbon Trail.

In 1805, Charles Burks started a gristmill and distilled whiskey with his leftover grain.

One hundred seventy-five years later, on June 14, 1980, the US Department of the Interior awarded the Maker's Mark Distillery the prestigious status as a National Historic Landmark. "These landmarks are awarded as visible reminders that persons, objects or events have in this spot effected broad patterns of American history, possessing national significance and commemorating the heritage of America," said Paul Hartig with the Department of the Interior at the ceremony.

An innovative public relations machine, Bill Samuels Jr. turned the National Historic Landmark status into several television appearances and newspaper stories. But these were planned events; his big media hit came by luck.

As soon as the Samuels family purchased the Burks Spring Star Hill Distillery, it invited tourists to the facility. It even solicited visitors on its first bottling from 1958.

Wall Street Journal reporter David Garino wrote about Maker's Mark on the front page August 1, 1980. Samuels Jr. now says his phone never stopped ringing after that story.

This is where the Maker's Mark legend truly begins. At this point, the distillery produced maybe 120,000 cases a year, with half sold in Kentucky and 25 percent sold in Indiana and Tennessee. After the *Wall Street Journal* story, Maker's Mark received calls from out-of-state liquor wholesalers, thousands of fan letters wanting to purchase the whiskey, airlines wanting to sell it as their in-flight bourbon, and three suitor requests a week. Fearing that its whiskey would quickly be drained, the small company publicly stated that it could only grow at a rate of 8 to 10 percent a year.

So, it did what any rational company would do (well, not really)—Maker's Mark advertised in the *Wall Street Journal* to explain it could not accommodate current demand, and in regional newspapers to inform longtime customers that it would not forget their loyalty. Maker's Mark also used the letters as a start of a major ad campaign, quoting real customers in advertisements and later creating a consumer loyalty program.

But the Samuelses were facing greater problems than just keeping up with demand. Marjorie Samuels died. Mrs. Samuels had owned half the distillery, while her husband, Bill Sr., owned the other half. Samuels Jr. was concerned not only about the pending estate tax, but also about a federal proposal on the floor that would increase distilled spirits excise taxes from $10.50 to $21 a gallon. Instead of waiting to see if the excise tax would double, Samuels Sr. opted to entertain the purchase offers his brand was receiving.

Maker's Mark received two significant offers, both for $15 million, from the Canadian company Hiram Walker and Norton Simon, which owned and operated the Old Fitzgerald Distillery (formerly Stitzel-Weller). The Samuelses worried that Norton Simon's motive for buying Maker's Mark was simply to improve Old Fitzgerald's standing. Their fear was that Norton Simon would purchase the brand name and its whiskey, then gradually downgrade Maker's Mark while Old Fitzgerald's stock rose. Old Fitzgerald, made with a similar recipe as Maker's Mark, was simply too similar to Maker's Mark.

Samuels Jr. also attempted to raise the capital to buy the brand himself; he was the director at the Marion National Bank in Lebanon. But he simply couldn't compete with the $15 million or the distribution and manpower of Hiram Walker. It was a bittersweet moment for Bill Samuels Jr., who negotiated a spot on the Hiram Walker board.

Still, in the early 1980s, Maker's Mark was the sexiest bourbon, and it targeted bourbon's biggest American whiskey rival—the Tennessee whiskey Jack Daniel's. A 1982 advertisement:

> Why can't I find Maker's Mark when I travel? I always see Jack Daniel's. The only way to truly solve the problem would be to go into mass production and we're not about to do that. Handcrafting is what makes Maker's Mark special. If we made much more than we do, well, it wouldn't be your Maker's Mark. Most of our production is taken up by our customers right here at home. There's precious little left for elsewhere. So if, in your travels, you have to search for a bottle of Maker's Mark—after seeing row after row of Jack Daniel's—we apologize. . . .

DEREGULATION

Prior to the Reagan administration, distillers worked alongside government gaugers who oversaw every aspect of the distillery and kept locks on stills and warehouses, making sure distilleries followed regulations and kept track of every drop of whiskey. In an effort to reduce government spending, Reagan initially attempted to deregulate the alcohol industry. But the distillery community fought this, as the government worker was considered a trusted ally.

"Those people knew the regulations and watched closer. If we had [government supervision] today, it would cut down on a lot of mistakes," said Leonard Riddle, longtime worker at Buffalo Trace Distillery.

The distillery gauger position disappeared through defunding.

Reagan also repealed stamp requirements as a part of the Deficit Reduction Act of 1984.

After Prohibition, government gaugers locked the stillhouse, cistern room, and all the warehouses. The agent had a key and the distillery had a different key, making each section double locked. If workers repaired equipment, the gauger crimped a metal tag after the job. This government oversight kept distillers on their toes, but was discontinued in the early 1980s.

This time in bourbon history is usually presented as the moment seized by Maker's Mark, at a time when the rest of the industry was on death's door. "By 1980, the skids would have been under bourbon," remembers Mark Brown, CEO of Buffalo Trace and someone who has worked in the spirits business since the 1970s. "Things like Bacardi, Cuervo, and Smirnoff were popular. They were always talking about bourbon being old and tired versus white goods not being old and tired."

Bourbon's sales gradually dropped by 50 percent from 1970 to 1985, amidst rising costs in advertising fees and increased taxes, but the industry was not dead. The early 1980s offered several bright spots other than Maker's Mark.

Jim Beam sold 4.2 million cases, up one hundred thousand cases, in 1982 and beat the number-two bourbon, Early Times, by a margin of two to one. Beam was even ahead of Jack Daniel's by eight hundred thousand cases. Much of this success was thanks to Vietnam veterans who purchased large quantities of Beam in the Post Exchange during the war and continued to patronize the brand when they returned.

At first, I didn't believe it myself.

Not too long ago, I received a phone call from a woman in Hattiesburg, Mississippi, whose real name is Mrs. Jack Daniel.

She told me that for years, and for obvious reasons, the only whisky her husband, Jack Daniel, would drink was the one with his name. Convinced her husband was too stubborn for his own good, Mrs. Daniel spent quite some time trying to get her husband to at least consider other brands. Finally, after years of friendly prodding, Jack consented to give our whisky a try. Now, according to Mrs. Daniel, Maker's Mark is the only whisky Jack Daniel drinks.

Well, I was so tickled by her story that for a brief instant I considered leaking it to one of those supermarket tabloids. Fortunately for Mr. and Mrs. Daniel, I came to my senses.

Of course, I'm not surprised that Jack Daniel prefers Maker's Mark. We've won over many converts to our smooth, handcrafted bourbon, once they tried it.

But, to like it enough to give up the chance to order a fine whiskey that bears your own name... well, I guess that says more about our bourbon than I ever could.

Bill Samuels, Jr.
Bill Samuels, Jr.
President
Maker's Mark Distillery

Maker's Mark

95¢/99¢ CANADA
Vol. 1 - No. 1 · 1993

Scam

Space Aliens Ate My Baby!

JACK DANIEL DRINKS MAKER'S MARK

MELON HEADED MAN SPEAKS ALIEN TONGUE
Uses hand signals to communicate with police and army officials

JESSE JAMES FOUND ALIVE IN LORETTO, KENTUCKY

Woman Marries Wildebeast!

Maker's Mark Distillery, Loretto, KY 40037, 45% Alc./Vol. (90 Proof). Fully Matured.

Maker's Mark had a way of taking shots at the category leader.

In 1983, Heaven Hill's Evan Williams—not Maker's Mark—was tagged as the fastest-growing bourbon brand, increasing 12.3 percent per year over five years. "We're sort of like a David among Goliaths—we have to look at niches," Heaven Hill's Max Shapira told the *Louisville Courier-Journal* in 1985. "We would have a difficult time spending $5 million behind a brand. We couldn't do it. So we have to offer brand characteristics that are hard to find." One of Heaven Hill's strategies was to change up how Evan Williams was served. They attempted to educate new-to-bourbon consumers that it's okay to mix with cola or ginger ale, the strategy that was helping Jack Daniel's and the white goods. "The image problem we have to overcome is the old cowboy running up to the bar and taking three ounces of bourbon and throwing it down," said Shapira.

Outside investors also saw the potential of bourbon. New York spirits businessmen Ferdie A. Falk and Robert C. Baranaskas bought the George T. Stagg Distillery and the flagship Ancient Age brand from Schenley Distillery. With new direction to Ancient Age, the brand chased the profitable high-priced segment, and longtime master distiller Elmer T. Lee also introduced the first commercial single barrel.

Named Blanton's, after Col. Albert Blanton, the single barrel was just that—a single barrel. While it was common practice for distillers to select barrels to bottle for private selection use, consumers could not go to a liquor store and buy a single-barrel product as they can today. At the time, single barrels didn't exist.

In 1984, Lee set the standards of Blanton's for future tasting panels: "An aroma that is a full rounded bouquet of caramel, vanillin, and alcohol that is pleasant and not raw or medicinal. Taste is slight caramel and vanillin semisweet alcohol that is smooth and pleasant, without bite or bitter taste. There is no lingering aftertaste or burning sensation." Blanton's was created for the Japanese market and entered the US market for $24, targeting baby-boomer pockets. When it launched in September 1984, Blanton's was advertised in the *New Yorker*, the *Wall Street Journal*, and Ivy League alumni newspapers. Falk told a reporter, "The high-priced segment is doing well in everything."

That was likely Falk spinning the new brand. Brown said the new bourbon was a domestic flop. In fact, the only thing positive about Blanton's was its popularity in Japan, a country that represented 51 percent of bourbon's exports and grew 349 percent in the 1980s.

The same can be said for the small-batch bourbons introduced by Jim Beam. Small batch was as misunderstood then as it is today. People believed "small batch" meant it was older bourbon and more delicious, but it is a mingling technique of selecting choice barrels in a batch rather than batching mediocre barrels with good ones.

The first of these small-batch bourbons was Booker's, named after the legendary Booker Noe, master distiller of Jim Beam. Beam's parent company, American

Brands, wanted a product to appeal to connoisseurs and requested Noe batch the very best barrels in the warehouse. "I searched warehouses and found these barrels. They were stored in the best possible location in the warehouse where they could age properly," Noe told the Associated Press. The whiskey was straight from the barrel, uncut, and unfiltered. It was $30 for a 750-milliliter bottle and 120.9 proof. "There are still people out there who like a strong bourbon. They'll like Booker Noe, but I tell them not to drink too much because it will nail you." Beam released about twelve thousand bottles in the fall of 1987. The whiskey sat on the shelves.

At this point, bourbon now ranked fourth in the spirits consumption charts, outranked by vodka, cordials, and Canadian whiskey.

The bourbon industry revitalized an old strategy—capitalize on its heritage. In 1989, the so-called Bourbon Information Bureau attempted to rev up enthusiasm using the legend of Elijah Craig in the two hundredth anniversary of his alleged invention of bourbon. But the publicity tactic failed, and reporters offered sales facts proving that bourbon was in great decline. Distilleries were closing and the popular culture was moving toward beer, wine, and white goods, maybe cordials—but bourbon was collecting dust.

Other than a few brands going strong, bourbon's best domestic story of the late 1980s was Rebecca Ruth candy maker, who was making bourbon candies and appealing to the American sweet tooth. As bourbon was domestically declining behind the bar, it was thriving in the kitchen with chefs and recipe developers frequently publishing bourbon cooking recipes.

Heaven Hill Distillery was a burgeoning brand in the 1980s and continues to make stellar bourbons.

JAPAN

Japan has long been a bourbon supporter. In the 1800s, the country sued a spirits company for shipping rectified bourbon mixed with unwanted liquids and calling it "straight bourbon." It won in court and gave America its first legal win in the fight against mislabeling whiskey.

Japan would continue to support bourbon but was disrupted through World War II because of being at war with the bourbon-producing country, and because distillers couldn't afford to export bourbon anyway.

Japan's true impact upon bourbon came in the 1980s, when bourbon exports increased 349 percent and Japan represented 51 percent of bourbon's total exports. Newer products, such as Blanton's and Booker's, did exceptionally well in Japan, while Japan was the largest market for Four Roses Bourbon.

As of 2016, Japanese companies owned Four Roses, Blanton's, and Jim Beam, among other brands. Their taste for bourbon has been one of the great godsends to the spirit. They loved bourbon in a time when Americans were moving toward vodka.

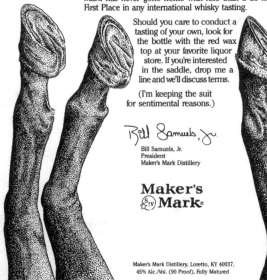

For sale: one (barely) used saddle.

Here in Kentucky, probably the only field more people claim expertise in than bourbon whisky is horse racing. So when a couple of friends came to me offering partial ownership of what they described as a "can't-miss," born-for-the-winner's circle thoroughbred, I just couldn't resist.

I paid my money, ordered some lovely racing silks, and bought a white suit to look good for the TV cameras come Derby Day.

Alas, not for us the blanket of roses. After finishing last, last and seventh in its first three races, the horse died. Leaving these three would-be syndicators with about 300 lbs. of uneaten oats and a nearly-new, custom saddle.

I did learn a valuable lesson, though: spend your time and money on things you know. Which in my case is crafting whisky and definitely not racing horses. For while our horse finished out of the money, Maker's Mark has never gone home with less than a tie for First Place in any international whisky tasting.

Should you care to conduct a tasting of your own, look for the bottle with the red wax top at your favorite liquor store. If you're interested in the saddle, drop me a line and we'll discuss terms.

(I'm keeping the suit for sentimental reasons.)

Bill Samuels, Jr.

Bill Samuels, Jr.
President
Maker's Mark Distillery

Maker's ⑤ᵢᵥ Mark®

Maker's Mark Distillery, Loretto, KY 40037.
45% Alc./Vol. (90 Proof), Fully Matured

In the 1980s, Maker's Mark showed the bourbon industry that profits could be made even though consumers were transitioning to white goods. They proved this with clever marketing and a delicious product, as well as revenue earned through visitor centers.

The modern Kentucky bourbon distillery keeps a manicured lawn to evoke a sense of unique place, but in the 1980s, the Kentucky Bourbon Trail didn't exist. Only Maker's Mark (pictured) had a strong visitor program.

Outside of the States, though, people could not get enough bourbon. Australia, the United Kingdom, South Korea, Italy, and Japan were paying upwards of $80 for Maker's Mark. As they watched sales drop domestically, distillers were eyeballing foreign markets. "Bourbon whiskey has become the 'in' drink abroad—really throughout the world. The ironic thing is that here in the US, it's just the opposite," Shapira told the Cox News Service in 1989. "Wouldn't it be great if the foreign demand set a domestic trend?"

At the time, Shapira and Heaven Hill master distiller Parker Beam were likely wishing, hoping this domestic decline would pass. Unfortunately, bourbon went from 36 million cases in 1970 to 15.6 million cases in 1989. Nobody really believed domestic bourbon sales would come back. "I can tell you 100 percent there was not a vision of bourbon staging a resurgence. I don't think anybody had delusions that we were going to buy the distillery and suddenly rebirth it," Brown says.

Maker's Mark, Glenmore, and Wild Turkey created international sales offices to increase foreign sales, while Brown-Forman and Jim Beam were already staffing the export market appropriately. They were all trying to appeal to the foreign consumer. Domestically, bourbon felt dead. Nobody was buying.

But salesmen kept pounding the pavement and new blood started entering the picture. New brands were buying stocks left over from defunct distillers and suddenly bourbon had life again.

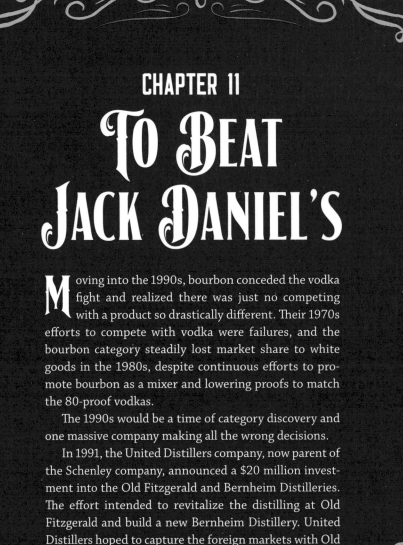

CHAPTER 11

TO BEAT JACK DANIEL'S

Moving into the 1990s, bourbon conceded the vodka fight and realized there was just no competing with a product so drastically different. Their 1970s efforts to compete with vodka were failures, and the bourbon category steadily lost market share to white goods in the 1980s, despite continuous efforts to promote bourbon as a mixer and lowering proofs to match the 80-proof vodkas.

The 1990s would be a time of category discovery and one massive company making all the wrong decisions.

In 1991, the United Distillers company, now parent of the Schenley company, announced a $20 million investment into the Old Fitzgerald and Bernheim Distilleries. The effort intended to revitalize the distilling at Old Fitzgerald and build a new Bernheim Distillery. United Distillers hoped to capture the foreign markets with Old Fitzgerald, Rebel Yell, and W. L. Weller, and believed, specifically, that Rebel Yell could compete with Jack Daniel's abroad and domestically. Within days of this announcement, master distiller Edwin Foote at the Old Fitzgerald Distillery drastically ramped up production of a wheated bourbon recipe to meet the forecasts.

Owensboro, Kentucky, was home to two major distilleries—Glenmore and the Medley Distilling Company (pictured here). Glenmore purchased the Medley in 1988 for $7 million and picked up Ezra Brooks Bourbon. Analysts called the Medley acquisition a sign that Glenmore was planning to grow, but Glenmore sold the company to United Distillers in the 1990s. Ezra Brooks would eventually be sold to the David Sherman Company, now Luxco, which also produces—in partnership with Limestone Distilling Co.—Yellowstone, a former Glenmore Brand.

Months later, United Distillers then purchased the Glenmore Distilleries for $161 million. For Glenmore, which operated facilities in Louisville and Owensboro, the time to sell was right. Glenmore was the eighth largest distillery company, and United Distillers moved up to number three.

All actions suggested that United Distillers would become a brilliant bourbon company when it launched Rebel Yell in the Australia market with a $6 million ad budget and publicly stated its plans to chip away at Jim Beam's and Jack Daniel's Aussie market share. After all, it managed to sell five hundred thousand cases of I. W. Harper in Japan in 1991.

But despite the investments and foreign momentum, United Distillers stopped distilling at Old Fitzgerald in 1992 and laid off seventy-five sales and marketing workers from the Owensboro operations. The company moved all distillation operations to the newly built Bernheim Distillery with the same goal as before—make more Rebel Yell to compete with Jack Daniel's.

Just four years after it purchased the Owensboro plant, United Distillers sold the two former Glenmore distilleries and thirty-seven brands to Barton for $171 million, saying the sale was a part of the global strategy to focus on Gordon's gin and vodka, Scoresby Scotch, and other premium brands. Despite this, they continued to distill large amounts of wheated bourbon at their Bernheim facility and aged this whiskey at the former Stitzel-Weller Distillery, which was known for its well-circulated warehouses.

Although United Distillers discontinued distilling operations at Old Fitzgerald Distillery in 1992, it continued to age whiskey on contract. Among its warehouse aging clients was Maker's Mark. Ironically, the former parent company of Stitzel-Weller, Norton Simon, once tried to buy Maker's Mark.

Over the course of the decade, United Distillers' American whiskey production and strategy created future stocks of Pappy Van Winkle, Jefferson's, Willett, Cyrus Noble, and many other brands that did not have their own distilleries. Other brands took notice, too, tasting the purchased stocks and deciding to increase their wheated bourbon production. "We were sitting in meetings going, 'That's not too shabby' and 'That's rather good' and 'This wheat is quite something,'" remembers Sazerac's Mark Brown. "It's quite a different whiskey. That whole project gave birth to the Antique Collection."

Both Heaven Hill and Barton Brands would broker the former Old Fitzgerald and Glenmore's whiskey stocks at a time you could buy a new fill barrel for $200. No existing distiller wanted older bourbon sitting in a warehouse.

But the foreign demand was just enough of a good thing that new blood thought a trend could be in the works. Plus, the publicity for bourbon had increased. Both *Whisky* magazine and *Malt Advocate* began covering bourbon whiskey along with other whiskey types; Chuck Cowdery released a film on bourbon; and Gary Regan published the *Book of Bourbon*. All the while, Booker Noe and Jim Beam hit the pavement trying to bring bourbon back to its former glory. Noe was educating the public about the nuances of bourbon like no one before. "A regular bourbon is made of good and bad whiskey to make it palatable," Noe told the *Cincinnati Enquirer*, "but there are no bad or immature whiskeys in a small batch."

Malt Advocate launched in the 1990s and built the whiskey following throughout the world. The magazine created WhiskyFest, where consumers taste bourbon and other whiskeys and hobnob with the distillers. Shanken Publications, publisher of *Wine Spectator* and *Cigar Aficionado*, purchased *Malt Advocate* in 2010 and renamed it *Whisky Advocate*.

Beam marketed its Small Batch collection of Booker's, Baker's, Basil Hayden, and Knob Creek; while Ancient Age promoted its collection of Blanton's, Rock Hill Farms, and Elmer T. Lee. Wild Turkey introduced Kentucky Spirit.

The distilleries argued that the whiskey was getting better, too, saying that this concentration on choice barrels yielded better bourbon. But that's the story they had to sell for the time. In fact, demand plummeted and they stopped producing

The Kentucky Bourbon Trail was formed in 1999, giving a tourism spark to bourbon. In the years to come, bourbon tourism became its own subindustry, eventually becoming the state's number-two tourist attraction, second only to the Kentucky Derby. Mint Julep Tours capitalized on this trend in the mid-2000s and began offering special adventures to the bourbon fan.

large quantities of brands and gallons. The single-barrel and small-batch marketing initiatives were not last-resort efforts, by any means, but they were measures aimed at markets such as Japan and Australia.

In fact, when the Nelson County Tourist Commission launched the Kentucky Bourbon Festival in 1991, it expressed a desire to make this an international festival. The festival included participation from most of the distilleries, but struggled to draw initial crowds. By 1998, though, the Kentucky Bourbon Festival's gala attracted 1,200 consumers from all over the world. That was enough for the *L.A. Times* to declare bourbon was the "drink of the decade." Perhaps this declaration was a little premature, but bourbon had life.

For aspiring young businessman Trey Zoeller, the slight growth and obvious interest in bourbon was enough for him and his father, Chett, to start the Jefferson's Reserve and Sam Houston brands. They bought leftover stocks from everybody they could, while others such as Tom Bulleit were establishing distillation contracts. These upstart brands were welcomed by distilleries sitting on large stocks of whiskey, much of which was left over from the United Distiller dealings. "People were thrilled to be able to get rid of older whiskey from their excess inventories," said Joe Magliocco, who resurrected the Pennsylvania Michter's brand with Kentucky whiskey in the early 1990s.

Meanwhile, newer brands had as their common mission to take market share away from Maker's Mark. Blanton's held a *Washingtonian* magazine tasting, in which Blanton's easily won. Maker's later complained of Blanton's wax use, which led to Blanton's giving Maker's Mark a little taste of its own medicine with a full-page advertisement:

> If Maker's Mark has a monopoly on wax closures, maybe Buckingham Palace should turn its royal seal and switch to self-adhesive envelopes. Or could their sudden obsession with wax betray a more legitimate concern with whiskey. Funny how it all surfaced after we ran an ad describing two independent blind tastings in which Blanton's was clearly preferred to Maker's Mark. . . . One taster called Blanton's "more grown-up and self-assured" while another found it "softer, consistently smoother and ever so much more wonderful." Wax or no wax, it seems some people think Maker's Mark doesn't hold a candle to Blanton's. . . .

Maker's Mark then held a one-on-one duel in Louisville, where it easily won, and another blind tasting was held months later.

At the "Shotglass Shootout" in Lexington, Blanton's won again; Maker's came in a close second. "It was a bad day, I guess," Maker's Mark's Bill Samuels Jr. said.

In a sense, it wasn't. This public feud was actually good for the category. If two brands claimed to be the best, the consumer just had to try them both and some might even ask, "Wait, what? Bourbon is good again?" Jack Daniel's, a Tennessee whiskey, had enjoyed a lifetime of publicity with its connection to Frank Sinatra, who was known to consume a bottle or two of Jack Daniel's and then sing about it. Brown-Forman employed somebody whose sole job was keeping Sinatra stocked with Jack Daniel's. But not even Ol' Blue Eyes could sustain the constant pressure Maker's Mark was putting on Jack Daniel's.

The premise of the Maker's Mark advertisements was basically to go as far as you could without getting sued. Bill Samuels Jr., a masterful marketer, signed a letter-style advertisement (see page 192) that read:

> At first, I didn't believe it myself.
>
> Not too long ago, I received a phone call from a woman in Hattiesburg, Mississippi, whose real name is Mrs. Jack Daniel.
>
> She told me that for years, and for obvious reasons, the only whisky her husband, Jack Daniel, would drink was the one with his name. Convinced her husband was too stubborn for his own good, Mrs. Daniel spent quite some time trying to get her husband to at least consider other brands. Finally, after years of friendly prodding, Jack consented to give our whisky a try. Now, according to Mrs. Daniel, Maker's Mark is the only whisky Jack Daniel drinks. . . .

The advertisement included a tabloid with headlines of "Jack Daniel Drinks Maker's Mark," "Jesse James Found Alive in Loretto, Kentucky," "Melon Headed Man Speaks Alien Tongue," and "Woman Marries Wild Beast."

You might think this would have been the straw that broke Brown-Forman's back, but it wasn't. According to a former Brown-Forman executive, Samuels Jr. invited members of the Brown family to a private party. Owsley Brown allegedly went to the party, only to see that Samuels Jr. had hired the Jack Daniel's Band. According to this source, Brown returned from the party and told his executive team, "Somebody, please create a bourbon brand to compete with Maker's Mark."

That brand was Woodford Reserve. Brown-Forman denied that it was Maker's Mark pressure behind the creation of Woodford Reserve, but an internal memo indicates there might be some truth to the story of Woodford Reserve originating to "compete with the likes of Maker's Mark." Brown-Forman master distiller Chris Morris says that any such competitive mentions would have been for the benefit of tourists. "Maker's Mark was really the only distillery doing anything," he says.

Nonetheless, Brown-Forman planned a distillery at the very site it once owned—Labrot & Graham in Versailles, in Woodford County. Nestled around seemingly endless bluegrass and horse farms, Woodford Reserve Distillery opened in 1996, and suddenly there was something to this bourbon uptick.

Then more people came to the Kentucky Bourbon Festival, more distilleries added visitor experiences, and Kentucky was attempting to make something special.

Woodford Reserve launched in 1996 and became one of the most important brands garnering new consumers.

In 1999, the Kentucky Distillers' Association created a brochure for the so-called Kentucky Bourbon Trail. The next year, it sent out a press release and a passport so consumers could get the experience stamped. It became an instant hit, albeit with some inside political scuffles. Buffalo Trace opted out of the KDA, but still claimed to be on the Kentucky Bourbon Trail, a KDA trademark. The KDA sued Buffalo Trace.

Nonetheless, the signs were pointing toward bourbon's return to glory.

At this point, sales were not yet what they once were, but the category's tourism and publicity indicated something special was happening. Whether by coincidence or strategy, distilleries began launching limited-edition products around the same time, driving new interest with the likes of the Heaven Hill's Evan Williams Vintage Single Barrels, Buffalo Trace's Antique Collection, and Jim Beam's masterpiece series.

By 1999, the industry still struggled, but an argument could be made that only a small percentage of the bourbon distillers were even trying to improve their brand's standings. Former president of the Kentucky Distillers' Association, Frank Dailey, said, "The larger companies, recognizing the problem of competition, own Scotch distilleries and wineries and produce vodka and gin because they see where the competition is so they acquire product in that area."

During the cocktail rise of the late 1990s and early 2000s, the mint julep was the bourbon world's cocktail of choice for the swanky populace. It's a simple cocktail that is traced back to the early 1800s and is the official cocktail of the Kentucky Derby. It's merely bourbon, sugar, water, crushed ice, and mint.

Perhaps the most disappointing distillery company from a bourbon perspective was Seagram. It was not placing stock in its bourbon distilleries. In fact, Joseph E. Seagram & Sons had closed numerous distilleries and was considering closing Four Roses in Lawrenceburg. In 1992, Jim Rutledge, who was then the area administrative manager and barrel warehousing manager, saved Four Roses. "Seagram was contemplating contracting with another distillery and closing Four Roses," Rutledge remembers, because they were not happy with the quality coming out of the distillery. "Everybody's jobs were on the line." With each passing year, under the control of Rutledge and distiller Ova Haney, the quality scored higher and higher until finally, "our corporate quality said we couldn't afford to close this distillery. The bourbon is too good."

Continued on page 208

MODERN DISASTERS

On November 7, 1996, the bourbon industry saw one of its most successful distillery companies engulfed in flames. Heaven Hill's Bardstown facility—seven warehouses and the distillery—burned an estimated 2 to 3 percent of the bourbon supply. Nobody was hurt, but it was a painful day for the bourbon community, and the competing distilleries offered their facilities so Heaven Hill could continue operations. After the fire, Max Shapira told all Heaven Hill employees that "nobody is going to lose their job."

Witnesses said the burning bourbon looked like flowing lava. The Alcohol, Tobacco & Firearms agent did not suspect foul play. Fanned by thirty-mile-per-hour winds, fire officials realized they could not effectively fight burning alcohol and decided to let it burn. Barrels exploded and shot into the air, and whiskey flowed down Kentucky Highway 49.

Heaven Hill was scrutinized for not enacting proper fire safety protocol. Bill Burger, the emergency response coordinator for the Kentucky Department of Environmental Protection, told the Associated Press that the fire might have been less severe if the warehouses had been surrounded by protective dikes to contain spills. In fact, the state regulations of the time required new warehouses to have drainage systems, fire-protection water, alarms, sprinklers, and several other safety measures. But these warehouses were built long before this 1994 regulation, and it was impossible for Heaven Hill or other distilleries to retrofit their mostly wooden and aluminum warehouses.

The federal government also sent agents to audit plant records to determine how much liquor was lost for federal taxes.

Heaven Hill's strategy of diversifying its portfolio to include more than just bourbon proved to be a fail-safe move. "Under no circumstances will Heaven Hill Distilleries be forced to shut down," Max Shapira said.

Three years later, Heaven Hill purchased the Bernheim Distillery, Old Fitzgerald, and Christian Brothers Brandy from United Distillers. And the company continued operations, putting the tragedy in the rearview mirror.

Unfortunately, Heaven Hill was not the last bourbon distillery to face fire.

A Wild Turkey warehouse caught fire May 13, 2000, destroying seventeen thousand barrels and sending bourbon into the Lawrenceburg city water supply. This forced local schools and businesses to close.

And in August 2003, a Jim Beam warehouse in West Point, Kentucky, burned, and more than eight hundred thousand gallons flowed into the retaining pond and then into a nearby creek, killing all the fish. Jim Beam reimbursed the state for the damages and cost of fighting the fire.

Neither the Wild Turkey nor Jim Beam fires caused human injuries.

But in May 2015, the Silver Trail Distillery still exploded and severely injured Jay Rogers and Kyle Rogers (not related). Kyle Rogers died days after the explosion, caused by a faulty still.

All of these incidents, especially the Silver Trail Distillery fire, outline the dangers of distilling and aging whiskey. Spirit is highly flammable.

Tornadoes and high winds have also regularly caused damage in recent years. In 2006, a tornado ripped open Buffalo Trace warehouses, leading to a later release of tornado bourbon and inspiring the Warehouse X experimental warehouse.

Neither Mother Nature nor fire cares if bourbon is popular again. Every warehouse is just a flame or tornado away from collapsing. This was a Heaven Hill warehouse taken down by wind gusts in 2015.

Continued from page 205

Rutledge attempted to buy Four Roses and campaigned for the brand's return to the United States as a bourbon. It had been exiled to foreign markets since the 1950s and only the Four Roses blended whiskey was sold in the United States.

Four Roses Yellow Label quietly returned to Kentucky-only liquor shelves in 1996 with two strong Seagram's caveats—no marketing dollars, and "we're only doing this so your employees can purchase it."

But the timing could not have been better.

Toward the end of the 1990s, Internet forums, magazines, and fan clubs were centering around bourbon. People were falling in love with bourbon all over again. But it was a slow process, and as they say, timing is everything.

Jim Beam launched a beautiful Distiller's Masterpiece twenty-year-old Cognac Finish bourbon in 1999. The packaging was beautiful and the whiskey was sublime, but the consumer base didn't understand the concept of finishing bourbon in a used cognac barrel. Had they just released the bourbon as a twenty-year-old product, it likely would have caught fire.

Around the same time, Pappy Van Winkle, the brand, was beginning to get noticed and *Malt Advocate* (now *Whisky Advocate*) named Sazerac Rye and George T. Stagg World Whiskey of the Year in consecutive years—2001 and 2002.

Nobody knew that these limited-edition products would be hits. "The antique collection was a complete flyer. In the deal with Diageo and looking at our own inventories there were these odd pockets of old whiskey. If I had any wisdom I'd have bought a hell of a lot more of it but we took twenty barrels of this or fifteen barrels of that or thirty barrels of that and said we'll try a flyer. Let's put them out as an Antique Collection, because the Heritage Collection had been around if you remember," Brown says. "We felt it would appeal to consumers at the premium end of the marketplace."

In addition to the birth of limited-edition products, bourbon started to show personality. The boisterous Booker Noe paved the way for master distillers to speak about bourbon in open forums, while the eccentric Bill Samuels Jr. offered flair and publicly complimented his competitors. Once hidden in yeast rooms and toiling with the still, late 1990s-era master distillers were getting outside their usual routines and spreading the gospel with their own styles. Wild Turkey's Jimmy Russell's shtick offered tongue-in-cheek comments about a Baptist minister inventing bourbon and Scotch being good because it's aged in used bourbon barrels. Heaven Hill's Parker Beam offered the savant palate and nose, with his boss, Max Shapira, saying that "Parker can pull whiskey out of a barrel, rub it between his hands, smell it, and know whether it's going to be good bourbon" in a

FAST FACT

A newly filled barrel from United Distillers in the early 1990s could have been used for a future Pappy Van Winkle release, at a cost of $250. Today, a barrel of Pappy Van Winkle has sold close to $10,000 at auctions.

The 1990s had the introduction of one of the most important brands—Pappy Van Winkle. Started by Pappy's grandson, Pappy Van Winkle is the only bourbon to receive a 99 from the Beverage Tasting Institute. The whiskey came from multiple sources in the 1990s, but mostly from the former Stitzel-Weller Distillery. Pappy would be a major player in bourbon's comeback.

Known as the "Buddha of Bourbon," Wild Turkey master distiller Jimmy Russell has worked for the company since 1954. He, Ancient Age's Elmer T. Lee, Heaven Hill's Parker Beam, and Jim Beam's Booker Noe were great friends and preached the bourbon gospel in a time when people were drinking vodka. Humble and true to the recipe and principles of his whiskey, Russell was honored by the Kentucky Distillers' Association in 2015 with the Lifetime Honorary Member award, an honor bestowed to only one other person—Bill Samuels Jr. Here, he hugs his brother, who said of Jimmy, "this is the best man."

2001 *Cincinnati Enquirer* article. Former Ancient Age master distiller Elmer T. Lee captured the room with his humble, yet bigger-than-life presence. The avuncular Al Young, a longtime Seagram's employee, became an industry historian, and a soft-spoken Woodford Reserve master distiller Lincoln Henderson used Brown-Forman's Kentucky Derby to discuss the passion of bourbon. "I look at the color of each sample, sniff the aroma, and swish some of the product around in my mouth. Then, I spit it out," Henderson told the Associated Press in 1999.

The publicity bourbon received in the late 1990s was drastically different from the decade before. The 1980s were a time of hardship, and eventual loss to vodka. Perhaps the industry could have spun it differently and shown the brighter side of bourbon, such as Blanton's and Maker's Mark, but they could not hide from the slipping sales. The 1990s were a decade of hope and desire. The sales were often soft, depending on the brand, but those bourbon distillers who stuck their neck out and tested fate would be rewarded. Somebody was listening.

UNITED DISTILLERS FALLOUT: WHO GOT WHAT

After United Distillers, now Diageo, offloaded its brands and eventually its Bernheim Distillery in 1999, their brands and whiskey injected life to the masses.

What happened to the whiskey? United Distillers continued operating the warehouses at the former Stitzel-Weller Distillery. From 1995 to 1999, United Distillers agreed to supply Barton Distillery in Bardstown with bulk whiskey, as well. These whiskey stocks would have been from Bernheim, Old Fitzgerald, and the Glenmore Distilleries. Some barrels were poured into stainless-steel drums so they would not continue to age and would not evaporate.

As part of their Weller and Charter sale to the Sazerac Company in 1999, United Distillers required Sazerac and its Buffalo Trace Distillery to buy every barrel allocated for these products from 1994 to 1998, and the company took all the aged whiskey distilled in 1992 as well as some of the 1991 barrels. This whiskey would be integrated into Buffalo Trace's inventory, including future Weller and Pappy Van Winkle bottlings. (Buffalo Trace and the Old Rip Van Winkle Company entered a partnership in 2002.) It would also be brokered to other companies.

Perhaps more importantly, the United Distillers closing made it apparent that Julian Van Winkle needed a new source for his whiskey. He had been operating out of the Old Hoffman Distillery in Lawrenceburg. "We were perfectly placed to bring everything to the party with Julian of consistency. I said, 'Look, you get first pick of the inventory. I mean when we run the barrel model your brands will go first.' We'll allocate all of that and make sure that Van Winkle is taken care of," Mark Brown said. "I think it was perfect and then Julian was freed up to go and spend time on sales and marketing and we took care of the back end. It's really been a fantastic marriage."

As for United Distillers brands, Rebel Yell, Yellowstone, and Ezra Brooks were sold to Heaven Hill, who sold it to David Sherman Company (now Luxco) in St. Louis; Old Fitzgerald went to Heaven Hill; but the company held onto George Dickel Tennessee whiskey and I. W. Harper, which was selling extremely well in Japan. Although it owned the Glenmore brands for only two years, United Distillers sold Kentucky Tavern in 1995 to Barton.

The United Distillers shakeup in the 1990s gave Heaven Hill a home after its horrific fire, and supplied Sazerac with its future award-winning stocks of Pappy Van Winkle, Weller, and other brands. It provided Jefferson's with whiskey to bottle and allowed the likes of Willett Distillery to acquire the stocks nobody wanted to later sell on the open market or bottle for themselves.

The executives may have mishandled the situation or misread the possible trends, but it's unlikely United Distillers gave the whiskey the same attention or marketing as it received under Sazerac, Willett, Barton, Jefferson's, and the dozens of other brands that bottled this whiskey.

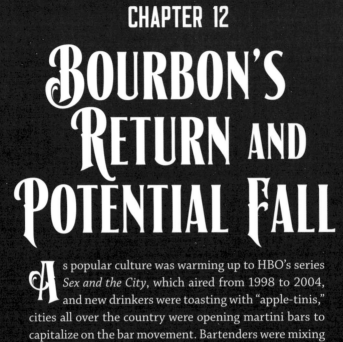

CHAPTER 12

Bourbon's Return and Potential Fall

As popular culture was warming up to HBO's series *Sex and the City*, which aired from 1998 to 2004, and new drinkers were toasting with "apple-tinis," cities all over the country were opening martini bars to capitalize on the bar movement. Bartenders were mixing with fresh ingredients as vodka's dominance continued. At home, people were adding tin mixing cans, strainers, small knives for cutting limes and lemons, and bar spoons—yes, can't forget the bar spoon. "The trend is away from beer and wine and toward cocktails when entertaining at home. People now want the sophistication of mixed drink," Beth Davies, a Distilled Spirits Council lifestyle director, said in 2002.

Other glamor consultants of the time gave their approval that drinking cocktails at home was acceptable. Their cocktails of choice were martinis, margaritas, and pitchers of frozen daiquiris. When referencing whiskey, they might recommend Scotch and soda, or a mint julep. But the home was no place for whiskey; no, it was vodka territory, according to pop culture.

Ignoring this martini trend was a punk rock bar in Chicago called Delilah's. Established in 1993, Delilah's opened the national doors for bourbon. Kentucky had its share of bourbon-centric restaurants, such as Old Talbott Tavern in Bardstown, but national media ignored them in the same way they largely dismissed bourbon. Delilah's founder, Mike Miller, started with 150 beers and 150 whiskies, easily the largest combined selection for the time. "My bar owner friends would ask me: 'Why would you carry all that booze?'" And of course the next question was, why bourbon? For Miller, he loved bourbon's people and didn't care if he went against the vodka craze. "Nothing on vodka, but I have never met Joe Stoli or Andy Absolut. In bourbon, they're all having drinks together. There's a nature about the whiskey business in general that everybody is on the same team," Miller said.

For its part, the bourbon business was thankful to have Miller on its team. He came up with simple ideas that nobody had considered before, like asking Maker's Mark for a neon light—a typical bar promotion for beer companies, but unusual for bourbon. Miller selected his first single barrel with Elmer T. Lee and carried nearly 100 percent of the available bourbon brands. In 1995, the *Louisville Courier-Journal*'s Susan Reigler, who later wrote several bourbon books, named Delilah's the best place in America to buy bourbon. Less than ten years later, the *Chicago Tribune* credited Delilah's with changing Chicago's fine-dining bars, asking, "How many restaurants carried Maker's Mark before Delilah's?"

Thanks to Delilah's and the subtle market growth, there were just enough outliers in the bar business to start a slight bubble trend. Around 2000, Louisville pizza restaurant owner Jason Brauner was enjoying bourbon with a friend and talking about their next restaurant concept. Brauner had grown up near National Distillery, where family members worked, and had smelled mash in the air for as long as he could remember; and a little piece of him missed that. Brauner had the wild idea of trying a bourbon restaurant. "Bourbon was struggling," he says. And for this reason, as well as the general risks of loaning to a restaurant, nobody would finance what is now called Bourbons Bistro.

"I remember laying on the couch very depressed that I had this great idea and couldn't get it financed," Brauner said. "Restaurants are typical losers from the get-go," but adding bourbon to it only made matters worse.

After incorporating, it took Brauner four years to garner financing. He had to offer up his house, "everything I owned," as collateral and refused to accept distillery sponsorships in exchange for in-restaurant promotions. People said that there's no way a bourbon restaurant concept would work; and if he had had to depend on only the Louisville market, they would have been right. "The locals didn't give two shits about it. Local people have been around bourbon forever," said Brauner, so Bourbons Bistro wasn't special to them. But for the outside-Kentucky bourbon fans, from Anchorage, Alaska, to Kinshasa, Congo, Bourbons Bistro was heaven with collectable whiskeys they'd never seen and a knowledgeable bar staff that could discuss the particulars between Weller made from Stitzel-Weller and

The legendary Bardstown, Kentucky, Old Talbott Tavern was serving bourbon long before it was cool, and before you were even alive. Abraham Lincoln once stayed here, and one of its former owners was the distiller Tom Moore.

Buffalo Trace. People flew into Louisville just to visit Bourbons Bistro, an oasis for people whose passion became bourbon. "Travelers from around the world would come in and be fascinated," Brauner says.

After it opened in 2005, Bourbons Bistro's success encouraged other local bar programs to capitalize on the Louisville bourbon scene, and the Louisville Convention Visitors Bureau soon was flying reporters into Louisville for the Kentucky Derby, then dinner at Bourbons Bistro, followed by nightcaps at the Brown Hotel Bar, Jockey Silks at the Galt House, or the Old Seelbach Bar. The Louisville CVB created the Urban Bourbon Trail, a program that included Louisville bars stocking more than fifty bourbons. Like the Kentucky Bourbon Trail, consumers received a passport to get stamped, and it motivated the restaurants in Louisville to add bourbons to their back bar, cook with it, and actually know what they were talking about.

But it all started with Bourbons Bistro. Without Bourbons Bistro anchoring bourbon's core market, there's a strong chance Kentucky's largest city would never have been motivated to support bourbon.

It took Jason Brauner four years to procure financing for Bourbons Bistro. But when he did, he created a bourbon dining experience the world had never seen.

The bourbon-centric bar movement coincided with the Internet explosion and the continued growth of the Kentucky Bourbon Festival. Before Twitter and Facebook, the bourbon world had two online social networks in the early 2000s— StraightBourbon.com and BourbonEnthusiast.net, where people in Alaska could chat with people from the Netherlands about their favorite bourbons. Now these enthusiasts could meet in Bardstown during the Kentucky Bourbon Festival— which attracted fifty-five thousand consumers in 2006.

An organic bourbon culture had been formed. Woodford Reserve, Maker's Mark, Heaven Hill's Bourbon Center, Wild Turkey's visitor experience, and Jim Beam's outpost offered travel destinations for regional travelers. "And then the blogs started coming around," says Jim Beam's Kevin Smith, former master distiller of Maker's Mark. Bloggers were talking about the whiskey, the history, and, soon, the politics of it all. Right in the thick of it was blogger and author Chuck

The bourbon bar movement exploded in the 2000s. Places like Hard Water in San Francisco (pictured) and Jack Rose in Washington, D.C., revitalized bourbon's popularity.

Cowdery, a once-employee of an agency of Brown-Forman, who produced a bourbon documentary and released the popular 2004 book *Bourbon, Straight*. Cowdery said in 2012, "The biggest change in 30 years is that people are actually writing about whiskey now. Thirty years ago, there were a couple in the UK but no one here. When I got into the business, whiskey was dead. I worked on many distilled spirits products but few whiskeys, because whiskeys were barely even promoted back then. Even when I started American whiskey writing about 20 years ago, I was a lone voice crying in the wilderness."

Cowdery and other whiskey writers were covering the legendary master distillers who endured bourbon at its worst. As the 2000s progressed, they were traveling to New York, Seattle, London, Dallas, really anywhere with decent distribution and where they were talking bourbon. Four Roses master distiller Jim Rutledge would speak the gospel in local VFW meeting halls. Woodford Reserve's Lincoln Henderson, who passed away in 2013, hosted guests and media during the Kentucky Derby, leading to multiple published accounts of his awesome life. "Just as cooks taste dishes over and over again to find the right blend, Henderson will keep sampling from various barrels until he finally gets each batch of Woodford Reserve to his liking," the *San Antonio Express* wrote in December 2003. Whether it was Heaven Hill's Parker Beam, Wild Turkey's Jimmy Russell, Buffalo Trace's Elmer T. Lee or later Harlen Wheatley, or the "baby faced" Greg Davis at 1792, the master distillers were becoming niche celebrities. People paid significant money to meet them at WhiskeyFest or Whisky Live or to fly to Kentucky to shake their hands at the distillery or the Kentucky Bourbon Festival. Consumers had master distillers sign bottles in the same way children solicit baseball players to sign baseball cards.

At some point a distillery company realized that its best story was not some trumped-up barn-fire legend or cocktail mixer; it was its own people. And they were sitting right there in the still house, placing milled corn in the cooker, turning knobs on the still, and rolling barrels into the warehouse. As the world was just warming up to the sweet brown spirit, the bourbon industry had a bullpen of talent just waiting to be unleashed.

And nobody was better at expressing his own bourbon way than Booker Noe, the first true rock-star master distiller. Elmer T. Lee and Jimmy Russell were arguably as big as the Jim Beam master distiller, but Noe's personality was just made for the spotlight, offering a side of Kentucky charm with an occasional curse word and defying whatever his corporate bosses told him. According to Cowdery, at a media event, a reporter once asked a Jim Beam official for the mashbill. The official said that's confidential, but Noe walked up to the reporter and whispered the Beam recipe into his ear.

When Booker Noe died in 2004, the *New York Times* and other major newspapers ran his obituary, rightfully crediting Noe with bourbon's comeback. "Small-batch bourbons like Booker's did for bourbon what single malts did for Scotch, creating a new market," the *New York Times* wrote. Noe's death marked a sadness for the entire bourbon industry; his appeal coupled with ingenious speaking ability made him the perfect bourbon ambassador at a time when it badly needed him. The fact that the *New York Times* found him worthy enough to run an unpaid obituary showed the renowned newspaper's appreciation for both Noe and his contributions to the spirit. He was the first Kentucky bourbon personality to receive a *New York Times* obit since Pappy Van Winkle in 1965.

Booker Noe was bourbon's first rock star. Although he perfected the so-called Small Batch technique, Noe was the first master distiller to constantly promote the product he made. Along with old-school master distillers Parker Beam, Elmer T. Lee, and Jimmy Russell, Noe transformed bourbon.

THE PASSING OF LEGENDS

A modern master distiller's life is unlike any other. They're often chemists, engineers, artists, and rock stars all in one package. The early 2000s were a special time for bourbon lovers, when they could sit and have a drink with the likes of Elmer T. Lee, Booker Noe, Jimmy Russell, Lincoln Henderson, Jim Rutledge, and Parker Beam. They were each amazing in their own right, but have slowly left us and each received a hero's applause in their obituaries. Of the old-school distillers, Russell is semiretired, Rutledge is starting a new distillery, and Beam is battling health issues. The torch has been passed to new distillers, who are in the ilk Booker Noe created. Part distiller, part marketer, part historian, modern master distillers must wear many hats.

Parker Beam, longtime master distiller for Heaven Hill, was a leading distiller in the bourbon revival. His Evan Williams Single Barrels were the first to feature a vintage year. When he announced his diagnosis of ALS, other master distillers united to create Parkers Unity, a composite of seven distillers' bourbon.

After his death, Noe's contributions were seen every spring and fall for years to come, as bourbon brands launched their highly anticipated limited editions; and Elmer T. Lee, who died in 2013, lived long enough to see people stand in long lines for special single barrels. The bevy of new releases caused wine magazines to review bourbons for the first time, and increased international coverage from *Whisky* magazine and *Malt Advocate*—which created consumer shows called Whisky Live and WhiskyFest, respectively. Consumers wanted to taste the new whiskeys either in their home, at an event, or in a bar; and then they wanted to read other people's thoughts on the new George T. Stagg, Four Roses Limited Edition Small Batch, Parker's Heritage Collection, or whichever. And then, after years of pounding the pavement and attempting to gain traction in bars and sell bourbon, Pappy Van Winkle bourbons began to catch national attention. The wine palates began writing reviews about the bourbon in the same columns that covered ports and Cabernet Sauvignon. Pappy received the highest rating for an American whiskey, a 99, in the late 1990s, and *Food & Wine* named Pappy the "American Whiskey of the Year" when it launched. Whiskey-tasting notes were calling it "elegant" and "sexy," as critic John Hansell wrote in 2005.

Pappy Van Winkle began selling out in the early to mid-2000s, and Julian Van Winkle stuck to his father's ideals of bottling less than you think you can sell. At the time, nobody knew much about the whiskey. But because the Van Winkle bourbons were winning so many awards and garnering so much publicity, others claimed to have the same whiskey as Pappy Van Winkle.

In the mid-2000s, few people knew about the United Distillers fiasco that put vast quantities of wheated bourbon into the open market pipeline. Some bourbon brands using this whiskey were telling distributors: "We bought from the same source that is used for Pappy." Then distributors told retailers and bars: "This is Pappy, just a different label." And retailers told their customers: "This is Pappy, just cheaper." The Pappy phenomenon became so great that people wanted to believe a non-Pappy bottle was Pappy.

The legend of Pappy and the whiskey grew with each passing year, until Pappy Van Winkle became hard to find and people had to turn to other bourbons. The trickle-down effect led to the discovery of new brands, as all distilleries were improving their brands and marketing reach.

As bartending became widely known as mixology—a vilified term to many old-school bartenders—bourbon and rye whiskey became the mixing base of choice. Tom Bulleit (profile below), founder of Bulleit Bourbon, views bartenders as "chemists behind the bar," and devotes valuable company resources to the cocktail culture. Also pictured: Charles Joly, right, who was named World's Best Bartender in 2015.

In 2005, nearly ten years after the spirits industry lifted its self-imposed TV ban, Jim Beam executed bourbon's first national television advertisement focusing on history. Both Brown-Forman and Buffalo Trace launched experimental collections that increased publicity and general interest in bourbon. And bartenders were now growing tired of the vodka trend and beginning to pick up bourbon.

By 2006, the sales data suggested bourbon sales were holding steady at about 3 percent annual increases and that the premium brands were even stronger at 8 percent sales increases. "People are drinking less, but they want to drink better. And bourbon is definitely figuring into the cocktail scene," Fred Noe, Booker's son, said at the time.

Finally, after years of dreadful, sagging sales, bourbon was up and distilleries began expanding. Exports increased 14.6 percent in 2007 and companies were building new warehouses, adding stills, and laying down promising whiskey. After building new warehouses at Wild Turkey in 2008, master distiller Jimmy Russell said, "As long as you see working going on—and the construction, and increasing your size— you know business is doing well." In fact, Wild Turkey expected to grow 12 percent that year through additional distribution channels, while Maker's Mark and Evan Williams rose 8 percent in 2007. Connoisseurs, bar owners, and retailers brought bourbon back from the abyss and into a promising category again. As Jim Meehan,

Constellation Brands launched 1792 Ridgemont Reserve in the mid-1990s, only to be sued by Brown-Forman for using similar packaging as Woodford Reserve. Brown-Forman won the case, stunting 1792's growth onto the bourbon scene. For distiller Bill Friel, the new product was the highlight of his career. Friel distilled it, and Ken Pierce, a chemist, mingled it in batches. It was given new life when Sazerac—owner of Buffalo Trace—bought it in 2009.

bar manager of the PDT bar in New York City, said in 2008, "You get a taste for bourbon, you don't stop drinking bourbon."

Seeing this trend, the brands began to expand and buy. In 2009, Sazerac bought 1792 Barton Distillery and Glenmore Distillery for $334 million from Constellation Brands; Campari purchased Wild Turkey for $581 million. Meanwhile, the Kentucky Bourbon Trail was growing at a rate nobody expected. Jim Beam alone received eighty thousand visitors in 2008, while Maker's Mark had about a hundred thousand. "This is the Napa Valley of this part of the country," Jim Beam's Fred Noe said.

But as soon as bourbon showed signs of recovery, an all-too-familiar foe returned—the taxman. Kentucky legislature wanted more money.

In March of 2009, the Kentucky legislature faced an unprecedented $456 million shortfall. Other states had increased cigarette taxes to make up for state deficits, and Kentucky did the same, also passing a 6 percent sales tax increase on all booze. After this, when you purchased bourbon in Kentucky, nearly 60 percent of your money went to taxes. "You rarely see a case where people campaign criticizing their opponents for taxing booze and cigarettes. Voters aren't going to show a lot of sympathy to the sin industry," Stephen Voss, political scientist for the University of Kentucky, told the *Associated Press*.

That's where Voss was wrong. Bourbon appealed to consumers at a much higher level than cigarettes. Bourbon was becoming the sexy symbol of Kentucky, and other states were building distilleries—ranging from Balcones in Waco, Texas, to Tuthilltown Spirits in Gardiner, New York—whose bourbons were garnering national attention.

As a protest against the tax hike, bourbon distillers poured bourbon on the state capitol steps. Having lived through the rise and fall of bourbon and being instrumental in its rebirth, they said enough was enough. The bourbon community—made of legacy distillers and new blood—chose to defend its industry with the same vigor shown by advocates in the late 1800s when passing the Bottled-in-Bond Act, and by the early 1960s distillers lobbying for bourbon's congressional declaration. Now, the plan was to study bourbon's impact and sell the merits to the masses through economics, a tactic even the non-drinker could appreciate. Bourbon makers were defending themselves by telling the world how much revenue they generated.

Bourbon had become a social media favorite. During the rise of social media—about 2007 to 2012—bourbon stories and pictures would trend at the highest rates of any beverage category. Right in the thick of it, as usual, was Maker's Mark. It created an ugly sweater campaign in 2011, in which it sent sweaters to its customers to put on bottles of Maker's Mark. They photographed bourbon bottles wearing sweaters, and people shared it on social media. In the same year, Maker's Mark's Bill Samuels Jr. retired.

At his retirement party, Samuels Jr. was credited with saving the bourbon industry by continually pushing the marketing envelope and thereby opening the door for other bourbon brands. If Booker Noe was the rock-star master distiller introducing

Maker's Mark never took its foot off the marketing pedal, launching an ugly sweater campaign in 2011. *Maker's Mark*

the world to the quality of bourbon, Samuels Jr. was bourbon's consummate salesman for an industry that badly needed one.

Always known as a showboater who "doesn't want attention," Samuels Jr. walked onto his retirement party's stage, his stringy pinkish-reddish-orange polyester wig glistened in the spotlight and his purple vest flashed like a Christmas tree. The packed Maker's Mark ambassador crowd erupted in cheers. "We love you, Bill!" a man's voice echoed. "Don't go!" a woman yelled.

Nursing a bad hip, the seventy-three-year-old Samuels tipped his small glass of Maker's Mark to the thousand brand ambassadors who had come from all over the world to see him one last time. "This party's about you all and not me," Samuels Jr. said. He looked into the sea of faces, paused for a few seconds as though taking it all in, and joked about the monsoon rains showering the party tents at that moment. With the wig brushing against his cheeks, it was hard to see signs of his emotion, but his voice slightly broke when he said, "It's been a long career, a hell of a time," tipping his glass toward the crowd. "Let's have a cocktail!"

Samuels Jr.'s son Rob took the company reins, and within two years Maker's Mark made a decision that spiraled into a negative story for the brand.

In 2013, Maker's Mark lowered their proof from 90 to 84. Perhaps this brand ambassador captured the loyalist sentiment best on Facebook: "Dear Maker's Mark, you told me you will never change my favorite whiskey, and I said I would never drink another. You lied, and now I'm leaving you." The story trended for several days, made above-the-fold stories in major newspapers, and became the butt of jokes for late-night talk show hosts.

Maker's tried to spin the proof lowering as the only option to meet demand without decreasing the age or increasing the price. Many spirits writers, including this author, came to Maker's Mark's defense, pointing out that Jack Daniel's had lowered its proof in 2004 to the minimum 80 proof and as a result saw case sales increase 30 percent over the next eight years. Wild Turkey, George Dickel, and Crown Royal all tried to slip their proof-lowering under the label, but at least Maker's Mark openly told its customers. Days after the proof lowering, as the negative publicity intensified, Samuels Jr., who was now retired two years, said the proof lowering was directly related to the bourbon growth:

> We did not anticipate the spike. My greatest accomplishment over the years has been managing inventories, managing growth—that was my first job and I held it. There was never a committee decision. How much whiskey to make and how much to allow out every year was my call for about 45 years: I spent a lot of time sitting on barstools listening to what was going on and asking people. We were short from time to time when it was . . . I mean, it was never anything like what we're experiencing right now.

Maker's Mark was a victim of its own success. In fact, the entire bourbon industry felt the pinch. As they attempted to expand overseas and in new markets, such as Bismarck, North Dakota, bourbon distillers were unable to fulfill 100 percent of their wholesale orders and longtime customers could not find their beloved everyday bourbon. This problem would grow every year.

Bill Samuels Jr. did not distill whiskey like his father. But he had a marketing flair unlike anybody before. This uniqueness carried over into his public wardrobe, which often included flashing lights.

As for the Maker's Mark proof debacle, customers were pissed, leading to Maker's reverting back to 90 proof and later saying, "We listened." Was it a publicity stunt? Just a bad decision? We may never know what the so-called proof debacle was about, but for industry insiders it was proof that bourbon had captured America's heartstrings again. Consumers loved bourbon so much they were willing to stand in long lines on a Tuesday in the cold, rain, and high winds just to put their name in the hat for a Pappy Van Winkle drawing that would give them the opportunity to spend $400 for a bottle. They loved bourbon so much that they formed drinking societies in cities as large as Los Angeles and New York and as small as Omaha, Nebraska, and Columbus, Ohio. They loved bourbon so much it gave birth to a new breed of fan—the conspiracy

Bottled from Barrel No.
% by Vol. (127. Proof)
Willett
Willett
Bourbon Whiskey

theorist—who spent his spare time debating the truth of the Maker's Mark proof debacle, arguing about whether or not Pappy Van Winkle was really just fancy packaging, and saying things like, "Did I hear somebody is storing bourbon in used barrels or distilling at illegal off-the-still proofs?"

Then, the fandom became so extensive that it spawned class-action lawsuits against Maker's Mark, Jim Beam, and Angel's Envy, a new breed of bourbon finished in used port barrels founded by former Woodford master distiller Lincoln Henderson, his son, and his grandson. Bourbon was no longer a slumping spirit. It was the "in" drink, preferred by millennials, mixed by bartenders, and beloved by all Kentuckians—even the politicians.

Just three years after the sales tax increase, Kentucky governor Steve Beshear announced that bourbon was a $2 billion gross state product that had added $338 million in new tax revenue from 2008 to 2012. Suddenly, bourbon was not the "sin" but the savior, and the state's legislature began to appreciate how much the spirit contributed to the state's economy. Bourbon built roads and schools, but the industry still bridled under a burdensome tax structure that didn't even allow it to write off certain taxes. Several distilleries were considering building warehouses outside of Kentucky; Jim Beam already owned warehouses in Ohio. "For Kentucky to maintain its dominance in the distillery industry, we must revise these burdensome tax policies that threaten to force distilling operations to move out-of-state," Kentucky Chamber of Commerce President David Adkisson said in 2012. "We cannot keep putting our bourbon industry over the barrel when it comes to global competition."

And so, like the distillers of years past, the bourbon industry again campaigned for lower taxes. In 2014, the Kentucky lawmakers passed a resolution allowing a tax credit on the distiller's corporate income, which up to that point had not been allowed until the whiskey went into the bottle. "Their bourbon was sitting there unusable for six to eight years and they're paying taxes on it. That's the only product like that you have. It wasn't fair," Kentucky Senate president Robert Stivers said in 2014.

By now, more than 1 million visitors toured Kentucky distilleries each year, distilleries were expanding with $1.3 billion in building investments, and Kentucky bourbon was championed as a $3 billion industry with 15,400 jobs and an average salary of more than $90,000. What's more, bourbon had a plan through 2020: to improve tourism laws, decrease taxes, and reduce the barrier to entry for smaller distillers. The so-called craft distillery industry was burgeoning, and many independent operations—namely MB Roland, Limestone Branch, Wilderness Trail, and New Riff Distilleries—opened between 2009 and 2015 despite the Kentucky economic

As the super-premium, highly collectable category developed, consumer groups formed and people shared tasting notes of their favorite bourbons. Willett became a cult favorite in the 2010s.

From the 1950s to 1970s, distillers commissioned ceramic makers to create decanters. Beam had a wide range of decanters, from political characters to banks; Old Crow had a beautiful chess piece that contained special whiskey; and Old Rip Van Winkle had a decanter of an old man "asleep many years in the wood" in 1977. The trend has since passed. Nowadays, bottlers are hand-blowing special releases, such as Angel's Envy (pictured).

Up until 2015, Kentucky bourbon distillers were forced to pay steep taxes on aging whiskey, but could not write off the tax cost until it was bottled. Here, Wild Turkey workers move barrels into the racks.

disadvantages compared to other states that offered tax credits to smaller-capacity facilities. In New York, small distillers were allowed to sell directly to restaurants, while smaller Kentucky bourbon distillers were forced to compete against the likes of Jim Beam for a distributor. In Oregon, a craft distiller license was only $100 in 2011, while Paul Tomaszewski paid an annual $3,090 license at his upstart MB Roland Distillery. But these Kentucky distillers opened in the Bluegrass State for the distilling culture and heritage, believing in better bourbon future.

Meanwhile, other states have seen bourbon distillers blossom. Despite a fall-out with founder Chip Tate, Balcones Distillery in Waco, Texas, continues to win awards with its whiskey, while Wyoming Distillery, Finger Lakes Distillery in New York, Tom's Foolery in Ohio, and others around the country are producing bourbon that offers stellar taste and small producer stories. The little guy also received its share of national attention.

As the "eat local" movement has progressed, so has "drink local." In a story promoting bourbon maker Hillrock Estate Distillery, where former Maker's Mark master distiller David Pickerell was creating stellar bourbon, the *New York Post* wrote in 2015: "There are now about 70 New York 'farm distilleries'—where at least 75 percent of the raw materials come from within the state—up from less than a dozen a few years ago. Some of these distilleries even grow the grains and botanicals for their liquors to control everything that goes into the bottle, and many offer tours and charming tasting experiences."

For these smaller distillers, they're making quality bourbon, brandy, rum, gin, and, occasionally, vodka. If anything, many craft distillers loathe vodka, because it offers less of an opportunity to show genuine craftsmanship. Oh sure, there are very good to great vodkas being produced at the likes of St. George Spirits in California and Cathead vodka in Mississippi. But the trends are against vodka for a smaller distiller to stake his or her livelihood on it. If bourbon's rise is to take on a broader appeal, it must have a stalwart bourbon distiller outside Kentucky, as it did after Prohibition with Hiram Walker in Peoria, Illinois.

Bourbon is in the middle of a diversification trend with new flavor profiles being formed by craft distillers using atypical grains such as buckwheat, quinoa, and rice, elements mastered by Corsair Distillery in Tennessee. Smaller bourbon distillers are smoking grains, such as King's County Distillers making a peated malt bourbon and MB Roland Dark Fired Bourbon. And they're finishing bourbon in used wine, port, sherry, and cognac casks, which the government allows as long as the label says the bourbon "finished in" whatever cask is used.

For the most part, the larger bourbon distillers understand that these little guys offer new styles to a once-struggling category. In fact, although they would never admit to it, the larger distillers have copied the unique secondary production methods of Corsair. And they've publicly dismissed the smaller barrels, claiming the five-gallon to twenty-five-gallon casks yield poor whiskey in comparison to the industry standard fifty-three-gallon barrel. Now that the nearly one-thousand-distillery-strong craft distiller market has four-year-old Rock Town Arkansas Straight Bourbon, Garrison Brother's four-year-old Texas Straight Bourbon, and five-year-old Town Branch Kentucky Straight Bourbon, the traditional bourbon distillers see these smaller brands growing and competing, lending to larger companies protecting their trademarks through legal efforts, which both Maker's Mark and Sazerac have consistently done, and investing in or buying popular bourbon brands. Smaller brands Nelson's Greenbrier, Angel's Envy, and Redemption either were purchased outright or sold a minority interest to grow the brand.

In 2015, for brands as small as 2Bar Spirits in Seattle and as big as the ever-growing Jim Beam, bourbon's stock was rising, while its nemesis, vodka, was falling.

"Taste profiles have moved to appreciate whiskey more," Ivan Menezes, Diageo's chief executive, told the *Wall Street Journal*. "It's a trend that's been building for a few years."

Unfortunately, the bourbon industry chose to once again let short-term profits get in the way of true perfection. In a case of déjà vu, as distillers enjoy their beloved bourbon's return, they've decided to invest into another category. Instead of investing in the creation of new vodka brands, bourbon distillers have pursued flavored whiskey—a regulated category defined as "Whisky flavored with natural flavoring materials, with or without the addition of sugar, bottled at not less than 30% alcohol by volume (60 proof). . . ."

Some argued that flavored whiskey was bourbon's savior by introducing people to the category. The liquors such as Fireball, made with Canadian whiskey, were replacing Jameson and Goldschläger for bar shots. And due to this fact, Fireball grew from $1.9 million in 2011 to $61 million in 2013. Every bourbon-affiliated distillery was lining up to create a flavored whiskey, and rightly so. From 2008 to 2013, the flavored whiskey category went from 108,000 cases to 54 million nationwide.

But unlike Fireball, which didn't have a straight bourbon connection, distillers slapped their brand names on flavored lines such as Knob Creek Maple, Evan Williams Cherry, and Wild Turkey Spiced, setting up potential brand confusion down the road. Any time a flavored whiskey proponent defends this strategy, they say, "Look at the sales. Numbers don't lie," and then add, "It's not like flavored vodka; we're not coming up with four hundred flavors." But they are. There are now cherry, bacon, cinnamon, apple, honey, and several other flavors of whiskey, with new ones being introduced every year. Cinnamon whiskey has become so popular that it has become its own category in the eyes of the novice consumer, with billboards touting "Cinnamon Whiskey." James Espey, former United Distillers North America president, says flavored whiskey hurts true whiskey and adds, "Brands are doing this because the executives want their fat bonuses."

He's not alone in the whiskey community in disliking the category; some brand CEOs refuse to place a flavored whiskey label on their premium brands. But the flavored whiskey phenomenon doesn't irritate the bourbon-drinking populace nearly as much as deceptive marketing practices, proof lowerings, and the discontinuation of age statements.

Experimentation has become such a common contemporary practice that distillers are releasing their experiments. Buffalo Trace introduced Warehouse X, an experimental warehouse, in 2014.

From 2008 to 2016, bourbon brands were lowering proofs and dropping age statements so they could meet demand. Very Old Barton, Jim Beam Black, Old Charter, Old Grand-Dad, Elijah Craig, Fighting Cock, and several others all made such changes. The distillers fixated on the age on the bottle—if the age statement said ten years old, that meant the youngest barrel in the batch was ten years old. The batch might include twenty-year-old whiskey, but if one barrel was ten years old, the age statement must reflect the youngest barrel age. Freed of holding themselves to an age, distillers could now bottle more of that particular brand. It also made the forecasting of future stocks much easier, but consumers found this tactic to be deceiving and have sometimes boycotted brands that changed the age statement. Consumers also dislike the price increases that have come along with bourbon's rise in popularity. The same bourbon geeks who brought about the rebirth of whiskey brands now feel betrayed.

The year before Heaven Hill dropped the Elijah Craig age statement, it moved the age toward the back label and publicly stated it was keeping the twelve-year-old age statement. Social media circles theorized that this 2015 back-label move was to make it easier to eventually drop the age statement completely, although Heaven Hill denied this. Popular blogger Steve Ury's "Sku Recent Eats" called the age statement dropping "extra slimy." Ury's complaint had more to do with Heaven Hill's initial denials of discontinuing the age statement.

However, Heaven Hill's belief was that it could not allow a twelve-year-old bourbon to continue at the $30 range while others were charging more than $50. Its options were to drop the age statement and grow the brand, increase the price, or come up with a new brand entirely and slowly phase out Elijah Craig twelve-year-old.

Heaven Hill had a long, impressive legacy. It started after Prohibition, scrapped away as an independent as the Big Four attempted to muscle out the little guys, survived World War II's governmental mandates, watched its Evan Williams flagship fight against cheaper-to-make vodkas, felt the 1980s plummet, and suffered a devastating fire in 1996, but still managed to scrape and claw back to the top and eventually found itself in extremely rare territory—popularity. Heaven Hill's Evan Williams was now the number-two bourbon on the market, and its brokered whiskey gave life to many products from non-distillers. By providing the most bang for the buck, Heaven Hill became the whiskey geek's most beloved distiller.

If anybody had earned the right to profit from the trends, it was Heaven Hill, but for a number of reasons the growing sentiment against distilleries remains. The most common reason for that hate: a phenomenon that formed after eBay shut down alcohol sales in 2012.

Before the eBay ban, collectors could buy and sell both rare and popular current products on the auction website, but the ban now forced an underground and unregulated sales practice known simply as the secondary market. So-called flippers purchased popular bottles, such as Pappy Van Winkle, and sold them for more than 500 percent over the suggested retail price. Whiskey hunters also went to estate

Most bourbon brands today do not carry age statements.

The new bourbon distilleries do not operate towering column stills. They usually begin with smaller stills, like that seen here at Paris, Kentucky–based Hartfield and Co., which opened in 2015. Nonetheless, these small stills are as important for capturing new bourbon consumers as Jim Beam's and Buffalo Trace's.

STILL
#2
26 gallon capacity

Franklin County Sheriff Pat Melton called the theft an "organized crime" effort that involved steroids, stolen Wild Turkey and Eagle Rare barrels, as well as cases of Pappy Van Winkle and Eagle Rare. A grand jury charged the nine defendants with several felony counts, ranging in a Class C felony of "receiving stolen property $10,000 or more" to second degree, first offenses of "complicity trafficking in a controlled substance."

sales to buy abandoned liquor from decades past. This black market became evident after Buffalo Trace distillery workers were caught stealing cases and barrels of whiskey from both Buffalo Trace and Wild Turkey. The liquor-thieving syndicate was also involved in selling steroids, but the Pappy Van Winkle heist led to several indictments and jail terms.

As the court system was playing out the Pappy heist drama, Buffalo Trace released a statement encouraging consumers to not buy whiskey illegally and promising to help authorities shut down the secondary markets. This was in December 2015, and it was likely too late to stop the trend, but there is irony in the fact that fifteen years prior, Buffalo Trace had no idea what to do with the whiskey stocks purchased from the United Distillers. Now, on Craigslist, people advertised sexual favors for a bottle of Pappy Van Winkle, which sells in auctions and in private sales for $6,000 a bottle.

The distillery community is aware that this popularity could go away any minute. Despite their growth and multibillion-dollar infrastructure investments, distillers fear the growing trend of health concerns tied to alcohol consumption. Canadian, British, and American health agencies have all discussed stricter alcohol consumption laws for the betterment of society. They also fight the comparisons of marijuana to bourbon—a common tactical connection made by marijuana proponents. Marijuana lobbyists argue that the Kentucky Bourbon Trail is "glorified," while marijuana users go to prison. The comparison, though unfair, is accepted by many. The bourbon industry also knows that the moment marijuana becomes legal at the federal level, there will be at least a dozen marijuana-flavored vodkas on the market, which could lead to blanket alcohol policy that impacts all spirits.

There's nothing the distiller fears more than government intervention, though it's unlikely that another Prohibition or conversion to industrial alcohol is coming. Given the climate of modern corporate culture, where billionaires seem to steal millions every day, governments are looking the other way as regards the claims of misleading consumers.

Founded in 2009, Pembroke, Kentucky–based MB Roland was the first Kentucky craft distiller and has introduced the first-ever "Dark Fire" smoked bourbon, for which the distillery uses a historic smoking technique on its corn before distillation. If bourbon is to reach the next level, new consumers must appreciate these newer aged bourbon styles.

Among the government's concerns about health, underage drinking, safety, and taxes related to the alcohol industry, it cares about the taxes most of all. If and when a distiller attempts to skirt proofs—place 90 proof in the bottle, but label it 80 proof—the government will crack down, hold hearings, and steeply fine them.

There's also the concern abroad. American whiskey has become a $1.6 billion export business. As tariffs have been reduced in Korea and Brazil, the industry has developed new palates. But they've also had to discontinue efforts in volatile markets, namely Russia and Ukraine. "We won't do business in Russia, because the distributors just disappear. You send them cases and the government seizes their assets. It's crazy," a distiller told me. If security and trade tensions close export markets, bourbon distillers will see a stiff drop in sales. But the world has greater problems to worry about if World War III occurs.

In the end, bourbon is the spirit that was American born, fought for attention, and largely stayed true to its recipes and heritage. It died during Prohibition and came back to life in 1934, and got punched in the kidneys in World War II only to land an uppercut in 1964 with its congressional declaration; it was on life support in the 1980s, but passion kept its heart ticking until, one day in 2008, bourbon was back. And it will grow as long as bourbon stays true to what it is. The only thing that can stop a further rise of bourbon's interests is the effort to make bourbon something it is not. It cannot compete with vodka. It should not become light whiskey or flavored whiskey. Bourbon is bourbon.

Sweet.

Precious.

Bourbon.

The Newport, Kentucky–based New Riff Distillery opened in 2014 and arguably offers the best night view in whiskey. New Riff is one of the larger "small" distilleries making strides; bourbon's success largely depends on these smaller companies earning consumer loyalty in the marketplace.

BIBLIOGRAPHY

Archives
Kentucky Historical Society: Catherine Spears Frye Carpenter Papers.

Oscar Getz Museum of Whiskey: Bourbon Institute, Jim Beam, Schenley, Seagram, W. A. Gaines, and Waterfill & Frazier collections.

Schenley Archives: 1933 to 1980

University of Louisville Archives: Brown-Forman, Cooperage Shops, Creel Brown, Crow Distillery, National Distillery, Old H. W. Coyte, and Samuel Thomas collections

Books
Bennett, Edmund H. <I>Fire Insurance Cases: 1865–1875<M>. Hurd & Houghton, 1877.

Cowdery, Charles K. *Bourbon, Straight*. Made and Bottled in Kentucky, 2004.

Farmer, John S. *Americanisms—Old & New*. Thomas Poulter & Sons, 1889.

Flanders, Harry. *A Treatise on the Law of Fire Insurance*. Claxton, Remsen & Haffelfinger, 1871.

Gunn's Domestic Medicine. J. Edwards & J. J. Newman, 1839.

Hirsch, Irving. *Manufacture of Whiskey, Brandy and Cordials*. Sherman, 1934.

Humfreville, James Lee. *Twenty Years among Our Savage Indians*. Hartford Publishing Company, 1897.

Marquat, John. *600 Miscellaneous Valuable Receipts, Worth Their Weight in Gold*. Christian Henry, 1860.

Meader, J. R. *The Cyclopedia of Temperance and Prohibition*. Funk & Wagnalls, 1891.

Mida, William. *Mida's Compendium of Information for the Liquor Interests*. Criterion Publishing Company, 1899.

Morse, Jedidiah. *The American Gazetteer*. S. Hall, Thomas & Andrews, 1797.

Pepper, James E. "American Distilleries." In *1795–1895: One Hundred Years of American Commerce*, D. O. Haynes & Co. 1895.

The Statutes at Large from the Magna Charta: Joseph Bentham, 1765.

Veach, Michael R. *Kentucky Bourbon Whiskey*. University Press of Kentucky, 2013.

Yasuda, Anita. *Louisiana Purchase through the Eyes of Thomas Jefferson*. Abdo Publishing, 2016.

Zoeller, Chester. *Bourbon in Kentucky*. Butler Books, 2009.

Corporate Literature
"Current Views on Prohibition and Forecast of Coming Events upon Which We Base Our Programme of Expansion." Ed. Schenley Products Company Inc., 1932.

"Schenley Industries, Inc. v. Nj Wine & Spirit Whole. Ass'n, 272 F. Supp. 872." 1967.

W. A. Gaines & Co. bylaws. Frankfort, KY: Geo. A. Lewis, 1887.

Government Publications
"An Act to Allow the Bottling of Distilled Spirits in Bond," 1897.

Alcohol Produced from Material Other Than Cereal Grains. Judiciary Committee, House of Representatives, 74th Congress, Mar. 17–Apr. 8, 1936.

"Amending Certain Provisions of the Internal Revenue Code Relating to the Production of Alcohol." Committee on Finance, 1942.

"Annual Report of the Commissioner of Industrial Alcohol Fiscal Year Ended June 30, 1931." Bureau of Industrial Alcohol, Treasury Department, 1931.

Appropriations Bill, 1929: Medicinal Liquor Withdraws, House Committee on Appropriations, 1929.

"The Code of Federal Regulations of the United States of America Having General Applicability and Legal Effect in Force June 1, 1938." 1937.

"Concentration of Economic Power." Temporary National Economic Committee, 2695-97, 1939.

"Concentration of Warehouses." Treasury Department, 1928.

Discussion in Congress: Debate upon Federal Prohibition Amendment in House and Senate, August 1, 1917.

"Designating 'Bourbon Whiskey' as a Distinctive Product of the United States." House of Representatives, 1963.

"Economic Concentration and World War II." Rose, Matthew; Houghton, Harrison F.; Blair, John Malcolm, 1946.

"Federal Alcohol Control Act," 1935.

"Industrial Alcohol Producers." *Victory Bulletin*, Sept. 1, 1942: 26. American Council on Public Affairs.

Investigation of the Department of Justice. Special Committee to Investigate the Department of Justice of the Committee on the Judiciary, June 26, 1952.

"Legislative History of the Federal Alcohol Administration Act." Russell, Wallace Alger. Federal Alcohol Administration, 1935.

Liquor Industry Hearings. Judiciary Committee, Senate, 1944.

Liquor Tax Administration Act; Taxes on Wines, Subcommittee hearing, 74th Congress, 2nd session, 1936.

The National Prohibition Law Subcommittee hearing, 79th Congress, 1st session, 1926.

"Report of the Commissioner of Indian Affairs." Office of Indian Affairs, 1863.

"Report of the Commissioner of Internal Revenue." Treasury Department, 1889.

Statement of Robert W. Coyne, President, Distilled Spirits Institute Inc. Ways and Means, Congress, July 12, 1968.

"United States vs. Fifty Barrels of Whisky (District Court, D. Maryland. October 26, 1908)." *Federal Reporter*, 165, 1909.

Interviews

Jason Brauner

Mark Brown

Bill Friel

Eric Gregory

Larry Kass

Mike Miller

Chris Morris

Fred Noe

Denny Potter

Eddie Russell

Jimmy Russell

Jim Rutledge

Bill Samuels

Max Shapira

Harlen Wheatley

Periodicals

A wealth of articles and vintage advertisements provided source material for this book—far too many to list here, but the newspapers and journals consulted were:

American Monthly Magazine and Critical Review

American Pure Food and Health Journal

American Wine and Liquor Journal

Antiques

Atlanta Constitution

The Bee

Bourbon News

Brainerd Daily Dispatch

Brewers' Journal and Barley, Malt and Hop Trades

Brooklyn Daily Eagle

Capital Times

Charleston Daily Mail

Cincinnati Enquirer

Coffeyville Daily Journal

Concord Times

Courier Journal

Daily Courier

Daily Notes

Daily Messenger

Decatur Herald

Delaware County Daily Time

The Distiller

Drug Trade Weekly

Eau Claire Leader

Evening Post

Evening Review

Fayetteville Observer

Federal Reporter

Fetter's Southern Magazine

Fort Wayne Sentinel

Freeport Journal-Standard

Gettysburg Adams Sentinel

Great Bend Tribune

Hall's Distiller

Hancock Democrat

Huntington Herald

Indianapolis Star

Journal of the American Medical Association

Lexington Transcript

Lincoln Star

Louisville Courier-Journal

Louisville Daily Courier

Louisville Times

Messenger-Inquirer

The Monroe News-Star

National Advocate

New Orleans Price Current and Commercial Intelligencer

New York Times

The News

News-Herald

North Carolina Journal

Northwestern Druggist

Oakland Tribune

Oregon Daily Journal

Palm Beach Post

Paris News

Pittsburgh Daily Post

San Bernardino County Sun

San Francisco Chronicle

St. Louis Post-Dispatch

State Journal

Sydney Morning Herald

Le Télégraphe

Le Télégraphe Commercial Advertiser

Tennessean

Times-Picayune

Troy Record

Waco News Tribune

Wall Street Journal

Washington Times

Wichita Daily Eagle

Wilkes-Barre Record

Wilmington Morning Star

Wine and Spirit Bulletin

INDEX

Page numbers in italics indicate items in illustrations or captions.

advertising, 38, 43, 160–161, 166, 220–222
age statements, 229–230
American Medical Association, 78, 93, 100–101
Ancient Age, 183, 193
Anti-Saloon League, 78, 97, 105
antitrust allegations, 153–158

Babcock, Orville, 45–46
Barton Brands, 182, 200
Beam, Jacob, 15, 17, *22*
Beam, Parker, 208, *210*, 216, *218*
Bernheim Distillery, 198–199
Blanton's, 193, 203
Booker's, 193, 195
Boone, Daniel, *16*, 25
Boone, Wattle, 21, 25
bootlegging, 84, 94–98, 107–108
Bottled-in-Bond Act (1897), 57–58, 60–63, 127
bourbon
  defining, 67–68, 71, 71–74, 133, 170–171
  early terms for, 36
  limited-edition products, 205, 208
  name, *21*, 27
  purity of, 38, 40–41, 44
  recipe for rectified, 48
  See also whiskey
Bourbon Information Bureau, 195
Bourbon Institute, 163, 166–170, 187
bourbon types
  blended, 152
  bottled-in-bond, 54, 57–58, 127–129, 152
  cognac finished, 208
  rectified, 40, 43, 48
  single barrel, 193
  small batch, 193
  wheated, 200
  See also whiskey types
Bourbons Bistro, 213, 215
Branham, Ernest L., 153–154
Brashear, Marsham, 21, 26

Brown-Forman Distillery, 135, 139, 143, 156, 168, 180, 204
Buffalo Trace, 205, *229*
bulk whiskey sales, 131
Bulleit, Tom, 202, *219*

Calk, William, 28
Canadian whiskey, 130, 132, 168
Chandler, Albert Benjamin "Happy," Sr., 120
charred barrels, *17*, 21, 28
Continental Distilleries, 154
cooperage industry, 117, 154
counterfitting, 84, 95
Cowdery, Chuck, 215–216
Craig, Elijah, 12–13, 18, 21
criminal activity, 41, 44–45, 230, 233. *See also* bootlegging
Crow, James C., 38, 40, 42

dairy farmers, 37
Delilah's (Chicago), 213
Distillers' Securities Corporation, 84
distillery fires, 41, 50–51, 206–207

Early Times brand, 172, 174
Emergency Price Control Act of 1942, 151–152
equipment, for distillers, 35–36, 36, 38
Evan Williams, 168, 193, 220
Evans, Walter, 57
export markets, 46, 82, 84–85, 163, 165–168, 170, 195, 197, 234

Federal Alcohol Administration Act, 131, 136
Federal Trade Commission, 134, 136, 161
Forman, Jacob, 28
Four Roses Distillery, 205, 208

Great Depression, 116
Great Whiskey Ring, 44–46

Hall, Harrison, 20–21, 40
Hamilton, John, 21, 25–26
Hayden, Basil, 15, 17
Heaven Hill, 168, 182–183, 193, 200, 206, 215, 230

Henderson, Lincoln, 210, 216, 225
Hiram Walker & Sons, 136, 153–155

industrial alcohol, 83, 138–143, 148

Jack Daniel Distillery, 168
Jack Daniel's, 175, 203
Jefferson, Thomas, 31–32, *33*, 35
Jim Beam, 43, 175, 182–183, 191, 200–201, 206–207, 208, 215, 225

Kentucky Bourbon Festival, 202, 204, 215
Kentucky Bourbon Trail, *202*, 205, 221
Kentucky Derby, 135, 215
Kentucky Distillers Association, 48, 52, 65, *145*, 163, 187, 205

Lee, Elmer T., 193, 210, 213, 216
Lindsay, John V., 171
Liquor Dealers Association, 57–58
Louisiana Purchase, 29, 32–35

Magliocco, Joe, 202
Maker's Mark, *14*, 15, 161, *165*, 167, 183, 189–191, 197, 203–204, 213, 220–223, 225
master distillers, 39, 43, *182*, 216–218
Mattingly, Leonard, 17–18
McDonald, John, 44–46
McKesson & Robins, 154
medicinal alcohol, 66, 86–88, 90, 92–94, *95*, 96–100, *99*–107, 109–112, 150
Mellon, Andrew W., 96, 98
Mexican bourbon, 91, 168, 170
Meyers, Jacob, 28
Miller, Mike, 213
monopoly investigations, 132, 134, 136–137, 149–153
Morton, Thruston B., 170

National Distillers, 43, 136, 153–155, 157, 168, 182, 184
National Wholesale Liquor Dealers Association, 57–58
New Orleans, 32–35, 37

Noe, Booker, 193, 195, 200, 208, *210*, 217–218, *217*

Old Crow, 38, 40, 42–43, 168
Old Fitzgerald, 198–199
Old Stagg, 172, 174

Pappy Van Winkle, 208, *209*, 211, 218–219
private label business, 179
Prohibition
  bonded warehouses, 114–115
  bootlegging and, 84, 94–98, 107–108
  chronology of, 92
  counterfeiting and, 95
  enforcement of, 92–94, 96, 98–99
  exports before, 82, 84–85
  incorporation of distilleries after, 119–123
  medicinal whiskey and, 86–88, 90, 92–94, *95*, 96–100, 99–107, 109–112
  repeal of, 111, 116–117, 119
  Tennessee state, 78, 80
proof, 187, 222–223, 229–230, 234
Pure Food & Drug Act (1906), 67–68, 70–71

Rebel Yell, 198–199
rectified whiskey, 40, 43, 48
regulation
  on advertising, 161–162
  of bourbon as American product, 170
  during World War II, 138
  post-Prohibition, 125–130
Reagan-era deregulation, 191
Ritchie, John, 21, 26, 28–29
Roosevelt, Franklin, 111, 116, *119*
Russell, Jimmy, 208, *210*, 216, 220
Rutledge, Jim, 205, 208, 216

Samuels, Bill, Jr., 189–190, 203–204, 208, 221–223, *223*
Samuels, Marjorie, 161, 188, 190
Samuels, Robert, 15, 17

Sazerac, 211, 221, 228
Schenley, 136, *144*, 153–157, 161–162, 168
Seagram & Sons Distillers, 132, 136, 153–155, 157–158, 168, 177, 182, 205
secondary market, 230, 233
Shapira, Max, 193, 197, 206, 208
Shawhan, Daniel, 21, 23–25, 29
Shawhan, George, 23–25
Sherwood Distilling Company, 157–158
shortages, 98, 146–148
small distilleries, 227–228
social media, 215, 221
sour mash technique, 42
sourced whiskey, 124
Spanish influenza, 86, *87*
Spears, Jacob, 21, 23, 29
Stewart, Daniel, 21, 25
Stitzel-Weller Distillery, 156–157, 168, 179, 183–184, 199

Taft, Alphonso, 40
Taft, William, 71–74, *75*
Tarascon, John and Louis, 28
taxation, 15, 21, 31–32, 35, 41, 44, 48, 55–56, 81–82, 125–126, 221, 225, 227, 234
Taylor, E. H., 42, *54*
temperance movements, 36–37, 41, 77–80, 105, 161–162
Thompson, John B., 57
Thorne Whiskey Bill (KY), 59, 64–65

United Distillers, 198–200, 211
US-Canada Trade Agreement (1935), 129

Van Winkle, Julian, 218
Van Winkle, Julian P. "Pappy," *154*, 156, 179
vodka, 176–183, 187
Volstead Act (HR 6810), 82, 85, 98

War of 1812, 44
War Production Board, 138–140, 142
Wathen, Henry Hudson, 28

whiskey
  defining, 67–68, 71–74, 98
  as medicine, 35, 65–66, 66, 86–88, 90, 92–94, *95*, 96–100, 99–107, 109–112, 150
  See also bourbon
Whiskey Rebellion, 15, 21
whiskey rings, 41, 44–47, 54
Whiskey Trust, 65
whiskey types
  blended, 130, 132, 152
  Canadian, 130, 132, 168
  flavored, 228–229
  light whiskey, 180, 182–183
  rye, 44
  straight corn, 133
  Tennessee whiskey, 168
  See also bourbon types
white spirits, 176. *See also* vodka
wholesalers, 38, 40–41, 57–59, 64
Wild Turkey, 183, 206, 215, 220
Williams, Evan, 28
women, 164
Women's Christian Temperance Union, 66, 77, 78, 105
Woodford Reserve, *14*, 42, 204, 215
World War I, 80–81
World War II, 138–143, *144–145*, 145–146

Acknowledgments

This book could not have been possible without several great people. Thank you to Buffalo Trace Distillery for unprecedented access to the Schenley Archives. A big thanks is given to Sazerac's archivist, Stephanie Schmidt, who took time out of her office-moving festivities to help me find history. Thank you to the wonderful University of Louisville Archives and Special Collections archivists, especially Pamela C. Yeager, for assisting my distillery research and the sorting through the Samuel Thomas collection. Thomas, who passed away in 2012, was a meticulous researcher, and his notes were invaluable to my work.

A big thanks to the staff of the Oscar Getz Museum of Whiskey who let me search through their files. I'm grateful for the Louisiana State University Archives and the Louisville Library for arranging the library loan of the early Louisiana newspapers.

To the Maker's Mark marketing team for allowing me to publish their hilarious advertisements.

Thank you to fellow bourbon author Michael R. Veach for proofing my manuscript and giving it his scholarly blessing.

Thanks to Erik Gilg, Quarto Group Publisher, for giving me another shot and to Bryan Trandem for the great edits; and once again, Madeleine Vasaly proves why she's one of the world's most dynamic editors. My agent, Linda Konner, continues to impress.

Most importantly, thank you to my family for enduring the long nights it took to write.

About the Author

Wall Street Journal best-selling author Fred Minnick wrote the award-winning *Whiskey Women* and *Bourbon Curious*. Fred writes about whiskey for *Covey Rise*, *Whisky Advocate*, and *Whisky* magazine. He is the official bourbon authority for the Kentucky Derby Museum and regularly appears in the mainstream media, including *CBS This Morning*, *Esquire*, *Forbes*, and NPR.